GERMAN EXPRESSIONISM

In the same series

SEVEN EXPRESSIONIST PLAYS
Murderer Hope of Womankind—Oscar Kokoschka,
The Guardian of the Tomb—Franz Kafka, *Squire Blue
Boll*—Ernst Barlach, *The Protagonist*—Georg Kaiser,
Awakening—August Stramm, *The Wolves*—Alfred
Brust, *Methusalem*—Ivan Goll

CARL STERNHEIM PLAYS
Scenes from the Heroic Lives of the Middle Classes
*The Bloomers, The Snob, Paul Schippel, Esq., 1913,
The Fossil*

VISION AND AFTERMATH
Four Expressionist War Plays
War, A Te Deum-Carl Hauptmann, *Naval Encounter*—
Reinhard Goering, *Antigone*—Walter Hasenclever,
Hinkemann—Ernst Toller

GEORG KAISER
Plays Volume One
*From Morning to Midnight, The Coral, The Burghers of
Calais, Gas I, Gas II*

Plays Volume Two
*David and Goliath, The President, The Flight to Venice,
One Day in October, The Raft of the Medusa*

THE ERA OF GERMAN EXPRESSIONISM
Editor Paul Raabe
Collection of the basic writings of the movement by its writers
and artists

FRANK WEDEKIND
Spring Awakening
The Lulu Plays
*Earth Spirit, Pandora's Box, Death and Devil, Castle
Wetterstein*

GERMAN EXPRESSIONISM
Series edited by J.M. Ritchie

PLAYS VOLUME TWO

Georg Kaiser

Translated from the German by
B.J. Kenworthy, H.F. Garten, Elizabeth Sprigge

JOHN CALDER · LONDON
RIVERRUN PRESS · NEW YORK

First published in Great Britain in 1981 by
John Calder (Publishers) Ltd
18 Brewer Street, London W1

and in the USA in 1982 by
Riverrun Press Inc
175 Fifth Avenue, New York 10010

© Verlag Ullstein GmbH, Frankfurt/Main, Berlin, Vienna 1970, 1971

© These translations John Calder (Publishers) Ltd 1981

BRITISH LIBRARY CATALOGUING IN PUBLICATION DATA
Kaiser, Georg
    Kaiser plays. – (German expressionism; 2) Vol. 2
    1. German drama – Translations into English
    I. Title II. Series
    832'912   PT2621.A33

ISBN 0 7145 3763 2 cloth
ISBN 0 7145 3899 X paper

Typeset in 9/10 point Press Roman by Gilbert Composing of Leighton Buzzard,
Beds, Great Britain.

Printed and bound in the U.S.A. by the Banta Company Inc. Wisconsin.

CONTENTS

INTRODUCTION

Georg Kaiser was born in Magdeburg on 25th November 1878. This was a time of rapid industrial and commercial growth in Germany; and it is symptomatic that in the year of Kaiser's birth the great ship-building yards of Blohm and Voß were founded in Hamburg and a liberal commercial policy was replaced by one of protective tariffs. The last quarter of the nineteenth century, when Kaiser was growing up, saw Germany finally change from a predominantly agrarian to an industrial economy, and in the process also becoming a more or less unified national state, rather than a collection of independent territories. The year of Kaiser's birth saw yet another element in the evolution of German capitalism: the introduction by Bismarck of the anti-Socialist laws which were to remain in force until 1890. Concomitant with the upsurge of industry was the creation of an urban proletariat and all that this brought with it: for instance, the population of Berlin rose from 1,122,000 in 1880 to 2,071,000 in 1910 (cf. Heinz Gollwitzer: *Europe in the Age of Imperialism 1880-1914,* London, 1969, p.20).

Such, in broad outline, was the background to Georg Kaiser's youth, though he left Germany between 1898 and 1901 to work for the General Electric Company in the Argentine, where he contracted the malaria that was later to prevent his serving in the German army in the First World War. On his return home he began to devote himself to writing plays, and it is on this genre that his literary reputation rests (although he also wrote two novels and a number of lyric poems). In 1908 he married and thereafter settled to a life of sometimes frenetic dramatic creativity, becoming in the 1920s, beside Gerhart Hauptmann, Germany's most frequently performed dramatist.

It was in the intellectual and emotional atmosphere of German Expressionism (whose heyday lasted from around 1915 to 1925) that Kaiser came to maturity. Virtually unknown until the overnight success of his pacifistic play *The Burghers of Calais (Die Bürger von Calais,* translated in Georg Kaiser: *Five Plays,* Calder & Boyars, London, 1971) in 1917–although it had been begun even before the outbreak of war in 1914–he had been evolving his individual style and diction. This was the time of the Expressionist literary revolt against Naturalism, which Kaiser condemns in the essay *Historical Fidelity (Historientreue,* 1923) as 'arid

7

copying from nature' (öde Abschilderei der Natur). Expressionism, with its accompanying experimentation, its formal innovation and its exuberant pathos was evidently congenial to Kaiser's talent. The aspiration for the regeneration of man, very much in the air at the time, was taken up enthusiastically by Kaiser, especially in the short-lived euphoria of the early days of the Weimar Republic in 1918-1919, when there was at least the chance that Germany might make a new social, political, and economic beginning. In 1918 Kaiser wrote in the essay *Vision and Figure* of this vision of the regeneration of humanity: 'This vision is a dangerous tempter: it arouses passion–which stifles the voice that should speak that it be heard . . . Cool speech advances against impassioned involvement–the hot-blooded must solidify into form!'

Here he anticipates a criticism that was long levelled at him and which is epitomized in the title of Bernhard Diebold's book *Der Denkspieler Georg Kaiser* (1924), which implies that he was a writer who toyed with ideas, that he was coldly noetic and devoid of emotional engagement. It is true that his reason remains in control even where he is concerned to portray the deepest passions and that he shows a propensity for symmetrically tailored dramatic forms; yet this does not invalidate his claim to genuine commitment–though it may be rather to his creative mission as a dramatist than to the immediate material of his plays. His work fluctuates between the apparent objectivity of social criticism in *The Burghers of Calais, From Morn to Midnight, The Coral,* and the two parts of *Gas;* and the more overtly subjective treatment in plays such as *One Day in October (Oktobertag),* which deal with individual human relationships, where love often serves as a kind of insulation against the harshness of the outside world–what Kaiser once called the 'hated reality' (die verhaßte Realität). But frequently his subjectivism supervenes, even when he seems to be pursuing a 'social' theme–the classic example is perhaps *The Coral;* and the ostensibly dispassionate objectivity is often the stalking-horse for a highly personal, subjective preoccupation.

The pacifistic, thoughtfully critical and generally left-wing–though non-doctrinaire–stance of Kaiser made him a natural target for suppression by the Nazis, and after their seizure of power in 1933 his plays were banned in Germany. Between then and 1938 he prudently restricted his dramatic writing to non-political plays dealing chiefly with love between the sexes, until in the latter year he escaped from Germany only hours before his planned arrest. He went first to Holland and from there made his way to Switzerland, where, although living in very straitened circumstances, he was at last able to give free expression to his anti-Nazi views. Some four weeks after the German capitulation that ended the Second World War in Europe he died in Ascona on 4th June 1945.

The five plays translated in the present volume represent Kaiser's work from its earliest phase through the time of his prolific maturity in the 1920s to the years immediately before his death. *David and Goliath* is one of a small group of plays set in Denmark (as they are subtitled 'comedies', it may be that a German setting seemed unpromising to Kaiser); they all deal with the power of money over men–and *David and Goliath*, for all its lightness, is not without its dash of social criticism. It is a play that must be seen against the background of the time when Kaiser was growing up and embarking on his career as a dramatist: the period from which it springs belongs very much to the days before the First World War. Its motivation depends in no small measure on *laissez-faire* capitalism and the commerical opportunities it offered the small businessman. In a version of the play earlier than that translated here, Sophus Möller proclaims: 'I, the small man, can step outside these walls of our penury and hurl a stone at the brazen giant wealth. It hits him on the head; it lays him low, and he has to yield up his treasure to me, without clemency or mercy, as it is written: And David drew his sword out of its sheath and smote the Philistine.' (Ich, der kleine Mann, kann hinaustreten aus diesen Mauern unserer Dürftigkeit und einen Stein gegen den erznen Reichtum schleudern. Er trifft ihn vor den Kopf; er schlägt ihn lang nieder und er muß mir von seinen Schäzten abgeben, ohne Gnade und Erbarmen, wie es geschrieben steht: Und David zog sein Schwert aus der Scheide und tötete den Philister.) This is reduced to the less circumstantial reference to the story of David and Goliath at the end of the play, and the signpost to Kaiser's theme thus rendered less obtrusive: '. . . You can conquer with your little finger, if your opponent has a weak spot. Merely to be on the attack is to be half way to defeat–you shall see that it's a dangerous game to make fun of dwarfs!'

In so much of Kaiser's work the plot turns upon the acceptance, occasionally by a whole community, more usually by an individual, of an idea–which can be based on self-deception and can emerge as an obsession, an extremity of subjectivism. Here the business community of the little town accepts as a fact that there is money to be made from the lottery winnings of the Möller family; Sophus accepts the existence of this belief as his working hypothesis: the perennially sensitive plant of 'business confidence' is brought into blossom by a confidence trick. It is revealed as applied avarice defeated by applied psychology and the stratagems of a not entirely disingenuous mind–Sophus, a typical product of his creator, is a master of sophistry.

The President (1905/6; revised 1926/7), a comedy–set this time in France–of a more derisively ironical tone, also depends for its plot upon a confidence trick, though one much more deliberately devised than that improvised by Sophus Möller as an answer to an aleatory challenge: the winning of the number once backed by his family in the state lottery. The schemes of the lawyer Blanchonnet are, by contrast, premeditated; the only chance element is the discovery among a deceased client's papers of documents concerning the defunct International Action League Against the White Slave Trade. He is motivated in resuscitating this League solely by the desire for social advancement–one must, as he says, be president of something or other to make one's way in society. What may appear as altruism is unmasked as arrant self-seeking. The father's deviousness is ironically confounded by the *ingénue;* his own daughter, armed with the unworldliness of her convent-school upbringing which was calculated to be one of her main assets in the marriage market, unwittingly thwarts his schemes, according to which she was to be bartered in marriage in exchange for his entrée into high society–a sardonic bourgeois modification of the very trade in flesh that Blanchonnet is ostensibly engaged in combatting. That Elmire, in her innocence, takes seriously a genuine social evil whose existence her father is exploiting for his own ends, and as a result helps a pair of hotel thieves to escape with all his ready cash, only makes the irony all the harsher. Yet Kaiser ensures that no harm comes to her, so that the end of the comedy remains unclouded and only the schemer is discomfited.

By the time *The Flight to Venice (Die Flucht nach Venedig),* was written in 1922 the Expressionist movement was at its height; many of Kaiser's most 'expressionistic' plays had already been completed. In this same year, too, he wrote one of his most 'ecstatic' dramas (the adjective enjoyed considerable favour with the Expressionist writers), *Gilles and Jeanne,* dealing with the moral regeneration and redemption of the sinner Gilles de Rais through the spiritual suasion of the saint, Joan of Arc. If this play has as its theme the beneficent influnece of the pure spirit, then *The Flight to Venice* examines the case against the intellect as a life-sapping succubus–a notion already treated by Kaiser in *Alcibiades Saved (Der gerettete Alkibiades,* 1919) and, since the turn of the century, a popular literary theme which was given currency by such writers as Thomas Mann and Hermann Hesse. Much of the vitalism prevalent at the time derives from Nietzsche's doctrine of the Dionysian release of the instincts and the senses–for instance, in *Thus Spake Zarathustra* (1883) he writes: 'Would that you were at least perfect as animals! But to the animal belongs innocence. Do I counsel you to kill your senses? I commend to you the innocence of the senses.' (Daß ihr doch wenigstens als Thiere vollkommen wäret! Aber zum Thiere gehört die Unschuld. Rathe ich euch, eure Sinne zu tödten? Ich rathe euch zur Unschuld der Sinne. *Von der Keuschheit.)* A further attack on the self-conscious, analytic intellect which undermines the *élan vital,* the life force, was launched by Henri Bergson in his *L'Evolution créatrice* (1907); and it is consonant with this thesis that, in Kaiser's *Alcibiades Saved,* Socrates is condemned to death for subverting the uncomplicated natural vitality of the gymnasia with his debilitating dialectic.

This contemporary concern was also a personal problem of Kaiser's. In his book *The Image of the Artist and the Artist Figure (Georg Kaiser: Künstlerbild und Künstlerfigur,* Frankfurt/Main—Munich, 1976, p. 94) Klaus Petersen writes: 'In discussing Kaiser's image of the artist, we have established that, in the Theoretical Writings, the dramatist recognizes two different types of artist: the artist who sets out from the idea and the one who sets out from the sensuous.' (Wir haben bei der Besprechung von

Kaisers Künstlerbild festgestellt, daß der Dramatiker in den Theoretischen Schriften zwei verschiedene Künstlertypen kennt: den Künstler aus der Idee und den Künstler aus der Sinnlichkeit.) While it is clear that Kaiser inclines to the former type, it is also evident that he feels at the same time some kind of moral obligation-arising, perhaps, from the pressures of the intellectual climate of the time-at least to genuflect in the direction of the latter type. Indeed, his essay *The Sensuousness of Thought (Die Sinnlichkeit des Gedankens,* 1925) attempts to find a synthesis of the two, as the very title indicates; and, in the year in which *The Flight to Venice* appeared, in a theoretical essay called *The Coming Humanity* (also published, revealingly, as *Poetry and Energy-Dichtung und Energie,* 1922) he seeks to vindicate creative writing as a vitalistic activity, both in its intention and in its practice: 'A form of energy is creative writing. With this affirmation the new aesthetics makes its appearance. The former one of terror and pity for the effect of poetry no longer obtains. Now we judge only according to the strength or weakness of the energy expended by the creator of the work. ' (Form von Energie ist Dichtung. Mit dieser Feststellung tritt die neue Asthetik auf. Die bisherige von Furcht und Mitleid für Wirkung von Dichtung besteht nicht länger. Wir urteilen nur noch nach Stärke und Schwäche der verausgabten Energie des Schöpfers von Dichtwerk.)

In the figures of Alfred de Musset and George Sand, Kaiser presents these two types of artist, though with a reservation, however, which makes the play a very personal one; though every artist, whether consciously or unconsciously, must in some measure determine the relationship between experience and imagination, between reality and vision, in his creative work. Musset is essentially the artist of the idea: he isolates himself, much as Kaiser did; his experience-such as his love for Sand-are not to be profaned as mere fodder to be gobbled up and regurgitated by his artistic genius. And his words: 'I lack perspective. I become obsessed with myself' have the ring of a personal avowal on the part of his creator. In this play the contrastive metaphor of cold and hot-which recurs in Kaiser's work, varying in implication from that of impotence as against sexual passion, of chill disillusionment following the chase after a life of fulfilment to the opposition of 'life' and intellect-is synthesized into the elaborate oxymoron addressed by Musset to Sand: 'Are you not frozen beneath your skin that breathes warmth? Touch it with your fingers: it burns-underneath ice is forming. In the mould of your body life and death is fashioned.'

Yet there remains the reservation: Musset, in an action symbolizing his emancipation from the 'vampirism of literary creativity' (Vampyrismus des Dichterischen, W. Huder) which he perceives in Sand, drops the locks of her hair into the canal. Similarly Sand, resolved to free herself from the inhibiting artist's compulsion to analyze each experience even in the experiencing of it, to overcome the element of objective detachment in her and to surrender herself utterly to the moment, drops her manuscript into

the water-a sort of parallelism typical of Kaiser's work. But both
symbolic gestures remain, ironically, gestures-Musset is drawn
inescapably to Sand, and at the end Sand is already shaping her latest
attempt at self-abandonment to instinct into literature. Neither can
maintain the extreme position originally allotted them, but each is
impelled into compromise with the other; the distinction becomes
blurred. It is as if Kaiser himself is propelled between these two poles of
his own artistic temperament, but cannot escape their traction: he is aware
that 'words are the death of life', yet remains devoted-equivocally,
perhaps, but absolutely-to the production of literature.

In his early plays-*Headmaster Kleist (Rektor Kleist,* 1903), *The Spirit
of Antiquity (Der Geist der Antike,* 1905)-Georg Kaiser had taken up,
with quizzical irony, the current concept of the mind/body dichotomy as
material for comedy; later he looks at it more seriously, and finally it
emerges in more metaphysical garb as the conflict between the outer
reality of the physical world and the inner world of the mind. And it is in
this sense that he developed a newspaper report of a paternity case in
France into his play *One Day in October (Oktobertag,* 1927). In this play,
as in so much of Kaiser's work, the idea triumphs over the crass
constraints of mundane reality. This drama of the interplay of outer and
inner reality might have taken as its motto the words of the Viennese
writer Arthur Schnitzler some thirty years earlier:

> More than the truth that **was** and **will be**
> Is delusion that **is** . . . the moment reigns supreme!
> (Mehr als die Wahrheit, die da **war** und **sein wird,**
> Ist Wahn, der **ist** . . . der Augenblick regiert!)
>
> from *Paracelsus* (1896)

In the play, Catherine, through the force of her own desire, has
mentally transmuted a chance series of events into a coherent pattern-her
betrothal and wedding to Jean-Marc Marrien and the consummation of
their marriage. But Kaiser further set himself the more difficult task of
demonstrating how, by a kind of psycho-osmotic process, Catherine's
version of the truth implants itself also in Marrien's mind. The catalyst of
this process, of course, is love, albeit of a somewhat startling suddenness.
That Kaiser recognized the difficulty of his undertaking-and opinions
may differ as to his success in it-is evident from Coste's words to Marrien:
'Everything is real and unreal at the same time. I am inclined to call what
brought you and Catherine together a mystical union. Doubtless of
heavenly origin-doubly difficult, therefore, to establish on the firm
ground of reality.' And the perilous seductiveness of surrender to
omnipotent fantasy which so readily transforms reality-and, like Sand's
genius, feeds upon the transformation-is recognized in Coste's warning:
'Lt. Marrien-there are limits to all transmutations of reality, the deepest
dream issues in death . . .' It is through death, through Marrien's brutal
killing of Leguerche under the impulsion of his deepest dreams-his

acceptance of Catherine's reality-that he attempts to break out of the limits imposed by the outward reality of the world: the 'objective' world, in the figure of Leguerche, is simply annihilated. *One Day in October* is a monument to its creator's own subjectivity.

In 1940, during his exile in Switzerland, Kaiser wrote to the Swiss dramatist Cäsar von Arx suggesting that they co-operate in writing a play; he goes on: 'read the enclosed newspaper report. From this report a play blossoms; in the life-boat are only children. The stage is the surging sea with this unique boat. We learn from the behaviour and the mouths of the children the extreme cruelty of events. The evacuation-the torpedoing... Now profound observations about life and the leaving of life . . . Condemnation of adults, who commit such infamies: leaving children to drift in a boat at sea . . .'

This play, then, which was in the end written without Arx's co-operation and which was not finished until 1943, also owed its inspiration to a newspaper report; the way Kaiser developed the account of the wartime torpedoing of a ship carrying evacuee children to Canada is indicated in his own prefatory note to the play, *The Raft of the Medusa.*

Whether it is entirely successful is open to debate-'profound observations about life and the leaving of life' from the lips of ten- and twelve - year - olds present their own problems; but Kaiser is not primarily concerned with naturalistic verisimilitude. That these observations are offered in an only slightly simplified version of Kaiser's stylized diction is a typical legacy of the largely undifferentiated language of the expressionist drama of his earlier days, where all the figures tend to speak with their creator's voice. Nevertheless, it does give rise to a certain tension between the language and the speakers.

The title *The Raft of the Medusa (Das Floß der Medusa)* was obviously suggested by Géricault's picture *Le radeau de la Méduse,* depicting the survivors of the French ship Méduse, which was wrecked off the African coast early in the nineteenth century. Kaiser, however, avails himself only of the name; his play revives a favourite theme of the Expressionist generation: that of the regeneration of man, of the so-called New Man. Here, however, the theme is overlaid with the misanthropic pessimism of Kaiser's last years; the morally reborn boy, Allan, is used, as the dramatist implies, as a vehicle for the condemnation of the adult world, whose follies and mindless cruelties are embryonic in the distorted and ill-digested superstitions that the children have picked up from their elders.

In the years during which *The Raft of the Medusa* was being written, Kaiser also completed his three 'Greek plays'. In one of them, *Pygmalion,* he formulates explicitly what had all along been latent in his work in connection with the theme of the regeneration of man: the admission that, however desirable it might be, it was nevertheless a utopian dream incapable of realization. The fate of Allan in *The Raft of the Medusa* is a further illustration of the impossibility of the regenerate man's survival in the world of empirical reality.

B.J. Kenworthy

DAVID AND GOLIATH

Comedy in Three Acts

Translated by B. J. Kenworthy

Characters

SOPHUS MÖLLER, Savings Bank clerk
HELENE, his wife
DAGMAR, his daughter
PETER MÖLLER, proprietor of a printing works
ASMUS EXNER, merchant
OTTILIE, his wife
MISS JUEL
JOCHUM MAGNUSSEN, brewer
AXEL, his son
LUNDBERG, book-keeper
BRANDSTRUP, landlord
MRS MACKESSPRANG
MAGNUSSEN'S FOOTMAN
SOPHUS MÖLLER'S MAID
GUESTS of the Magnussens

The action takes place in a small Danish town.

ACT ONE

The top-floor flat of SOPHUS MÖLLER: *the cramped room at once living-room and dining-room. A window in the sloping wall right. A glass door at the back. In the centre the table is laid for supper.* AXEL MAGNUSSEN *is leaning against an armchair and drumming heavily on its wickerwork.* DAGMAR *at the piano-playing and singing.*

DAGMAR. Stately bird that far above us flies —
          thou art rich but I am poor —
          all thy gold falls from the sun —
          thou art rich but I am poor —
          and silver showers on thee the moon —
          thou art rich but I am poor —
          here below thy darker shadow flies:
          here, where gold and silver lose their lustre —
          I am poor-yet thou so rich!

AXEL *puts the chair noisily in its place and goes to the piano.*

DAGMAR. Haven't you the patience to hear the end of it? Isn't it beautiful, the way the tune is repeated here: thou art rich-I am poor?

AXEL *(removes the music).* You're wasting your time and your voice on it!

DAGMAR. It's a song I like.

AXEL. How can you like a piece of nonsense that-

DAGMAR *(laughing).* Made the composer world-famous!

AXEL. I'm not bothered about the music-but I am criticizing the words. 'Stately bird that far above us flies-here below thy darker shadow flies!'—Why, it's a soothing shadow the bird casts into this hell-fire that is life. Why does it have to be a dirge? Someone has to sacrifice himself-and bear the burden of wealth for other people. Or do you think that it's any pleasure?

DAGMAR. Songs can't be told in words, Mr Magnussen.

AXEL. But songs **are** words!

DAGMAR. Am I to sing nothing but doh ray me fah soh?

AXEL. Must you always be playing the piano and singing, Miss Dagmar?

MRS HELENE MÖLLER *enters from the left with the lamp, which she puts down on the table.*

HELENE. Dagmar, you'll have to stop now. It's high time you got dressed for the concert.

DAGMAR. I've already stopped, mother-Mr Magnussen was objecting to my going on.

AXEL. I was certainly objecting to-

DAGMAR. Piano, song-the lot!

AXEL. Only just a poem!

DAGMAR *has already gone off left.*

HELENE *(turning up the lamp)*. Why didn't you like it?

AXEL. Because-Miss Dagmar was trying to let me know with that silly chorus about 'thou art rich-I am poor' that—*(he hurls the music book down on to the sofa.)*

HELENE. Finish what you were going to say, Mr Magnussen.

AXEL *(in front of her)*. Mrs Möller-don't you feel it-as clearly as the blind feel-you and Dagmar-that the air is full of unspoken declarations?!

HELENE. Does your father know that you are a frequent visitor under our roof?

AXEL. I have nothing to confess to him.

HELENE. And if you were to tell him?

AXEL. I'd get a more or less unnecessary answer!

HELENE. No-your father would be right.

AXEL. Mrs Möller!

HELENE. Let me have my say. It's true enough: **so** rich doesn't belong with **so** poor. The son of Magnussen of the Royal Brewery doesn't belong with the daughter of Möller, a mere clerk in the municipal savings bank. We don't want to bring fairy-tales into this workaday world. We should wake up with headaches.

There is a knock on the glass door. HELENE *opens it-to* MRS MACKESSPRANG, *the charwoman.*

MRS MACKESSPRANG *(notices* AXEL-*curtsies)*. Mr Magnussen junior himself in person-it's enough to take my breath away. I don't suppose Mr Magnussen knows me-I'm Mackessprang the charwoman. But is there anyone in the building who doesnt know young Mr Magnussen? It's a great honour for the stairs I scrub-and when Mr Brandstrup the landlord fusses about the amount of soap I use on the scrubbing, then I tell him the stairs a Mr Magnussen junior walks up have got to be as bright as a new pin!

HELENE. Was there something you wanted to tell me, Mrs Mackessprang?

MRS MACKESSPRANG. I really wanted to ask you something, Mrs Möller. I hope you won't mind, in the presence of-

HELENE. Well, what is it?

MRS MACKESSPRANG. I'm a bit short of money–just until the first of the month. Of course, my wages aren't due for three days yet, but I'm in a bit of a fix. I wonder if I could ask for the money for doing the stairs today? *(With a glance at* AXEL*)*. Maybe it could be arranged.

HELENE *(quickly)*. I can't possibly manage it today, Mrs Mackessprang. I pay on time–but not a day earlier or a day later. You'll get what's due to you on the first. It's a waste of time asking me. You've come all the way up here for nothing. *(She edges* MRS MACKESSPRANG *out and shuts the door.)* I have you to thank for that, Mr Magnussen!

AXEL. For your charwoman's visit?

HELENE. That and more. Mr Brandstrup is putting the rent up. People think we're well-off–since young Mr Magnussen has been coming here. Now we have to pinch and squeeze even more–we may have to exchange this attic flat for the basement. That's the language of harsh reality which we all have to obey!

AXEL. But–a single word can change all that!

HELENE. In a world of make-believe, where money falls from the sky and rich fathers are angels!

AXEL. I swear to you that I shall marry only the poorest of girls– because that's what I want to do now! That's a binding oath—or I'll go and be a labourer in my father's brewery!

HELENE. That's your fate, Mr Axel–Dagmar's way leads through the conservatory to music teaching. I shall thank the Lord if only Möller can pay for that!

AXEL. Yes–it must be costing him a lot to have her study singing and piano together.

HELENE. Is it expensive?

AXEL. Don't you know anything about it?

HELENE. Möller never mentions it. She is his only daughter, after all.

AXEL. It's a remarkable achievement for a man earning a clerk's salary.

HELENE *(attentive)*. How much do you think the lessons are swallowing up?

AXEL. I should reckon at least four-hundred crowns a year.

HELENE. Four hundred crowns? Why, that–that's impossible!

AXEL. Mr Möller is making it possible.

HELENE. Mr Magnussen–are you helping my husband out with money?

AXEL. No, Mrs Möller.

HELENE. Then I can't understand it . . .

AXEL. You're getting quite worked up about it!

HELENE. No–that's not what we were going to talk about. Möller works in the savings bank, so he ought to know about money matters. He'll know where to get the money from–and how to make his money go round!

AXEL. He'll have learnt to account for it in the savings bank!

HELENE *(close to Axel)*. Mr Axel-you must say goodbye to Dagmar today, this very evening. She'll have to give up-and she can now-she knows enough to stand on her own feet. She can go to Copenhagen and teach beginners.

AXEL. And what about me?

HELENE. You will find a girl from your own circle.

AXEL. Do you want to make me break my oath?

HELENE. Give Dagmar up-I beg you!

AXEL. The moment Dagmar becomes rich-as rich as I am-I shall be separated from her. We shall be oceans apart, Mrs Möller.

HELENE. Our daughter won't embarrass you by making that come true. Well then-*(DAGMAR enters left-still pulling on her gloves.)*

DAGMAR. Are you bringing me home from the concert?

AXEL. When I've taken you there!

DAGMAR. Let's go!

HELENE. Aren't you going to have something to eat first?

DAGMAR *(by the table)*. Cold sausage-cheese-beer?

HELENE. Were you expecting to find something more when you came back from the concert?

DAGMAR. This meal will be completely transformed with the help of the magic of Brahms and Beethoven. That's what music does for **me,** Mr Magnussen. Then the sausage will become pheasant-the cheese pineapple-and the beer champagne. That's the way we live in the lap of luxury, whenever we want to!

AXEL. I'm sorry not to have been invited too!

DAGMAR. So you see, mother, I'll have a delicious meal today. I'll see you again at suppertime! *(Kisses her quickly on the cheek. Exit with AXEL, who kisses HELENE'S hand.)*

HELENE *(at the table-pressing her hands to her temples-stammering)*. Four . . . hundred . . . that-that just isn't possible . . . four-hundred a year . . .

*The glass door is opened cautiously-*BRANDSTRUP'S *podgy face under a peaked cap peers into the room.*

BRANDSTRUP. May I?

HELENE *(starting and turning round)*. Mr Brandstrup!

BRANDSTRUP. That's right-it's yours truly! *(Sits down at the table.)* Those stairs-those damn awful stairs!

HELENE *(also sits down-staring at BRANDSTRUP)*. What-about . . . Has anything happened?

BRANDSTRUP *(looks at her, nodding and grinning-pushes his hand across the table and grasps HELENE'S hand)*. . . . I congratulated the young lady on the stairs.

HELENE *(with a sigh of relief-deprecatingly)*. My daughter is not engaged to the gentleman!

BRANDSTRUP. That was Magnussen the brewer's lad, wasn't it?

HELENE. And she isn't going to get engaged to Mr Magnussen either, Mr Brandstrup.

BRANDSTRUP. Why ever not? Magnussen, however rich he is, won't be able to say no now!

HELENE *(standing up)*. What can I do for you, Mr Brandstrup?

BRANDSTRUP. Well now, Mrs Möller, you see I really should have had to give you notice to leave-

HELENE. You wanted more rent.

BRANDSTRUP. That's a sore point with everyone. All my life no-one's ever given me a penny-I've raked it together from a bit of interest here and a bit of interest there. And you weren't exactly on a bed of roses either-

HELENE. And we're determined not to do anythng that could harm you, Mr Brandstrup. We'll be out of the flat by the first of next month!

BRANDSTRUP. Of course, it goes without saying that you'll be looking round for somewhere else to live now. I'm not the sort of man who says a lot-but I'm happy when others are happy-I'm not one to be jealous. My second floor's empty and all ready for occupation. Now how would you like to move down into my nicest flat?

HELENE *looks at him in surprise.*

BRANDSTRUP. Four rooms at the front, the back rooms all newly papered. A lift for coals-water closet. I'll attend to any special wishes you may have.

HELENE *(wearily)*. How do you think Möller is going to pay for that?

BRANDSTRUP. Quarterly-and at the end of the quarter-not in advance-at the end! I'd trust Mr Möller like the king of Denmark!

HELENE. If you imagine that we are getting any advantages from young Mr Magnussen, whom you met on the stairs with my daughter, then you're making a mistake, Mr Brandstrup! Let it suffice that Möller and I never wanted these visits and that we have forbidden them for the future. I'm not interested in whether Mr Magnussen is rich or not. We aren't, and that's something I know well enough!

BRANDSTRUP. *(laughs uproariously)*. You're not—no, that you aren't! Old Magnussen has been sweating away all his life-brewing, filling bottles, sticking on labels. Mr Möller sits in his office giving people receipts for the few coppers they deposit-

HELENE *(trembling)*. Has something—happened to Möller?

BRANDSTRUP. He's made fools of the whole savings bank, of sweating Mr Magnussen and of the untiring efforts of the townsfolk to put something by. He's won eight-hundred-thousand crowns in the Danish state lottery. That's the first prize!—what a celebration there'll be in the town!

HELENE. Möller doesn't hold his ticket alone: he shares it with four other relations: Peter Möller, the owner of the printing works, Exner and his wife, who have a shop–and Miss Juel. That's our aunt!

BRANDSTRUP. Five more wealthy people!

HELENE. But I know nothing about–

BRANDSTRUP. Yes, it does take time for it to get right up here under the roof!

HELENE. Möller isn't back from the office yet–

BRANDSTRUP. Then I must go and meet him! Put in a good word with him for my flat. After all, I was the first one to bring you the good news. One good turn deserves another. Quarterly, and at the end of the quarter—at the end, Mrs Möller. Tomorrow you can have a look at the rooms. You'll like them—I know what well-to-do people like, I do!

HELENE. Without Möller I can't commit myself to anything.

BRANDSTRUP. I'll make the contract with Möller—*(at the door he bumps into* OTTILIE EXNER; *shaking her hand.)* Congratulations! *(Exit.)*

OTTILIE *(hat askew, jacket done up in the wrong button-holes—rushes to the table and bangs down a fistful of money on it).* Here's my money—counted out to the last penny! There it is, all together and above board, just as I've reckoned it up!

HELENE. Whatever money is that?

OTTILIE *(alarmed).* You don't mean you won't take it now?

HELENE. I don't know what you've brought the money for.

OTTILIE. It's my contributions to the lottery ticket. Latterly I hadn't been paying them on time. I'd forgotten to—as true as I'm standing here, it had completely slipped my mind. By almighty God, Helene—it was only that I was forgetful. It never entered my head to give up my share in the family ticket!

HELENE. But Ottilie, you surely don't believe your brother would wish to do you out of a share in the winnings?

OTTILIE *(relieved).* You check it over and see if it's all right. I've been through all my pockets—and it was just enough!

HELENE. How long is it since you last paid?

OTTILIE. Ten years, Helene. I'd given up hope of winning anything. For sixteen years we'd been putting up our money, and never saw a penny of it again!

HELENE. And Möller never reminded you about it in all those ten years?

OTTILIE. No, Helene, never!

HELENE. Möller is a good-natured man.

OTTILIE. And that's why he won't let me down now! It's what I've always wanted—the dream of my life—what I've always longed for. And now it's happened: at last it's put an end to that—the church-mouse's tail is cut off!

HELENE. Are you the church-mouse?
OTTILIE. That's what Asmus calls me-he used it to keep me quiet. It was his trump card. What did you bring into our marriage? One bale of Danish cloth? I brought you into a whole shopful of bales! Did you have a single hank of wool to show for yourself? I opened up a whole store-room of wool for you!—I held my peace and he held the floor!
HELENE. You never said anything about Asmus throwing that in your face.
OTTILIE. Church-mice don't dare come out in the daylight!
HELENE. Aren't you fond of your husband?
OTTILIE. Who said anything about that? I worship him! But you get tired of crawling round on your knees all the time. There comes a time when you have to stand up and confront your god face to face! You can't be happy unless you do! Now I can stand up to Asmus—I'm as big as he is now—I've got as much behind me as he has! Now we'll change the name of the firm: Asmus **and** Ottilie Exner, Cotton and Woollen Goods. What do you say to that, then?
HELENE. Your hat's on crooked.
OTTILIE. I don't care—rich people's clothes are always right. Over one eye or perched straight up on top: our money sets the fashion! *(She goes out like a whirlwind.)*
HELENE *(shakes her head, puts the money away. There is a repeated knocking with the handle of a walking-stick on the glass door).* Peter!

PETER MÖLLER *enters—waves portentously to* HELENE—*puts down hat and stick—goes to the table, takes a newspaper from under his coat and spreads it out.*

PETER. There it is-there. Column three, page three: one hundred and forty thousand two hundred and forty-two!
HELENE *(reading with him).* That's our number!
PETER. One-four-nought-two-four-two! Am I seeing straight or not?
HELENE. So it **is** true, then?
PETER *(shrugging).* Figures don't lie! You must get used to the idea. There's nothing we can do about it. We've won.
HELENE. But it's—much too much!
PETER. We gambled—now we must bear the consequences.
HELENE. Sophus—is a rich man.
PETER. Hasn't Sophus come in yet?
HELENE. Surely nothing can have happened to him—in the first excitement of it?
PETER *(sitting down).* I've got a queer feeling in my legs, too. Damn it all, what's it got to do with our legs?
HELENE *(also sitting down).* I'm as tired as if I'd been for a long walk!
PETER. Suddenly you emerge into the broad daylight: there is the treasure! I'm sitting there at my desk, and the office - boy brings me the paper straight from the press. It's still wet. I read the political news: the Emperor of Japan has died—

HELENE. Is he really as bad as that?

PETER. I feel sorry for the man even when he's dead! I get to the local news: it really is high time they stopped the St. John's church clock striking thirteen. A quick glance at the stop-press: the Holy Father is suffering from a nasty cold—

HELENE. Is he really bad?

PETER. A cold can develop into all sorts of troubles! The draw for the first prize in the state lottery took place this morning, and the winning number—as yet I notice nothing, though there's something at the back of my mind—like when you have a word on the tip of your tongue and can't get it out. I read on: this year the colorado beetle seems—

The glass door is thrown open suddenly: MISS JUEL *breezes in.*

MISS JUEL. Well, my dears, we really seem to have struck it lucky! Is Sophus here? I must feel this lucky ticket in my hand, stroke it—give it a kiss! What's become of Sophus, our faithful ticket-keeper?

HELENE. Sophus still has his office-hours.

MISS JUEL *(rummages in her knitting-bag and takes out some pastilles).* My throat's dry! *(She sucks one.)* Come on, have a cough-drop! Always suck a cough-drop! The Holy Father's got a cold, too. Did you read the late news, Peter?

HELENE. Auntie—we are only interested in another piece of news at the moment!

MISS JUEL. Has something else been happening in the world then?

HELENE. Our lottery ticket, auntie!

MISS JUEL. Oh, I know about that, dear!

HELENE. The world might be standing still now, as far as I'm concerned.

MISS JUEL. Nelly, my cough-drop must have rolled over to you!

PETER. Yes, auntie, you're right. We mustn't forget we're still living in this world. That would seem ungrateful, after we've been living in it for so long without any particular fuss.

MISS JUEL. Why aren't the Exners here yet?

HELENE. Ottilie has been here already.

MISS JUEL. What had she got to say for herself?-Peter, my cough-drop must be somewhere near you.

HELENE. Ottilie laughed and cried!

MISS JUEL. Nelly, there's someone coming. It'll be your Sophus bringing us the ticket!

ASMUS *and* OTTILIE *enter.*

OTTILIE. Asmus and Ottilie Exner, Cotton and Woollen Goods–the new firm!

ASMUS *(disengages himself from* OTTILIE—*embraces* MISS JUEL, PETER, HELENE *in silence. Then suddenly businesslike).* How much is due to each of us? There are eight-hundred-thousand crowns—

and five partners. I take it the contributions have been paid regularly to Sophus?

OTTILIE. Yes, on the dot to—

HELENE. Sophus!

ASMUS. That means eight-hundred-thousand to be divided into five. Fifteen percent is deducted from the total sum.

MISS JUEL. Why?

OTTILIE. Whatever for?

ASMUS. A statutory deduction paid to the state.

OTTILIE. We won't stand for it!

ASMUS. Be quiet, Ottilie!

OTTILIE. You be quiet, Asmus!

MISS JUEL. After supporting the lottery for sixteen years, I should think we had every right to make a fuss if they deduct anything!

PETER. Yes, Asmus, I must say I find it a bit of a nerve.

OTTILIE. It's a swindle! First they inveigle us into gambling our precious money—*(She breaks off.)*

MISS JUEL. For sixteen years we've been living in a perpetual state of excitement—

PETER. I wouldn't object if they deducted something from the small winnings—but it's another matter to pester winners of the big prizes like us with tricks of that sort!

ASMUS. I think we'll put up with it, and not bring any action against the state. We all know that the king has more people behind him—

OTTILIE. We can afford the fattest lawyer's fees, too!

MISS JUEL *(less sure of herself)*. Asmus, Peter—promise me there'll be no court case! Not for all the money. I'd rather go empty-handed!

PETER. Don't worry, auntie. A sensible person knows when to stop!

SOPHUS MÖLLER *appears in the glass door; seeing the gathering he waves his straw hat.*

SOPHUS. Long live the King of Denmark!

PETER. Long live his majesty the King of Denmark! *(All join in.)*

SOPHUS *(going to the table—bending over the newspaper).* Whereabouts is it, then?

PETER. There: number one hundred and forty thousand two hundred and forty-two!

SOPHUS. Haven't you had any telegrams?

ASMUS. From you, Sophus?

SOPHUS. From the lottery office in Copenhagen! That's impossible, though—the ticket will be in my name, Sophus Möller!

MISS JUEL. A telegram from Cophenhagen—what charming official manners!

SOPHUS. It's only to be expected—we're not mere nobodies they can afford to ignore.

PETER. Have you had a telegram, Sophus?

SOPHUS. At four-thirteen this afternoon!

MISS JUEL. Thirteen—that's an unlucky number!

SOPHUS. Four-thirteen—I was just booking three crowns eighty öre to old Mrs Gillerup's credit—

OTTILIE *(disdainfully)*. Three crowns eighty ore!

SOPHUS. Each according to his means, my dear sister!

ASMUS. Be quiet, Ottilie!

OTTILIE. You be quiet, Asmus!

SOPHUS. Then the telegraph-boy came in. For Mr Möller of the municipal savings bank! I close my counter and shut myself off from the outside world. I read it—and I don't mind admitting that it made some impression on me—then I put it with the other papers and opened my counter again. I'll give a prize of a thousand crowns to anyone who noticed anything from my face or from anything else!

MISS JUEL. Sophus—I can't wait to see your telegram from Copenhagen!

SOPHUS. If I'd only thought that I'd find you all here—but who can think that far ahead in the first moment of surprise!—I'd have put it in my pocket.

PETER. The telegram isn't as important as all that!

OTTILIE. Oh, Peter!

PETER. Our fingers are itching to get hold of the—

OTTILIE. Let's pass the ticket round!

MISS JUEL *(groping about in her knitting-bag for her pince-nez)*. It belongs equally to everyone!

SOPHUS *(turning to ASMUS and laying a hand on his shoulder)*. Asmus, you're a sensible businessman—do you carry eight-hundred-thousand crowns about in your pocket? Or do you stuff valuable documents into the pockets of your working clothes? You entrusted our syndicate ticket to me—and so I had a special responsibility to be careful with it. It is lying in the iron safe at the savings bank with the telegram.

ASMUS *(shaking his head)*. You're the only one who has kept his head. Now I'm very glad we chose you as our lottery supervisor.

SOPHUS. What are you looking for, auntie?

MISS JUEL. My pastille's rolled under your shoe!

SOPHUS. And how did you come to hear the great news?

PETER. I read it.

SOPHUS. Your paper, of course.

PETER. If you'd let me know right away, I'd have put in a note that the prize had gone to someone in the town—and that we are the lucky winners!

SOPHUS. Is the whole town to hear about it?

MISS JUEL. My maid came rushing in from the street, where Mr Brandstrup had just—

OTTILIE. Brandstrup pulled open the shop door just when I was measuring five yards of Danish cloth from the roll—

HELENE. Brandstrup was up here visiting me—

SOPHUS. How does Brandstrup know?

PETER. He was in my office wanting to put an advertisement in the paper about his magnificent flat. I simply burst out with the news. Brandstrup is a good customer. He's always putting in advertisements about his flats. But he suddenly changed his mind and withdrew the advertisement—

HELENE. He wants you as his second floor tenant!

SOPHUS. Then it's certainly no secret any more, if Brandstrup is spreading it about!

PETER. Are we to make a secret of our wealth? *(To* ASMUS*)* Have you made any plans yet?

ASMUS. I think it's about time I bought a house in Oster Street.

SOPHUS. Quite right too—Oster Street. That's the only district for a businessman.

OTTILIE. And after all this time I'm marrying into my husband's business; Asmus and Ottilie Exner, Cotton and Woollen Goods!

SOPHUS. You're a fine couple. And your five children. You know how to build up a company! Yes, Peter, I suppose you'll be getting above yourself as well?

PETER. I shall build.

SOPHUS. That'll make work for the tradesmen!

PETER. I'm sick of printing the local paper. You know, Sophus, one must work at something artistic—you can learn from it. If I print the work of our great writers I combine business and pleasure. I read them over in proof. That means I have to be doubly attentive—and that's the way to develop critical judgment. And a person must have critical judgment—or he isn't worthy of having a share of eight-hundred-thousand crowns!

SOPHUS. Splendid idea, Peter—you want to earn in order to learn! Auntie, it's your turn now!

OTTILIE. Aunt Juel will get married!

MISS JUEL. Me?—captivate a man?

SOPHUS. They'll be there like flies round a honey-pot, or I'm a Dutchman!

ASMUS. Aunt Juel must have her wedding within a month!

SOPHUS. It's all settled, then: Aunt Juel is to get married.

MISS JUEL. First let's find out what Sophus is going to do with his money!

PETER. Come on, brother Sophus—we're waiting!

ASMUS. As your brother-in-law, I think I deserve to know!

SOPHUS. I shall leave it all to my only daughter, Dagmar.

MISS JUEL *(after a short pause—preparing to leave).* Well, the rest of us are keeping what we've got. Helene, if you find any cough-drops on the floor tomorrow—

HELENE. But auntie, you can buy as many as you want now.

OTTILIE. Asmus, we'll go round by Oster Street!

PETER. I'm off to have a look at the town-plan!

ASMUS *(at the door—in a low, foreboding tone)*. We'd better keep close together! *(The four of them go off.)*

HELENE. I took Ottilie's money for you—her contributions for ten years. I haven't counted it. Must be a few hundred crowns there. *(She puts the money on the table.* SOPHUS *has sat down on the sofa—takes out a battered wallet and searches about in it for something)*. It was nice of you not to let on that she really has no right to a share in the lottery. She was like a cat on hot bricks! ·

SOPHUS *(has found a piece of paper, folded up small—unfolds and smooths it)*. Push the lamp over this way a bit.

HELENE *(does so)*. What are you looking for?

SOPHUS *(comparing ticket and newspaper)*. One hundred and forty thousand two hundred and forty two.

HELENE. Have you got—the ticket?

SOPHUS *(nods)*. One-four-nought-two-four-two!

HELENE. But just now you told the others—*(suddenly sitting down—faltering)*. Didn't it win?

SOPHUS. It's the right number.

HELENE *(confused)*. And is the ticket—?

SOPHUS. I've—not been backing it for the last ten years!

HELENE *(looks at him speechless)*. Sophus—you're joking—it's gone to your head—you're rich now! You did get a telegram, didn't you?

SOPHUS. No, dear, I didn't get a telegram.

HELENE. But you told us about it down to the last detail: old Mrs Gillerup—the telegraph-boy?

SOPHUS. Yes, it was marvellous, imagining it all: me closing my counter—opening the sealed telegram—that falls like a beam of light into the greyness of the bank!—I just can't believe it could be nicer, if it were really to happen! And then, when you were all so happy, here, I hadn't the heart to be a kill-joy. Helene, could you have done it?

HELENE. But Sophus—it—it's dreadful!

SOPHUS. There you are—I knew you wouldn't have screwed up the courage to do it!

HELENE. Whatever gave you the idea of giving up the lottery?

SOPHUS. Why, that wasn't at all difficult for me. First Ottilie gave up paying—and I really couldn't go dunning my own sister for the money, especially as she isn't exactly living in the lap of luxury. And I hadn't enough to make up the extra ten crowns every month! And then I regretted all that money we were always sending off—and none of it ever coming back again!

HELENE. Then you ought to have told Peter, Asmus, and Aunt Juel, and advised them to stop too.

SOPHUS. No, Helene, it wouldn't have been right to do that. I couldn't rob them of their hopes. And in any case they'd have gone on gambling

among themselves and wasting their money! No, I was right to save
them from the demon of gambling!

HELENE. But you went on regularly taking their money?

SOPHUS. I had to do that—otherwise they'd have guessed they weren't
gambling any more!

HELENE. How much money was it, then?

SOPHUS. Including my share, which I always paid up, about four
hundred crowns a year.

HELENE. And you've been spending it on yourself?

SOPHUS. I just told you—I always paid my share.

HELENE. Whatever for?

SOPHUS. Well now, Helene, that's always been my own business
really—I paid for Dagmar's training with it! *(Quickly).* Promise me
that Dagmar shall never hear a word about it. My daughter is very
proud. It would make her ashamed of her father. You wouldn't want to
estrange father and daughter?

HELENE. Sophus—I can't understand it: you were the happiest of the
lot when you came in.

SOPHUS. I said: 'Long live the King of Denmark.'

HELENE. But that couldn't fail to give the impression that it was all
true!

SOPHUS. Oh no, it doesn't commit you to anything! It can never do any
harm to say: 'Long live the King!' There's mostly some reason for it,
too. A prince has been born—the King has died—long live the new
one—

HELENE. Sophus, all that doesn't matter. What's to be done now? Our
relations firmly believe they've won!

SOPHUS. They'll hardly get the money with this ticket. *(He starts to
clean the paper with a rubber.)*

HELENE. At this moment Asmus is strolling along Oster Street and
Peter is looking at the town-plan! Sophus, you must go to Peter and
Asmus right away and make a clean breast of it. Tell them the ticket
has lapsed–

SOPHUS. Ten years ago!

HELENE. You must pay them back–

SOPHUS. For the whole ten years?

HELENE. They'll get over it–it was only a gamble, not money earned for
honest work. Let it remain a gamble that failed!

SOPHUS. No, Helene, it's not a gamble any longer. Good fortune is
always taken very seriously. If you bury a loved one, you'll forget it in
time. But good luck that slips through your fingers will drag you to the
grave.

HELENE. Are you going to keep up the deception?

SOPHUS. It's my duty to! If I failed once, I must be on my guard a
second time!

HELENE. Surely you won't be able to—without the money, and you haven't got that?

SOPHUS. Would they get it from the lottery office now? No. The draw goes on for another fortnight yet.

HELENE. You propose to leave them a fortnight-

SOPHUS. And a fortnight after that the official list of winners will be published. No payments will be made till then. We shall have four weeks. Four weeks for them to revel in their dreams of grandeur—does that mean nothing?

HELENE. Sophus—you're joking again.

SOPHUS *(stops rubbing out)*. Ooh, I've cleaned a hole in it now! Right where the tens come in the date. I've rubbed out a whole ten years!— Who could see if there was a one or a nought there now?

HELENE. Surely you're not going to-

SOPHUS. Look at this—it really looks quite presentable. Fit for anyone to look at, isn't it? As if it had just been printed?

HELENE. You're not going to pretend that the old ticket is a new one?

SOPHUS. Well, at least it's clean. That's the main thing—for anything you carry in your pocket or your head. A solid foundation to build on! *(He puts the ticket carefully away in his pocket.)* Tell me, what was that about Brandstrup? He wants me to rent his second floor, is that it? What has he in mind?

HELENE. The rent to be paid at the end of each quarter.

SOPHUS. It's worth considering! *(He gets up.)*

HELENE. Where are you off to, Sophus?

SOPHUS. I'm gong to see if the flat is suitable for our changed circumstances.

HELENE. You're going to rent the second floor?

SOPHUS. It's the least we can do, if Asmus is going to buy a house in Oster Street and Peter is studying the town-plan. Pass me my coat out of the cupboard!

HELENE. Sophus, I really can't make out-

SOPHUS. What's so strange about it? Brandstrup is letting me his splendid flat-have I shown him my money?

HELENE. But you haven't any!

SOPHUS. Then he must have thought over his proposition all the more carefully. I don't want to keep him waiting. *Exit left.*

HELENE *follows him.*

BRANDSTRUP *peers through the glass door—then he enters silently. Behind him* MRS MACKESSPRANG. BRANDSTRUP *carries a bottle of champagne under each arm, and champagne glasses between his fingers.* MRS MACKESSPRANG *carries a heavy basket. Both tiptoe to the table, clear away the food standing on it and replace it from the abundant contents of the basket. Then they go off quickly.* PETER, MISS JUEL, ASMUS *and* OTTILIE *return.*

OTTILIE *(looking round)*. The birds have flown.

ASMUS. Not a sign of Sophus.

PETER. You're not trying to suggest that Sophus might take the ticket and go to Copenhagen–or to America?

ASMUS *(shrugging)*. Well, the ticket's worth eight-hundred-thousand crowns!

PETER. My brother is certainly no thief!

ASMUS. I don't believe he is, and I hope he's not. Anyway, he wouldn't be the first to have his head turned by a tidy sum of money. Human frailties are given by the Lord, like hair and fingernails. Don't forget the minister who betrayed his trust and the confidence of the king and embezzled millions of other people's money. And here it's not a matter of millions, but of eight-hundred-thousand crowns. So you see, I'm not doing your brother any injustice–I'm putting him on the same footing as the minister!

PETER. Sophus doesn't lose his head.

ASMUS. That's not the impression I have.

PETER. He's just a steady civil servant!

ASMUS. No, there's a streak of fantasy in him. Just look at the way he worships Dagmar!

MISS JUEL *(by the table)*. Look: pheasant—champagne—pineapple!

PETER. What does it all mean?

OTTILIE. It's a fabulous supper!

ASMUS *(to PETER.)* There you are—he's got a streak of gluttony in him too. It confirms my belief that we must act now, before it's too late for Sophus and us! *(SOPHUS–in his dark coat–comes in from the left; surveying the others and the laden table in surprise.)* We've invited ourselves to your house, Sophus, and we want to stay the night with you.

SOPHUS *(by the table)*. Well, there's certainly enough for everyone!

PETER. That's what I call a real spread–I admire your appetite!

SOPHUS *(catching on—animated)*. I was on the very point of asking you round. I had the little celebration all ready–I was going to let you stay at home long enough to change into your best clothes. Look at me–I'm all dressed up ready!

MISS JUEL. I'll be back in ten minutes!

ASMUS. You stay here, auntie. In any case, it would take forty minutes. Before we sit down, Sophus, there's something Peter has to tell you.

PETER. I . . . can hardly bring myself to say it!

ASMUS. Then as the third male member of our lottery syndicate–

PETER *(bursts out)*. Sophus–we want to get the ticket from you!

ASMUS. More accurately: we feel it our duty to relieve you of the responsibility for the ticket, which today is worth a not inconsiderable sum of money. We will stay with you until the morning, then we'll accompany you to the savings bank. Then Peter, as the eldest, will take

charge of the ticket and keep it under his heaviest type-setting machine.
Does our suggestion meet with your approval?

PETER. It really makes me feel quite ashamed–after all, you are my
brother, Sophus!

ASMUS. Sophus can always refuse–he's the one with the ticket.

SOPHUS *(puts his hand into his pocket–lays the ticket on the table).*
I didn't make any fuss earlier in the evening, and you can sleep in your
own beds tonight: here is the ticket!

MISS JUEL *(snatching up the ticket).* My beautiful ticket–come and be
kissed!

OTTILIE. You'll spit out your cough-drop!

PETER. It's already got damp and crumpled!

ASMUS. Why did you tell us that you'd left it in the safe at the
savings bank?

SOPHUS. To protect the document from destruction–the sort of thing
Aunt Juel has just given us an example of. Wouldn't you all have
grabbed at the ticket in your first ecstasies and not let it go till it fell
under the table in worthless shreds? You've got over it a bit by now–
you've even started thinking out ways to keep your treasure safe. Under
Peter's type-setting machine–it'll be safe there till the Day of
Judgment!

PETER. Sophus, what a good chap you are!

ASMUS *(pats him on the head).* You know what you're doing all right—
eight-hundred-thousand crowns!

OTTILIE *(holding the ticket up to the light).* It's got a hole in it—here.
(Looking through it and laughing) Peep-bo, Asmus!

ASMUS *(examining it).* A good job it's in the date and not the number.
That would well and truly have put paid to our hopes!

PETER. No one is likely to deny that we are living in this year!

MISS JUEL. Anyway, the paper's all crumpled and rough!

PETER. You know nothing about it, Aunt Juel. Paper is part of a
printer's business. It's my job. That is best quality paper. My
newspaper is smooth—but the state prints on rough—it's more
appropriate!

ASMUS. We'll hand over the ticket in a sealed envelope to Peter. In four
week's time we three men will go to Copenhagen to collect the prize.

OTTILIE. To Copenhagen, without me–

ASMUS. Be quiet, Ottilie!

OTTILIE. You be quiet, Asmus!

ASMUS. I suggest we get on sealing it now. *(To* SOPHUS*)* Give us an
envelope, a light and sealing-wax.

SOPHUS *brings everything to the table.*

ASMUS. We have the ticket here! So strike a light, Ottilie! Aunt Juel,
hold the envelope! Do you see the ticket? Now I'll push it into this
strong envelope! Five seals—we'll put on one each.

In solemn silence PETER, MISS JUEL, *and* OTTILIE *fix on their seals.*

ASMUS *(counting).* One-two-three. *(Affixing his own).* Four-

SOPHUS *(sealing).* Rest in peace!

ASMUS. Five!

MISS JUEL *(with tears in her eyes).* Yes, it's every bit as solemn as a funeral!

ASMUS *(gives* PETER *the envelope).* Keep it as faithfully as your brother has done until now!

OTTILIE. Asmus!

SOPHUS *(clapping his hands).* Now the serious business is over, let's enjoy ourselves! Take your seats and let the corks pop!

They seat themselves noisily, the corks fly out of the two bottles. DAGMAR *appears through the glass door.*

DAGMAR *(amazed).* Whatever does all this–whoever thought–*(At the table–to* SOPHUS*)* Are you serving all this for me?

MISS JUEL. Pheasant!

OTTILIE. Pineapple!

ASMUS. Champagne!

PETER. You're a rich girl now!

DAGMAR. I–am rich??

SOPHUS. Aren't you glad?

DAGMAR. I don't know–

SOPHUS *(hugging her).* You shall come to no harm. That's the stake I've gambled for all of us. Now I really do feel like staking everything on a gamble!

HELENE *has come in left, and is watching apprehensively.*

ACT TWO

A round pavilion in choice baroque style on MAGNUSSEN'S *estate. The wide French window opens upon a prospect of the park: a well-mown lawn stretches away, bounded by shrubberies at whose edges white statues mark the entrance to bright gravel walks. In the room, to left and right, sofas, small armchairs, low tables. The squares of the walls covered with mirrors. Above a rocking-chair hangs a large photograph of the king. Small doors right and left down stage.*

MAGNUSSEN *the brewer stands in the centre: his large body is in white trousers and a white silk shirt; on the breast of this shirt the insignia of an order.*

At one of the low tables sits the stunted figure of LUNDBERG, *the book-keeper, who is writing at* MAGNUSSEN'S *dictation.*

MAGNUSSEN *(as he dictates hammering his right fist into the palm of left hand).* I, Jochum Magnussen, brewer by appointment to His Majesty the King—make over by deed of gift—

LUNDBERG *(starting).* —gift?!

MAGNUSSEN. —gift! *(A* FOOTMAN *comes in from the back, bringing a newspaper which he lays down on the small table down stage right.* MAGNUSSEN *notices him.)* Call my son Axel!

FOOTMAN *leaves at the back.*

MAGNUSSEN. Where had I got to?

LUNDBERG *(reading).* I, Jochum Magnussen, brewer by appointment to His Majesty the King, make over by deed of gift—

MAGNUSSEN. —to Peter Möller, printer, the piece of land adjoining the brewery. In return Peter Möller undertakes—

LUNDBERG. —Peter Möller undertakes—

MAGNUSSEN. —to begin at once with the erection of a building on it!—A new piece of paper, Lundberg! *(Dictating)* I, Jochum Magnussen, brewer by appointment to His Majesty the King, make over by deed of gift—

LUNDBERG *(starts again).* —gift?!

MAGNUSSEN. —by deed of gift to the firm of Asmus and Ottilie Exner my house in the middle of Oster Street. In return the firm of Asmus and Ottilie Exner undertakes—

LUNDBERG. —Exner undertakes—

MAGNUSSEN. —to begin immediately with the conversion of two storeys into shops! Now type that out on two separate sheets and wait in the next room—with pen and ink ready for my signature!

LUNDBERG *leaves left.*

AXEL *comes in from the back.*

AXEL. Did you wish to speak to me, papa?

MAGNUSSEN. Sit down, my boy! You won't mind if I keep on the move? If I don't I shall burst like a boiler without a safety-valve!

AXEL. Either we both stand or we sit together. I can't imagine how we can have a serious talk otherwise. Or isn't it important? In that case—*(he makes as if to leave.)*

MAGNUSSEN. I'll sit down—and I'll burst. Just as you please, my boy! It is important. Otherwise I wouldn't bother with such ridiculous performances!

AXEL. You're the one who is giving a formal garden-party with plenty to drink and gramophone records.

MAGNUSSEN. I intend—to get engaged!

AXEL. You've got yourself overheated, papa.

MAGNUSSEN. Not in order to give you a second mother—or myself any pleasure—but as a matter of business!

AXEL. You know how little interest I take in—

MAGNUSSEN. You will this time! There's an important item in it for your attention. I've got something arranged for you!

AXEL. I'm not even curious.

MAGNUSSEN. A whole shower of money has fallen on the town. Money paid out by the state—so it's as safe as houses!

AXEL. Safe even from you?

MAGNUSSEN *(grinning).* Are you beginning to catch on? *(AXEL shrugs).* I'm after the money the Möllers and their partners won in the lottery! *(AXEL looks up.)* I'm not letting it go! I'll stick to the scent like a retriever and not let up till the game is in the bag!

AXEL *(controlling himself).* Explain your plan to me.

MAGNUSSEN. I've invited the five winners to this party.

AXEL. Are you intending to rob them behind a hedge in the garden?

MAGNUSSEN *(shaking his head).* They haven't got their money yet— it won't be paid out for another month!

AXEL. Then what's the point of inviting them today?

MAGNUSSEN. Today we shall make the contracts! But you don't understand these things. Anyway, that's how I shall make sure of three out of the five shares. That leaves two outstanding. Of these my fiancée will bring me-

AXEL. You sound as if you were engaged already!

MAGNUSSEN. You can consider it as good as done! That leaves the remaining fifth.

AXEL. How do you propose to collect that?

MAGNUSSEN. That's where you come in! One of them is some sort of clerk—at the savings bank, I believe—he must be a funny chap. He's given away the whole lot of his winnings to his daughter!

AXEL *(between his teeth).* Very funny.

MAGNUSSEN. And it's up to you, Axel, to hook the girl with the cash. Then we'll have the lot in our pockets—and it won't be sticky with the sweat of our brows! Yes, my lad, I've got what it takes to take what they've got!

AXEL. I shan't be getting engaged.

MAGNUSSEN *(taken aback).* Why not?

AXEL. Because the girl is as rich as I am.

MAGNUSSEN *(flabbergasted).* Because? Because? What on earth?

AXEL. I have sworn only to marry a poor girl.

MAGNUSSEN. Have you been in the cellar drinking a drop too much of the ale?

AXEL. Let that be my last word on the subject. I don't interfere in your affairs, either.

MAGNUSSEN *(annoyed).* It is my affair, my lad!

AXEL. You're going too far!

MAGNUSSEN. You'll be engaged to the girl by six o'clock!

AXEL. Not even by twelve o'clock!

MAGNUSSEN. Very well, then I'll need to give you a bit of help!

AXEL *(roused)*. One ill-chosen word from you, papa–

MAGNUSSEN. Not another word until six. But then I must ask you not to make your father and the young lady look silly!

He leaves down right. AXEL *storms out into the park.*

Through the centre door come SOPHUS, HELENE, DAGMAR, PETER, MISS JUEL, ASMUS, *and* OTTILIE—*dressed up in their Sunday best. They gaze about them in astonished awe.*

OTTILIE *(steps forward—looks upwards)*. The chandelier!

PETER *(crossing to the wall—feeling)*. The mirrors!

ASMUS *(sliding across the floor)*. The marble!

MISS JUEL *(beneath the photograph)*. The King! *(Once more a reverent silence.)*

PETER. Have you nothing to say, Sophus?

SOPHUS. Where can Mr Jochum Magnussen be? *(They all look at him in alarm.)* Are you afraid to look at him? He won't eat us. I can't believe that that's the purpose of his invitation.

ASMUS. I must admit the magnificence of these surroundings makes me feel rather uncomfortable.

OTTILIE. Your first moment of weakness, Asmus!

PETER. I can't rid myself of a certain sense of oppression, either.

MISS JUEL. It makes me feel thoroughly dizzy. I'd like best to sit down.

SOPHUS. How do you feel, Helene?

HELENE. It's no good asking me about anything!

SOPHUS. Then I shall turn to Dagmar, who is unscathed by this shimmering magic. Or are you trembling?

DAGMAR. Not because everything is strange and beautiful.

SOPHUS. Then I shan't disturb the rest of you in your humility. Kneel down before what you can't help yourselves worshipping. But I'll help to raise you up from the dust, if you forget to stand up again. You can conquer with your little finger, if your opponent has a weak spot. Merely to be on the attack is to be half way to defeat—you shall see that it's a dangerous game for a giant to make fun of dwarfs!

MAGNUSSEN *comes in from the right.*

MAGNUSSEN *(surprised)*. Who are you?

SOPHUS. Your guests, who have arrived—the Möllers!

MAGNUSSEN. Which of you is Miss Juel?

MISS JUEL *(taking refuge behind Sophus)*. Oh no! My tablets!

SOPHUS *(leading her over to Magnussen)*. You have the honour of making the acquaintance of our Aunt Juel. I am Sophus Möller.

MAGNUSSEN. Later!

SOPHUS. And this gentleman is my brother, Peter Möller, the printer.

MAGNUSSEN. Later!

SOPHUS. Allow me to present Asmus and Ottilie Exner, my brother-in-law and my sister, who are in the cotton and woollen goods trade.

MAGNUSSEN. Later!

SOPHUS. This is my wife and my only daugher, Dagmar.

MAGNUSSEN. Later! *(Remembering and correcting himself)* Which is your daughter? *(In front of* DAGMAR*)* So you're the daughter. Wait a moment. *(He goes to the door at the back, claps his hands and calls).* Axel!

DAGMAR *(to* SOPHUS*).* Father—I'm going straight out into the park—it's too airless here in the pavilion!

MAGNUSSEN. Where are you going?

DAGMAR. I'd like to look at your lovely park, Mr Magnussen.

MAGNUSSEN. Yes, yes, go along—all of you go and have a look at the park. You'll find something to drink, and the gramophone will be playing. *(To* MISS JUEL*)* No, Miss Juel—I must ask you to stay here!

MISS JUEL. I couldn't walk in any case—my legs are too wobbly!

SOPHUS. Aunt Juel will have to take a little rest. Come on, auntie, I'll settle you in the rocking-chair—it'll feel as if you're cradled in heaven! *(To the others)* We'll disappear.

Except for MISS JUEL *and* MAGNUSSEN, *all go off into the park.* MAGNUSSEN *closes the French window—fans himself with his hand.*

MAGNUSSEN. First I'll have to get my breath back a bit.

MISS JUEL. Your house is full of visitors.

MAGNUSSEN. Yes—quite a collection!

MISS JUEL. The park's swarming with them. We're not in the way, are we?

MAGNUSSEN *(bursts out laughing).* How delightfully you put it! Enough to make a cat laugh. No, you're not in the way—only the others could manage to be in the way at the moment. But I wouldn't advise anyone to try butting in here just now!

MISS JUEL. Do you like being here alone? *(Goes to get up from the rocking-chair.)*

MAGNUSSEN *(pushes her back—laughing again).* The words drop from your lips like pearls—one need only pick them up—and one has the string in one's hand! Yes, I like being alone here—with you!

MISS JUEL. That's very flattering for me, Mr Magnussen!

MAGNUSSEN *(at a loss).* Now—you must say something again.

MISS JUEL. I've—often seen you in the distance, Mr Magnussen.

MAGNUSSEN. That's all the confounded coachman's fault! The pace the man drives at—I've told him about a million times! But I've had enough—the fellow'll get his notice, and before the evening's out, at that!

MISS JUEL. Because you haven't noticed me, little Miss Juel, as you went dashing past in your carriage?

MAGNUSSEN. Then are we—not to dismiss our coachman? *(Already the hulking man is going down on his knees.)* Is he to drive us at full gallop to the registry office?! *(Resting his hands on the arms of the rocking-chair, he tips* MISS JUEL *forwards—and she lands on his breast.)*

SOPHUS, *carrying a glass of wine, pushes open the French window. The sound of the gramophone blares in.*

SOPHUS. Auntie—you really must try it—Rhine wine with peaches— *(He lapses into silence.)*

MISS JUEL. Sophus—I'm falling—give me some firm ground under my feet!

MAGNUSSEN. We've no need of a firmer foundation in this case!·

SOPHUS *(behind* MAGNUSSEN*).* The first glass to your new-found happiness, with an accompaniment of gramophone music! *(He drains his glass.)*

MISS JUEL. What are you two up to with me?

MAGNUSSEN *(has started to lead* MISS JUEL *off at the back).* The bridegroom—

SOPHUS *(following).* And the incorruptible witness!

The three go off. DAGMAR *comes in quickly.* AXEL *enters slowly.*

DAGMAR *(breathless).* What does—that mean?

AXEL. My papa is providing a striking example of the fact that my attitude is the right one.

DAGMAR. To what?

AXEL. It leads to painful situations when money plays a part in love. Or can you imagine anything more ridiculous than those two out there?

DAGMAR. Your father didn't even know Aunt Juel half an hour ago-

AXEL. -but he's always been on the best of terms with money!

DAGMAR *(haltingly).* Is your father—marrying Aunt Juel—because Aunt Juel—has just—won some money?

AXEL. Do you think he'd let anyone else snatch anything as tempting as that from under his nose?

DAGMAR. Mr Axel—you must do me—do us—a service!

AXEL. Since you have become a rich young lady, I am no more than your cavalier. I am at your command, dear lady!

DAGMAR. Don't talk like that! Not now. Now I'm worried to death about Peter, about Asmus and Ottilie!

AXEL. Why are you putting your own heads into the noose? You could have refused the invitation to come here.

DAGMAR. My relations weren't keen to come—but my father insisted.

AXEL. He's dazzled by his sudden wealth.

DAGMAR. He has given it all to me, so he's as poor as he was before.

AXEL. Then he has definite plans in mind.

DAGMAR. Have a talk with him. Point out the dangers threatening us here. We must leave. Something terrible is bound to happen if we don't turn back. Already Aunt Juel is–

MAGNUSSEN *appears in the centre door–leading* PETER MÖLLER *by the hand. Seeing* DAGMAR *and* AXEL, *he pushes him aside;* PETER *disappears again.*

DAGMAR *goes quickly past* MAGNUSSEN *out into the park.*

MAGNUSSEN *(to* AXEL*)*. How far have you got?

AXEL. Kindly shut the door, if you want to exchange confidences with me.

MAGNUSSEN *(slams the door)*. None of your fooling—I'm your father. I've already shown you the way to set about such matters— have I got engaged or haven't I got engaged?

AXEL. You should know best. At the moment I'm only interested in the business side of it.

MAGNUSSEN *(stares at him in astonishment)*. What—are you interested in?

AXEL. I require a guarantee that the final accounts will balance up without any deficit.

MAGNUSSEN. Are you—my book-keeper?

AXEL. Your business partner in the matter of Möller and associates. You're trying to force me to co-operate, so I'd be glad if you'd convince me that you can bring it off. I don't come in on a deal unless it's worthwhile.

MAGNUSSEN. Aren't you satisfied with the sample I gave you by the way I hooked the Juel woman?

AXEL. But you won't be able to marry Peter Möller or Asmus and Ottilie Exner.

MAGNUSSEN. I won't, thank God! It would be asking a bit much of anyone to undergo that for each of the five shares!

AXEL. You'll put a more subtle noose round Peter Möller's neck?

MAGNUSSEN. You young scoundrel—what a way to put it! Peter Möller is going to build—he needs a piece of ground for the building—and that's what I'm going to give him!

AXEL. You're giving it to him?!

MAGNUSSEN. I have the place behind the brewery where the bottles are dumped.

AXEL. And he is to build on the rubbish-heap?

MAGNUSSEN. He wants to—and he'll have to! Castles in the air shoot up like lightning on ground that costs nothing. He builds his money into it—he overreaches himself—and he'll do that all right!—he can't carry on—he's at his last gasp—then I jump in and finish the building: a new brewery adjoining my brewery, so that beer may flow more abundantly in Denmark!

AXEL *(after a pause)*. How are you proposing to pick the pockets of Asmus and Ottilie Exner?

MAGNUSSEN. I'm making a present of my house in Oster Street to Asmus and Ottilie Exner!

AXEL. That's not a house—it's a delapidated pigsty!

MAGNUSSEN. And so it needs to be rebuilt. Large, bright rooms in two storeys. Make a nice restaurant. They'll be tapping my beer-barrels there!

AXEL. But surely the Exners aren't in the catering trade?

MAGNUSSEN. Oh, they'll never move in. They'll get the establishment about half built—you leave the calculations to me!—then I take over. They'll take comfort from Peter Möller, who didn't build his way to heaven either!

AXEL. You're—a genius—

MANGUSSEN. ́Well, I don't just sit around!

AXEL. —in your own way!

MAGNUSSEN. It wouldn't do for us all to be alike!

AXEL. Anyone who wanted to keep up with you would need the help of the Lord at least! Otherwise I can't imagine there being any sort of fight at all.

MAGNUSSEN. No more can I, Axel! Anyone who tried to block my path would have to be enormous—I'd trample down a giant if one suddenly stood in my way! Heaven help anyone who doesn't get out of my way when I make a leap forward!

AXEL *(by the door)*. There's your Peter Möller lurking outside the door.

MAGNUSSEN *(still bawling)*. Send him in!

AXEL *goes off*—MAGNUSSEN *mops his brow.*

PETER *(eventually showing himself in—picking up the newspaper from the low table—clearing his throat)*. The Copenhagen paper!—Yes, now there's a real paper for you! The lay-out, the advertisements— folk like us just can't compete!

MAGNUSSEN. But the future might bring it!

PETER. Exactly my sentiments! The future might bring it. It **must** bring it, Mr Magnussen! *(Goes up close to him, fingers the decoration on his chest.)* Do you see what I mean? We must have a big newspaper in the town. With political news and articles. We must be able to read about events throughout the length and breadth of the country. What's the King doing at this minute? Where is the Princess dancing this evening? Do we know a word about it? Nothing! You have to get your information from Copenhagen—I can't provide it for you. The town needs a big newspaper just as much as it does sewers or the fire-brigade!

MAGNUSSEN. And you need a sizeable printing-works for it!

PETER. A big printing-works! Cheese-paring won't get one anywhere. A newspaper building has to make an impression. It must give the town its stamp and impress, as it were, and provide a reservoir of local talent!

MAGNUSSEN. Have you been looking out for a building-site?

PETER. I have been studying the town-plan. There's a great choice of sites all over the place. *(Laughing)* Why, the whole world's a building-site, come to think of it!

MAGNUSSEN *(joining in)*. True enough—the whole world's one!

PETER. Wherever you look—

MAGNUSSEN. —you see building-sites! A printing-works can be put up anywhere—you don't read the paper right on the spot!

PETER. You're right again!

MAGNUSSEN. Get hold of the space behind my brewery!

PETER. That would be too much to aim at!

MAGNUSSEN. Free and gratis! After all, I'm doing business with a relation, aren't I? *(PETER stares at him.)* I'll make a present of the site to you. You clear away the rubbish that's accumulated there—level off the ground—and then up goes your building—up and up, until you're overcome when you're standing outside your own building!

PETER *(stammering)*. I—can—build—

MAGNUSSEN. You must build—the first shovelful of earth will be flying tomorrow!

PETER *(whispering)*. I must even—

MAGNUSSEN. The contract signed and sealed!

PETER. I can print a morning and an evening edition!

MAGNUSSEN. And a midday special in between!

PETER. I can print the classics—

MAGNUSSEN. And cookery-books and school-books and account-books. Your presses will be running day and night!

PETER *(pinching himself)*. Am I really Peter Möller? Well, am I? *(Turning to a mirror and putting out his tongue)* Can you see me, Peter? Do you recognize me? Peter Möller, proprietor of the printing-works—and neighbour of Jochum Magnussen? *(To* MAGNUSSEN*)* Good morning, neighbour, I trust you slept well?

MAGNUSSEN *(drawing PETER to him)*. Call me Jochum, my dear friend—it will make the formalities easier. Come with me—Lundberg is waiting!

He almost carries him off, back right. Exeunt.

SOPHUS *and* HELENE *come in from the back.*

HELENE. Axel keeps on talking to you, and looking deadly serious about it. And now you come dashing in here!

SOPHUS. I want to congratulate Peter.

HELENE. On what?

SOPHUS. Jochum is giving him a building-site at the back of his brewery.

HELENE. Will Peter accept it?

SOPHUS. He won't put up much resistance.

HELENE. Will Peter build there, too, then?

SOPHUS. As high as the church!

HELENE. How will he pay?

SOPHUS. Aren't all the wealthy people in the town gathered here?

HELENE. Is he to go round begging from the guests?

SOPHUS. Did he come with empty pockets?

HELENE. Yes, Sophus—he has nothing! Not a farthing to pay for such grand schemes!

SOPHUS. What about the building-site? Isn't that worth something?

HELENE. It's worthless, because he can't build on it. He'll have to refuse the gift—you must make him. Or we shall all have to hide our heads in shame.

SOPHUS. I carry my head upright on my shoulders, the way I was made. Has any one of us done anything wrong? We didn't gate-crash our way in here. It's an undeniable fact that Jochum Magnussen sent us invitation cards with gold edges!

HELENE. The others were against accepting.

SOPHUS. They were wrong. It would have been cowardice that would not have plucked us a single leaf from the tree of fame!

HELENE. Mr Magnussen believes we are rich—and we aren't!

SOPHUS. If that's how he's made his bed, he'll have to sleep on it. Everyone makes his bed the way he likes it. I have the courage to bear other people's faith in me. If he's worshipping a golden calf, then he'll get his punishment. I'm taking no hand in the whole business—but hundreds of hands are stretched out to us. I only propose to shake them—and you just watch what falls out of them! *(PETER returns left.)* All fixed up?

PETER. Do you know about it?

SOPHUS. The site at the back of the brewery!

PETER. Might have been made for my printing-works!

SOPHUS. Helene's delighted about it.

PETER. I'm on intimate terms with Jochum.

SOPHUS. Won't Asmus be jealous?

PETER. Oh, Jochum wants to see him.

SOPHUS. About the house in Oster Street?

PETER. Do you know everything?

SOPHUS. Yes—Axel let me into all the secrets!

HELENE. Peter—

SOPHUS. We mustn't keep it to ourselves. Jochum's infinite generosity mustn't be hushed up for a second. We must trumpet it forth! Come on out into the park: we'll let them know that you, Peter, have become the owner of the ground behind the brewery, and that you're going to build on it. Then we'll listen to the echoes it raises! *(The three go off. ASMUS and OTTILIE EXNER enter.)*

ASMUS. Peter must have misunderstood. There can't possibly be any question of a present and of the house in Oster Street.

OTTILIE. Peter has got the ground at the back of the brewery, and the gift is all set down in writing!

ASMUS. Then Peter's a lucky devil.

OTTILIE. But not a bit luckier than you or me or Aunt Juel—we've all won the first prize.

ASMUS. I'd be in a dither if I had to sign anything at the moment. The letters would swim in front of my eyes.

OTTILIE. So we'll go in together and place the firm of Asmus and Ottilie Exner, Cotton and Woollen Goods, at the disposal of Jochum Magnussen. *(MAGNUSSEN enters left.)*

MAGNUSSEN. Where is—

OTTILIE. Asmus, do you hear how anxious he is to see us?

MAGNUSSEN. Only one—the man! I can't reach an understanding with a woman!

ASMUS. Be quiet, Ottilie!

OTTILIE. Off with you, Asmus!

MAGNUSSEN *and* ASMUS *go off left.* MISS JUEL *enters from the back.*

MISS JUEL. Wherever's Jochum all this time?

OTTILIE. He has to attend to all his guests, auntie.

MISS JUEL *(almost in tears).* What sort of engagement party is that? Is this the way the dreams turn out when they come true?

OTTILIE. They've turned out splendidly for Peter and Asmus!

MISS JUEL. What are they all up to out there in the garden with Peter? They're crowding round him calling out numbers. They're not offering him money, are they?

SOPHUS *enters.*

SOPHUS *(to OTTILIE).* Is Asmus with him?

OTTILIE. Behind closed doors!

SOPHUS. Then don't disturb them!

MISS JUEL. Sophus, tell me what's going on. There was I, alone and God-forsaken on the lawn, and Peter was the centre of attraction!

SOPHUS. Then Ottilie had better go and give him some competition! Ottilie, you're part of the firm on whose behalf Asmus is just accepting the house in Oster Street. You run into the garden and get together the money to convert two floors of it into shops. They'll shower it on you— for when a Jochum Magnussen gives presents, there must be more to be got hold of than in the Emperor of China's treasure-house!

OTTILIE *leaves.*

MISS JUEL. Jochum hasn't even given me a bunch of flowers.

SOPHUS. He can't be bothered with trivialities. The whole park's yours. Find Helene and pick some flowers together. It'll pass the time for you, and in the end you'll look charming.

MISS JUEL *leaves.* ASMUS *staggers in from the left.*

SOPHUS. Are you all right, Asmus?

ASMUS *(dumbfounded).* The house in Oster Street. Centrally situated. Two floors converted into a shop. Twenty arc-lamps!

SOPHUS. Thirty, Asmus!

ASMUS. I won't let fifty scare me off!

SOPHUS. Sixty, Asmus!

ASMUS. There are illuminations all along Oster Street. The sign of our firm—Asmus and Ottilie Exner, Cotton and Woollen Goods—will shine like the sun!

SOPHUS. One can't ask for more, Asmus! They're going to buy us the sun. It doesn't shine brightly enough—it must be brought closer to many of God's creatures!

ASMUS *leaves.* SOPHUS *now shuts the garden door—takes up his stance by the rocking-chair.* MAGNUSSEN *comes in from the left, jauntily swinging his arms in the exuberance of his consciousness of victory.*

SOPHUS. —It keeps you young to get plenty of exercise.

MAGNUSSEN *(pausing—looking SOPHUS up and down).* You're— the one with the daughter!

SOPHUS. So you haven't forgotten that?

MAGNUSSEN. I forget nothing. There's room in my head for everything. Like a whirring machine, I register everything—that might come in useful. All the waste is flung out!

SOPHUS. Someone else will be clearing them away!

SOPHUS. Yes, a syndicate is already being formed to clear it and to finance the printing-works.

MAGNUSSEN. Whatever nonsense is this you're talking?

SOPHUS. They're offering Peter Möller all the capital he wants.

MAGNUSSEN. Who?

SOPHUS. Your guests.

MAGNUSSEN. Where?

SOPHUS. In the park.

MAGNUSSEN. Offering—Peter Möller?!

SOPHUS. And the firm of Asmus and Ottilie Exner for the shop in Oster Street.

MAGNUSSEN. The firm—of Asmus and Ottilie Exner?

SOPHUS. Cotton and Woollen Goods.

MAGNUSSEN. On my plot of land—in my house in Oster Street?!

SOPHUS. On your plot of land that you made over by deed of gift to Peter Möller—and in your house in Oster Street that you made over to Asmus and Ottilie Exner.

MAGNUSSEN *(reeling)*. Damnation! The devil take the lot of them!

SOPHUS. Gently now, Mr Magnussen, you'll do yourself no good.

MAGNUSSEN. Have they started giving you credit on the strength of .my gifts?! Am I launching you on your trip to Eldorado?! Am I, Jochum Magnussen, brewer by appointment to the King, to be cheated of my reckoning and draw a blank out of the crock of gold?! *(He looks about him almost helplessly.)*

SOPHUS *(leads him to the rocking-chair)*. Get your breath back, Mr Magnussen—don't excite yourself.

MAGNUSSEN. It's enough to choke—

SOPHUS. It's too soon for that yet.

MAGNUSSEN. Are **you** going to get my land and my house back for me?!

SOPHUS. It's up to you to decide that.

MAGNUSSEN. Out there the stock-market is in full swing—and I'm sitting here powerless!

SOPHUS. You must spare yourself. The difficulties are not insurmountable.

MAGNUSSEN. But they're piling up horribly!

SOPHUS. If you concentrate on one point, you'll master the situation. No venture was ever lost that was tackled without tied hands.

MAGNUSSEN. How are my hands tied?!

SOPHUS *(rocking him gently in the chair)*. They're too full—you have too much business in hand.

MAGNUSSEN. I own the biggest brewery in Denmark!

SOPHUS. Now do you see where the snag is?

MAGNUSSEN. And I want to expand still further!

SOPHUS. That you must—and you shall, Mr Magnussen!

MAGNUSSEN. Is anyone thinking of trying to stop me?

SOPHUS. Your own worst enemy is rocking in this chair!

MAGNUSSEN. Well, keep it still, then!

SOPHUS *(continues to rock him)*. It has become quite clear to me that you are your own enemy. Even your strength has its limits. Who's winning the game out in the garden now? The others—if you don't stop dissipating your energies in time. The brewery and all these new transactions—even a giant like Jochum Magnussen won't be able to cope with it!

The merriment and tumult from the garden comes nearer.

MAGNUSSEN. They're damn cheerful!

SOPHUS. They seem to have reached agreement. They're coming!

MAGNUSSEN *(extricating himself from the rocking-chair)*. I won't be
  defeated! I'll shout the lot of them down! We're only just
  beginning! This is my house—and I'm master here–and I'll forbid
  whatever I like! Everything we arranged is revoked! I'll free my hands!
  Who wants to have the brewery?! *(*SOPHUS *holds out his hand.)*
MAGNUSSEN. What do you want?
SOPHUS. What you are offering.
MAGNUSSEN. What do you know about beer?!
SOPHUS. All that a director of your brewery needs to know!
MAGNUSSEN *(looks at him closely)*. You are a director—on one
  condition!
SOPHUS. Collateral?
MAGNUSSEN. Your daughter as my son's wife!
SOPHUS *(clasps his hand)*. And may God bless them!
MAGNUSSEN *(triumphantly)*. The last fifth! I've got it! Is any of it
  missing?! Is there any gap between one and five? Come along now, and
  pay the piper all you've got—I'll be graciously pleased to accept it!
  (Laughs thunderously.)

*The French window is flung wide open before the following procession;
at its head the liveried* FOOTMAN, *carrying the blaring gramophone—
behind him* MISS JUEL, PETER, ASMUS *and* OTTILIE EXNER,
*garlanded and decked with wreaths and flowers. At a slight distance
on the right* AXEL—*on the left* HELENE *and* DAGMAR. *The crowd
of guests brings up the rear. The noise of the gramophone and the
approaching procession dies away.*

MAGNUSSEN *(with a magniloquent gesture)*. Are you looking for
  me?! Here I am—Jochum Magnussen, brewer by appointment to the
  King! All of you: look at me, listen to me! Axel, come over here!
  (He makes no move.) There stands my son Axel! Look at him! At
  present he is standing alone–*(looking for* DAGMAR—*beckoning
  to her)*—but in a moment—
AXEL *(in his great embarrassment had hidden his face behind the
  newspaper. Now looks up–calls out)*. Stop! Listen! I must read this out
  to you! *(Stands up on a chair–reads.)* We understand that the first prize
  of eight-hundred-thousand crowns in the draw for the state lottery this
  year has remained in the capital, where it has been won by the
  proprietor of a slaughter-house. We offer the lucky prizewinner our
  congratulations—but venture to hope that meat prices may at last come
  down! *(Astonished silence reigns.)*
PETER *(looks at* ASMUS*)*. Asmus—
ASMUS *(to* MISS JUEL*)*. Aunt Juel—
MISS JUEL *(to* OTTILIE*)*. Ottilie—
OTTILIE. Our lottery prize—
AXEL *(flourishing the newspaper—laughing)*. Gone to a butcher!

THE GUESTS. In Copenhagen!!

MAGNUSSEN *(to* SOPHUS—*purple).* I demand an explanation!!

SOPHUS *(calmly).* Give me the Copenhagen paper! *(He smooths it out.)* Right enough. Word for word—I had the announcement put in myself. It's my notice. I sent it—to nip any sordid suspicions in the bud. They were bound to crop up, weren't they? Mighn't they even now come buzzing out like a swarm of wasps—and distress our dear Jochum Magnussen with spiteful slanders? This Jochum Magnussen, who has made such haste to get engaged to our aunt Juel—who has presented my brother Peter Möller with the building-site at the back of the brewery—who has given my brother-in-law and my sister, Asmus and Ottilie Exner, the house in Oster Street—who is trying to keep a firm hand on his son Axel—who has made me a director of his brewery! Is it to be said that this man, Jochum Magnussen, has been concocting this or that or the other scheme, simply to get his hands on the eight hundred thousand crown prize?! I'll protect Jochum Magnussen by holding this newspaper in front of him—and whoever casts the first stone at him will hit this brazen wall of paper!

MAGNUSSEN *(clenching his fists—grinding his teeth).* Even if they haven't won anything—there's nothing I can say against that!

ACT THREE

The large living-room in SOPHUS MÖLLER'S *house. New, solid furniture—grand piano. High windows at the back—door right and left. The chandelier shines with the light of a thousand candles. A neat* MAID *enters from the left, crosses the room and opens the door on the right.*

MAID. The director will see you now.

LUNDBERG *comes in with a briefcase. The* MAID *goes off left.* LUNDBERG *opens the briefcase and takes out some papers.* SOPHUS *enters from the left.*

SOPHUS. Here as late as this, Lundberg?

LUNDBERG *tentatively takes* SOPHUS' *hand and bows low before him.*

SOPHUS. Have you brought some letters for me?

LUNDBERG. From Mr Magnussen.

SOPHUS. Why to my private house?

LUNDBERG. Because you're travelling to Copenhagen tonight, Mr Möller.

SOPHUS. Did Mr Magnussen make such a careful note of the precise time?

LUNDBERG. He has a square of cardboard hanging above his desk with the date written in red!

SOPHUS *(after a short pause).* I'm not going to Copenhagen.

LUNDBERG. Not going to Copenhagen, Mr Möller?!

SOPHUS. No, Lundberg. I've changed my plans. Put your papers away again. I can't take anything to Copenhagen. I shall be at the brewery tomorrow morning as usual. Good night, Lundberg.

LUNDBERG *(shaking his head, he puts everything back into his briefcase).* Good night, Mr Möller. *(Exit right.)*

DAGMAR *(enters from the right—putting her arms round his neck).* Are you a good father?

SOPHUS. The questions you ask—

DAGMAR. Are you?

SOPHUS. Judge for yourself.

DAGMAR. Aren't you then?

SOPHUS. Have you ever had cause to doubt it?

DAGMAR. Will you take me to Copenhagen with you tonight?

SOPHUS. Is that the evidence on which you're going to condemn me?

DAGMAR. If you say no!

SOPHUS. No.

DAGMAR. Why are you refusing my request?

SOPHUS. Because–I'm not going myself!

DAGMAR. You're staying at home?

SOPHUS. There's too much work at the brewery for me to get away. Lundberg was here only a few minutes ago. Magnussen thinks my presence is essential.

DAGMAR. Then let me go with Peter and Asmus!

SOPHUS. If Peter and Asmus go, you shall go with them. I promise you that!

DAGMAR. A promise is a promise! *(Kisses him.)*

SOPHUS. To Copenhagen with Peter and Asmus–but only—

DAGMAR *(running off left).* I'm off to pack ready to go to Copenhagen!

HELENE *(enters left; worried).* The child's getting ready to go to Copenhagen.

SOPHUS. I had to let her.

HELENE. How is she supposed to be getting to Copenhagen?

SOPHUS. She was so keen to go.

HELENE. Who is she to travel with?

SOPHUS. Yes–who *is* going?

HELENE. At this time of night?

SOPHUS. I'm not going.

HELENE. Neither are Peter and Asmus!

SOPHUS. Nobody—

HELENE. Sophus–I'm worried that the time has come when you'll have to make your confession to them.

SOPHUS *(with a sudden show of interest)*. About the worthless lottery ticket and the lost winnings?

HELENE. The money's being paid out tomorrow.

SOPHUS. You're wrong, Helene—it's not being paid out.

HELENE. Not to us–I know that. But Peter and Asmus and Aunt Juel and Ottilie are all worked up in anticipation. They haven't been sleeping for a fortnight.

SOPHUS. Yes–it's high time they got a proper night's rest again. I wouldn't want to be responsible for ruining their health.

HELENE. Do you believe it can possibly go off without an explosion?

SOPHUS. Why should they explode? Because this windfall isn't dropping into their laps? Are they misers who hoard up their money? I'm quite sure they wouldn't know what to do with all that extra money–so what good is it to them?

HELENE. I'm prepared to listen to you, Sophus–but you'll have a harder time with the others. *(She listens in the direction of the door.)*

SOPHUS. Who's that coming?

HELENE. It's Peter's step!

SOPHUS. I'll open the door to him!

HELENE *is about to hurry off left.*

SOPHUS. Aren't you going to stay?

HELENE. No, Sophus–I can't do it!

HELENE *leaves.* SOPHUS *goes off right—returns with* PETER.

PETER *is got up in peculiar fashion: he wears an antiquated, worn-out cloak; a cap is pulled low over his eyes; a long scarf wound round about him; he carries a brightly coloured carpet-bag.*

PETER. Well, Sophus, here we are!

SOPHUS *(staring at him)*. Have you taken leave of your senses?

PETER *(portentously)*. I'm travelling in disguise, Sophus. It took some thinking up, I can tell you!

SOPHUS. Have you got a job as a night-watchman?

PETER. I'm like the watchman who guards the town at night. And I'm guarding more. Our lottery-ticket! *(He gropes about in his cloak and at length produces a capacious leather case.)* Help youself, Sophus!

SOPHUS. I don't smoke.

PETER. No, no–just put your hand in!

SOPHUS *(pulls out the sealed envelope)*. What's all this supposed—

PETER *(chuckling)*. No-one would expect to find the treasure there. You wouldn't find a brand worth taking in the cigar-case of a man of my appearance. No pick-pocket would bother about it. Isn't that a cunning way to hide it, eh?

SOPHUS. You're a great chap, Peter, and no mistake!

PETER *(surveying SOPHUS)*. Aren't you going to get ready?

SOPHUS. No, Peter, I'm not.

PETER. You're putting off important matters to the last moment.

SOPHUS. You're right enough about that!

PETER *(taking out his watch)*. Do you think Asmus—

SOPHUS. There's Ottilie chattering–that means the firm is on its way!

SOPHUS *goes off right—returns with* ASMUS *and* OTTILIE. *He is wearing a tight-fitting black coat, black kid-gloves, top hat; carries a small case.*

ASMUS *(businesslike)*. Have you provided yourselves with some means of proving your identity? Have you got the sealed envelope? Are the seals unbroken? All right, then–off to the station. Eight-thirty. No time to lose!

SOPHUS. Asmus–go and stand beside Peter!

ASMUS. What's the point of doing that?

SOPHUS. Aren't you afraid of being stopped by the first policeman you meet in Copenhagen?

ASMUS. Why?

SOPHUS. Walking arm in arm in that get-up?

ASMUS. The opposite will happen. We shall travel separately. I'm going first class–you second–and Peter third. I deliberately chose these clothes, to make it impossible for anyone to realize we belong together. One person is always less likely to be noticed than several. We'll communicate by signs–perhaps an inconspicuous movement of the lower part of the left arm! *(He demonstrates–PETER practises it.)*

SOPHUS. You ought to have been a pair of detectives!

OTTILIE. Tell me, Sophus, doesn't Asmus look a picture? What will the fine ladies of Copenhagen think of him?

SOPHUS. My dear sister, you can put **that** worry right out of your mind!

ASMUS *(severely)*. Ottilie, the timetable!

OTTILIE *(hands it over)*. It's hard to say good-bye!

ASMUS. Brush my hat!

OTTILIE *(brushing it)*. With tears in my eyes! *(The* MAID *enters left.)*

SOPHUS. Was that the door-bell?

MAID. Yes, sir. *(Exit right.)*

PETER. Shan't we miss the train?

ASMUS. Are you going to receive a visitor now?

MAID *(at the door)*. Mrs Magnussen!

PETER. What on earth—

ASMUS. —can auntie want at a time like this?

AUNT JUEL *enters—elegantly dressed.*

AUNT JUEL *(surveying them in surprise through her lorgnette)*. Aren't you sitting in the night train to Copenhagen? It's high time! You asked me to come, Sophus–I suppose it's to keep Helene company while you're away.

ASMUS. Eight-fifteen!

PETER. The train leaves at eight-thirty!

ASMUS. We'll still just manage to jump on!

SOPHUS. It's twenty-five past eight, Asmus. You set your watch by St. John's church–and churches are always a bit behind the time.

ASMUS. Then we can't possibly catch the train now!

SOPHUS. Don't get excited about it–it would have no point if you did! Sit down, all of you–make yourselves as comfortable as you can. Would you like a cushion, auntie?

They all sit down—and stare at Sophus.

PETER *(faltering)*. But–the lottery money–is due tomorrow!

SOPHUS. Yes, Peter, that's true: the four weeks between the draw and the money being paid out to the winners are over.

ASMUS. The money can be collected tomorrow!

SOPHUS. It will be duly collected tomorrow, Asmus!

PETER. Without us—

ASMUS. Peter–myself–and you?!

SOPHUS. I assume–that the butcher in Copenhagen won't turn down the prize!

ASMUS *(dully)*. The butcher—

OTTILIE. The butcher—

SOPHUS. Simply in the interests of lower meat prices, it's highly desirable!

AUNT JUEL *(clapping her hands together)*. Why–it was all in the paper!

SOPHUS. And newspapers never lie. You ask Peter.

ASMUS *(coming to life–abruptly to* PETER*)*. Have you lost the ticket?

PETER *digs out the cigar-case.*

ASMUS. You can keep your cigars!

PETER *(lays the envelope on the table)*. Check the seals!

ASMUS. There were five–one for each of us!

SOPHUS. Open it!

ASMUS. You all agree? *(They all nod mechanically.)* Then I'll open it! Here's the ticket, safe and intact!

SOPHUS. Intact?

ASMUS. Just as it was on the day we had our little sealing ceremony. It's even got the same hole in it!

OTTILIE. Yes, it did have a hole in it!

ASMUS. Even the hole is intact!

PETER. It was in the year of the date of issue.

SOPHUS. As round as a nought, where there ought to be one–to represent the decade we're living in!

ASMUS. A hole can't take ten years off the date!

SOPHUS. Suppose the hole is a nought, and always was–and the butcher has the proper ten on his coupon?

PETER. Then–we're ten years short of the first prize?

SOPHUS *(takes the ticket and tears it up)*. The ticket is ten years old. So much waste paper!–I've not been backing it for ten years!

AUNT JUEL *(dissolving)*. A cushion, Ottilie!

SOPHUS. Look after auntie! Were you about to say something, Peter?

PETER. We–haven't won anything?

SOPHUS. Not a thing!

ASMUS *(stuffs the timetable into his top-hat)*. We backed a loser!

SOPHUS. A complete outsider!

OTTILIE *(blowing the fragments of the ticket into the air)*. Fly away bubble!

SOPHUS. Burst!

AUNT JUEL. And I'm Mrs Magnussen!

SOPHUS. You are!

PETER. And I have the printing-works behind the brewery!

SOPHUS. You have!

ASMUS. Ottilie–we own the house in Oster Street!

SOPHUS. You do!

AUNT JUEL. Without a farthing!

PETER. Without a single farthing!

ASMUS AND OTTILIE. Everything without a farthing!

SOPHUS. And in the same way I'm a director of Jochum Magnussen's brewery!

AUNT JUEL. —And I've been set on a throne of money-bags, with Jochum kneeling before them!

SOPHUS. That isn't true! What you're saying is a lie. You never jingled your money when Jochum was paying his respects to you. You hadn't even the courage to face him–I had to introduce you to him by force. You were shaking so much that your cough-drop slipped down your throat!

AUNT JUEL. Jochum assumed I was rich!

SOPHUS. Which is not in the least to his credit–let's not talk about his little weakness. We mustn't say things about people behind their backs. You've been his wife for two weeks–has he been a disappointment to you?

AUNT JUEL *(blushing)*. What do you mean by that?

SOPHUS. That's all right, then. It doesn't matter how a marriage comes about–what does matter is how it goes on. Are you satisfied with each other?

AUNT JUEL. Jochum is happy–he's calmed down a lot. He needed a woman to take him in hand!

SOPHUS. Keep him in hand–and you'll bring him the blessings that only women can bring. That takes care of your worries, auntie. Why are you getting up, Peter?

PETER *(behind his chair—earnestly)*. We have lied and cheated!
SOPHUS. Whom have we cheated?
PETER. All those who gave Asmus and me money to build with, when Jochum Magnussen had made us a present of building-sites.
SOPHUS. Peter, listen: you'll make me say harsh things about Jochum– but the presence of our aunt, his wife, seals my lips!
PETER. Jochum believed we possessed eight-hundred-thousand crowns!
SOPHUS. And gave you nothing, until you had money yourselves! Why didn't he shower you with gifts when you were poor?
PETER *(uncertain)*. What do you say, Asmus?
ASMUS. I'm also beginning to wonder why he never gave us anything when we were penniless!
SOPHUS. You're touching on a sore point there. But now I'm here to shield Jochum Magnussen–the director protecting his chief! I won't let you pursue the matter and hunt through old washing for specks of dirt. Where we find weaknesses, we must show forbearance. Custom demands that of relatives. Where Jochum is concerned–and he's a good friend of us all–let's have no quarrelling. If he should have made a mistake, then he has paid dearly enough for it. Auntie is married–you are building, Peter–Asmus and Ottilie are rebuilding:you pay interest on the money and so none of those who advanced it will come to any harm!
PETER. —You ought to have told us the truth on the first day.
SOPHUS. No, Peter–it was my moral duty to say nothing!
PETER. You ought not to have left us lulled in our dreams for four weeks.
SOPHUS. Isn't that the whole secret? To dream of happiness? Happiness brings out abilities that otherwise remain hidden. Didn't I ask you about your plans that evening? You flexed your muscles: you were all ready to set to work. You wanted to build something, not to stand idle! It was then that I knew I must let events take their course–and I flung the bait out in a great sweep for the gold-fish to snap up!

ASMUS *silently shakes* SOPHUS *by the hand, as do also* OTTILIE *and* AUNT JUEL.

SOPHUS *(to* PETER*)*. Aren't you going to?
PETER. I can understand it all, Sophus–but there's one thing I find hard to say to my brother: you've been collecting our money for ten years, and you haven't sent it off. That's embezzlement.
SOPHUS. Yes, I embezzled it. I know I did! The end doesn't justify the means. But there are ends which make wrongdoing appear in a milder light. I used it to pay for Dagmar's music lessons.
PETER *(grasps his hand)*. Sophus, I'm rather ashamed of what I just said!
SOPHUS. Aren't children the paradise in which we older ones can still walk in innocence?

OTTILIE *(to* ASMUS*).* We have five of them tucked up in their cots!
ASMUS. Let's go back to them–and bear in mind what Sophus said. *(To* SOPHUS*)* Goodbye!
OTTILIE. And thanks, Sophus, because Asmus won't have to go to Copenhagen now!
PETER. Sleep well, Sophus!
SOPHUS. The best wish from a brother's heart!
AUNT JUEL. What am I to say to Jochum, since none of you is going?
SOPHUS. Take no thought for the morrow; for the morrow shall take thought for the things of itself!
AUNT JUEL. That saying fits you like a glove!

All go off right. SOPHUS *returns–with* AXEL, *who carries a bag and is dressed for a journey.*

SOPHUS. Are you going away?
AXEL. To Copenhagen!
SOPHUS. Why all the rush?
AXEL. Today was the last straw!
SOPHUS. A scene between you and your papa?
AXEL. Don't speak of it! I'm capitulating and running away. For ever. I'm here to take my leave of you–Mrs Möller–and of Dagmar!
SOPHUS. No, Axel. We can't shake a hand held out in anger. Tell me all about your troubles. You'll breathe freer if you talk about it.
AXEL *(bursts out).* Am I to obey his orders–and marry a girl just because she has money?!
SOPHUS. If the voice of love doesn't tell you—
AXEL. It's not a question of love–the decisive thing is that she is poor!
SOPHUS. Must you choose someone poor?
AXEL *(angrily).* Because of a solemn vow I made!

DAGMAR *enters left—dressed for a journey.*

DAGMAR. Have Peter and Asmus left already?
SOPHUS. Long ago.
DAGMAR. Without me?!
SOPHUS. They're in their beds!
DAGMAR. Why aren't they on their way to Copenhagen?!
SOPHUS. They don't want to have a row with the butcher, when he presents his ticket at the lottery office!
AXEL *(stares at him–begins to understand–radiant).* Mr Möller—
SOPHUS. The prize will benefit the whole population and bring meat prices down. The common good stands above our appetite for lobster and champagne!
DAGMAR *(stammering).* You're not–getting–any money?
SOPHUS. Not from the state–but that's hardly surprising, is it?
DAGMAR *(looking at* AXEL*).* Then–I'm poor–*(she opens her arms.)*
AXEL *(draws her to him).* —and I'm so rich!

SOPHUS *(listening towards the door on the right).* Whoever can that be at this time of night? *(Exit right.* AXEL *kisses* DAGMAR–DAGMAR *kisses* AXEL. SOPHUS *enters from the right—with* LUNDBERG.) Didn't you give Mr Magnussen my message?

LUNDBERG. Yes, I did! And he shouted at me: the fellows must go–otherwise there'll be trouble–if no-one goes to Copenhagen! *(*SOPHUS *looks at* AXEL.)

AXEL *(defensively).* I'm going to Copenhagen! *(To* LUNDBERG*)* Run and tell my father that I've gone to Copenhagen–and I shall return with the most precious of treasures! *(Presses* DAGMAR *to him.)*

LUNDBERG. That'll make him as gentle as a lamb! *(He leaves, right.)*

DAGMAR *(unbelieving–blissful).* At night–to Copenhagen?

AXEL *(to* SOPHUS*).* Was I telling lies?

SOPHUS. No–from now on we must stick to the truth. Especially as it comes so easy! Is there another train?

AXEL. The slow train!

DAGMAR. Is it fast enough for you?

AXEL. What are we waiting for?

He gives SOPHUS *a quick hug;* DAGMAR *hugs him as well. Then both hurry off right.* HELENE *enters left.*

HELENE. Where—

SOPHUS *(going to her—with a gesture).* Don't break the great silence! Two lovers are going out into the night. Under the twinkling stars.

HELENE. Dagmar—

SOPHUS. —and Axel! The final triumph. Don't ask about it. The details fall away into nothingness. The essential remains! *(He sits down in the middle of the sofa.)* Bring me Dagmar's Sunday-school Bible!

HELENE *(fetches it from the bookcase and puts it on the table).* What do you want it for?

SOPHUS. Let me find it–and sit down here beside me.

HELENE *sits by him on the sofa.*

SOPHUS. Here it is. The story of David and Goliath. I'll read it to you! *(He bends over the book.)*

THE PRESIDENT

Comedy in Three Acts

Translated by B. J. Kenworthy

Characters

BLANCHONNET
ELMIRE
MRS BROWN
RAVANINI
SECRETARY
JOURNALIST
PHOTOGRAPHER
RADIO REPORTER
POLICE OFFICER
HOTEL MANAGER
HOTEL PAGEBOY
Two DETECTIVES

ACT ONE

BLANCHONNET *and the* GENTLEMAN *are sitting in armchairs facing one another.*

GENTLEMAN *(after a pause-politely).* Someone knocked.

BLANCHONNET *hears nothing: motionless-leaning slightly forward, he gazes bright-eyed into the face of the* GENTLEMAN.

GENTLEMAN. That was a knock.
BLANCHONNET *(returning from his flights of fancy).* Where?
GENTLEMAN *(pointing).* On the door there.
BLANCHONNET *(making an effort to collect himself).* Come in!
(A hotel pageboy comes in left and presents a visiting-card to BLANCHONNET). For me?
PAGEBOY. Yes, sir.

BLANCHONNET *takes the card from the tray-reads-puts it into his pocket, and turns his full gaze to the* GENTLEMAN *again.*

PAGEBOY. Shall I show the gentleman up?
BLANCHONNET *(completely preoccupied).* What? Who?
PAGEBOY. Is the gentleman to wait?
BLANCHONNET. Of course he must wait! I'm much too busy at the moment. Under no circumstances can I receive a visitor now. Quite impossible. Where's he waiting?
PAGEBOY. Down in the hall.
BLANCHONNET. Then I must ask him to be patient for ten minutes. *(To the* GENTLEMAN *in the armchair)* Forgive me, but that is assuming our discussion is finished.
GENTLEMAN. It won't take another five minutes.
BLANCHONNET *(gets up-goes to the door with the pageboy).* Then tell the gentleman I'll be at his disposal right away. Tell him I'm in a very important conference-a vitally significant one. I regret the delay-but it arises from the nature of my business. I'll phone as soon as I'm free.

The PAGEBOY *leaves.* BLANCHONNET *returns to his chair and assumes his former attitude once more.*

GENTLEMAN. So it is the Prefect's wish—
BLANCHONNET *(nodding)*. —the Prefect's wish—
GENTLEMAN. —since he happens to have come over for the day—
BLANCHONNET *(as before)*. —happens to—
GENTLEMAN. —from Paris—to collect documents from the administration of the department for his speech at the ministry—
BLANCHONNET. —at the ministry—
GENTLEMAN. —to take advantage of his presence here to welcome members of the congress. He suggests an informal meeting this evening under the trees in the prefecture garden. That means informal dress—and no speech-making either on the part of the Prefect or on your part.
BLANCHONNET. Beginning at—
GENTLEMAN. Nine o'clock.
BLANCHONNET. On the dot.
GENTLEMAN. The Prefect would be happy to make the acquaintance of the president of the congress beforehand. The Prefect receives visitors at midday.
BLANCHONNET. I'll be there at midday.
GENTLEMAN. That is all I had to tell you.

He rises, bows.
BLANCHONNET *also bows-without moving from where he stands.*
The GENTLEMAN *leaves.* BLANCHONNET *remains standing stiffly.*
Then he suddenly comes to life: he does not know which impulse to follow. He is on the point of knocking at the door down left—hesitates and changes his mind. Finally he rushes to the desk: with hurried movements he spreads papers about on the desk-telephones 'Send the gentleman up!' *He then seats himself in the armchair at the desk and pretends like one possessed to be immersed in his work. There is a knock left.* BLANCHONNET *calls loudly.* Come in!

The PAGEBOY *admits the* JOURNALIST. *The* PAGEBOY *leaves. The* JOURNALIST *waits.*

BLANCHONNET *(glancing up from the papers he is pretending to work at)*. Yes?
JOURNALIST. I sent up my card-
BLANCHONNET *(looks at him in preoccupied fashion)*. Card?
JOURNALIST. By the pageboy.
BLANCHONNET *(raising his hand to his forehead)*. I put it down somewhere-heaven knows where. Buried under these papers. To look for it would be virtually hopeless. Never mind about that. You are from the newspaper?
JOURNALIST. A representative of the local paper and a national press correspondent.
BLANCHONNET. Do sit down. What did you wish to know?

JOURNALIST *(on a chair-with a notebook)*. Information of general interest about the congress that begins tomorrow. What can I write down?

BLANCHONNET *(gets up-walks up and down. Taking a deep breath)*. The congress begins this evening.

JOURNALIST *(looks up)*. This evening?

BLANCHONNET. With a prelude in the gardens of the prefecture.

JOURNALIST. In the prefecture gardens?

BLANCHONNET. Under the beautiful old green trees.

JOURNALIST *(writing)*. A social gathering of the congress delegates in the prefecture gardens. Without the Prefect.

BLANCHONNET. With the Prefect!

JOURNALIST. But the Prefect's in Paris.

BLANCHONNET. The Prefect arrived from Paris this morning.

JOURNALIST. To open the congress?

BLANCHONNET. He has interrupted his negotiations at the ministry, although a number of important items were still awaiting his consideration-as his secretary, who was with me until a moment ago, explained to me.

JOURNALIST *(taking it down)*. -negotations-broken off-items awaiting consideration.

BLANCHONNET. The official nature of the reception is stressed by the fact that the Prefect is to deliver an address, to which I shall reply.

JOURNALIST. -official nature-address-shall reply-

BLANCHONNET. I don't wish to make any further statement at the moment. In any case, the details will unfold before your eyes. You will be present at the garden-party? Have you a pass? Here's a card that will admit you to all the public functions. From secret sessions the press-in particular the press-is excluded.

JOURNALIST. Of course.

BLANCHONNET. But I shall be glad to see a detailed account of the garden-party given in the presence of the Prefect-in the national dailies as well. I'll let you have the text of my little speech this afternoon. It could then be read in the morning edition.

JOURNALIST. Excellent.

BLANCHONNET *(concluding the interview)*. It's been a great pleasure.

JOURNALIST. I'd be glad to have a few short notes on the agenda for the congress.

BLANCHONNET. This afternoon-or rather come back tomorrow. The preparations are getting too much for me-you can see for youself how it's piling up on my desk. I have no assistance-the whole burden of work and responsibility falls on my shoulders alone!-by the ton! *(he sinks into the chair at the desk.)*

JOURNALIST. In the interests of the public I regret my lack of success.

BLANCHONNET. Write about the prefecture gardens. That'll be of interest. Or is a prefect only a cipher? To me he's not-to me the Prefect is–*(Breaks off with a smile.)* My nerves–all this muddle–then suddenly the secretary stirring things up–lighting up new horizons as a flash of lightning does! Leave me to myself. Grant me the quarter of an hour that a man needs to sort out the chaos that he calls his world!

The JOURNALIST *has retired to the door–he leaves in bewildered silence.*
BLANCHONNET *clears the desk and stuffs all the papers into the drawer. Then he goes to the door left and knocks gently. The door is quickly thrown open and* ELMIRE, *her light frock billowing round her, rushes to* BLANCHONNET's *bosom.*

BLANCHONNET *(laughing).* You'll knock me over.
ELMIRE. I'm going to hang on tight—you shan't shake me off.
BLANCHONNET. You certainly have more strength in your arms than I'd have expected in a girl like you.
ELMIRE. I shan't let go.
BLANCHONNET. Now I can't breathe–Elmire, your father's choking.
ELMIRE. Give me your word first.
BLANCHONNET. What about?
ELMIRE. Not to leave me by myself again for a single second.
BLANCHONNET. What a thing for me to–
ELMIRE. By the Holy Virgin!
BLANCHONNET –to have to swear, and by the most sacred oath into the bargain!
ELMIRE. Because it's the most sacred!
BLANCHONNET. Then I'll have to consider whether I can promise. Let me go.
ELMIRE. No. Promise me now!
BLANCHONNET. Can't you bear being alone, then? *(*ELMIRE *shakes her head.)* Because it's boring? *(*ELMIRE *shakes her head more vehemently.)* Then what's the reason?
ELMIRE. I'm–afraid!
BLANCHONNET. Afraid? Of what?
ELMIRE. Of–the room.
BLANCHONNET. There aren't any ghosts in it!
ELMIRE. Of–the furniture!
BLANCHONNET. But it doesn't pull faces at you!
ELMIRE. Of–the curtains.
BLANCHONNET. There are windows behind them–not burglars!
ELMIRE. Everywhere there's a creaking and the trampling of feet!
BLANCHONNET. Yes, dear–it's not like the convent you've just left. A hotel has all sorts of noises. A foretaste of the world you are soon going to enter. There'll be rattling and roaring that'll give you plenty to think about! The symphony of life is played with full orchestra! But for you it shall have only pretty tunes. I have chosen the score for it myself –would you like to hear it?

ELMIRE *(cautiously)*. Are you going to stay with me?

BLANCHONNET. If I'm to give you a glimpse into the future, then I can't help being here, can I? *(He looses her arms from his neck.)*

ELMIRE. I'll keep hold of your hand!

BLANCHONNET. So long as it isn't too uncomfortable for you—*(He stands in front of a chair.)*

ELMIRE. I'll push my chair close to yours. *(She does so; both sit down. BLANCHONNET gazes in front of him.)*

ELMIRE. It's nice like this.

BLANCHONNET *(clears his throat)*. How old are you, Elmire?

ELMIRE. Seventeen.

BLANCHONNET. Seventeen already

ELMIRE. Is that very old? At the end I was the oldest in the convent school. The Mother Superior finally believed I should stay there. If you hadn't brought me away, I'd have become a nun.

BLANCHONNET. But we did fetch you away in time!

ELMIRE. Why did you leave me in the convent for such a long time?

BLANCHONNET. It's the best recommendation to good society—if one wants to be counted as belonging to it—to marry off one's daughter direct from the convent school.

ELMIRE *(gazes at him—her confusion is boundless)*. I—am to be—married?

BLANCHONNET. To a man you'll like, too.

ELMIRE *(staring)*. My love belongs to Jesus Christ, not to any man!

BLANCHONNET. You'll learn to love your husband, just as you learnt your reverence for Heaven.

ELMIRE *(her face in her hands)*. Take me back to the convent!

BLANCHONNET. That's over and done with—it's a closed chapter for you. Forward now in good heart! We can only go forward—but it demands effort from all of us. Otherwise the chariot on which the goddess of success is enthroned rolls on over us. To be her vassal is—to be human. Everything else is trash on which we should turn our backs.

ELMIRE *(whispering)*. Why isn't mama here?

BLANCHONNET. She's coming—and she won't be alone!

ELMIRE. I don't want to talk to anyone but mama now.

BLANCHONNET. You shan't appear with eyes red from crying—first impressions are what counts. And Gaston demands high standards.

ELMIRE. Gaston?

BLANCHONNET. That's your fiancé's name. A Sillon-Dudet—an old family. It's an honour to be connected with it. It's a name that will throw Paris open—to you and to me. It is a step that may have unimagined results. I've already some idea of the consequences. But you don't need to hear about that. In your heart there must be only devotion to the chosen man. Now it's my turn to ask for your promise. Will you promise to be sensible and to love him?

ELMIRE. I want–to meet him–at home–not here–not in a hotel–in a strange town!

BLANCHONNET. This is where Gaston is going to see you–and me! Here I'm somebody, not just a mere nobody! What glamour is there about a lawyer in Paris? He fades into the ill-lit background. Here I'm presiding over a congress. I occupy the platform. I decide who's to speak and who isn't. In all the languages of the world. I wield the gavel —hurl resolutions! There's magic in the word: president. Doesn't it force you to your knees? (ELMIRE *remains in awed silence.*) And that's not all: my words will get into print. The newspaper will fill its columns with my speeches and counter-speeches. I shall be read in the villages and in Paris alike. Who underestimates the power of the press? (ELMIRE *is silent.*) My greatest moment will be this evening: at nine o'clock precisely. Shaking hands with the Prefect. An exchange of pleasantries between equals. The gardens and the darkness will conjure up a mood for confidences. We shall stroll arm in arm up and down the avenues–and as we turn a corner I shall introduce Gaston–a member of the Sillon-Dudet family–to the Prefect. Mutual pleasure on the same social plane. And I shall have introduced them. Can I possibly be ignored after that? I hold some precious trumps in my hand. I'll play them like a skilful card-player and break the bank. Between the two fires I'll forge my iron into bright steel, with which I'll conquer Paris– blow by blow. Blanchonnet to the fore–promise me by that motto which your mother also holds sacred. Your hand on it!

ELMIRE *unresisting, lets him take her hand.* BLANCHONNET *gets up.*

ELMIRE *(alarmed).* Are you going away?

BLANCHONNET. On a state visit, my dear: the Prefect is expecting me to call on him. The man has come from Paris to meet me. Am I to decline because a little girl is cross when her father is invited to see high dignitaries of the republic? (ELMIRE *contradicts weakly.*) Be reasonable, dear–you're beginning to get the idea of thinking out your course of action. Be a true Blanchonnet. Eyes on the target–and the legions fall around you. A formidable battle-cry–but unambiguous. I need my top-hat. *(Goes into the room down left–returns with top-hat and kid-gloves.)*

ELMIRE. Will you be long with the–

BLANCHONNET. That's up to the Prefect. No room for sentiment in these matters. With top-hat and kid-gloves. How do you like your father now?

ELMIRE. You look–handsome.

BLANCHONNET. Well turned out. *A la mode.* Not too much individuality. That doesn't help one's career. A trifle above the average on the outside–but a volcano inside. That's what does it. I'll open the balcony for you. *(Does so.)* There's a deck-chair. Read something. Here–I've still got your English magazine you had on the train–even the convent didn't object to that. *(ELMIRE reclines in the deck-chair.)* All right? *(Kisses her hand. ELMIRE looks at him imploringly.)* Afraid? *(ELMIRE nods.)* Then I'll lock you in—so that the savage robbers can't come and carry Elmire away. Satisfied? *(ELMIRE nods.)* At all events you have the telephone to sound the alarm in the hotel. *(ELMIRE is silent.)* Now, don't worry youself about anything-until mama arrives-and *(he wags a finger at her)*-Gaston!

He takes the key out of the lock-goes off. From outside the sound of the key turning in the lock.
ELMIRE attempts to immerse herself in her magazine. Once more there is the sound of a key in the lock. ELMIRE quickly lowers her book, looks towards the door. After some difficulty, the door is successfully opened: RAVANINI-youthful, supple-slips in silently, closes the door behind him. ELMIRE stares petrified.

RAVANINI *(turns, sees ELMIRE. The slightest suggestion of surprise-then a polished bow).* M. Blanchonnet was in too much of a hurry to come back up himself—so he cut matters short by handing me the key to his room. Would you like to take charge of it now? As far as I'm concerned, it's served its purpose. *(ELMIRE remains motionless.)* Then I'll keep it—and hand it in to the porter. *(He drops it into his waistcoat pocket. ELMIRE is still unable to speak.)* No doubt it would be simpler to knock and be asked to come in, if there had been anyone who could have opened the door. Instead of that I gave myself all that trouble with an obstinate lock that almost prevented me getting in. Did you hear the fearful din I unleashed out there? *(ELMIRE is silent.)* The hotel management ought at least to make sure their locks work properly, if they're taking first-class guests. I shall make a complaint—the more effectively, as I have a witness. I wonder if you'd mind coming with me to see the manager?
ELMIRE *(in a small voice).* No-
RAVANINI *(laughing).* Anyhow, what I said is a lot of nonsense. If I have the key, you can't unlock the door from the inside. Right?
ELMIRE. I—have no key.
RAVANINI. So I let myself in with the key, unless there's a duplicate. But that would be unusual in a hotel. Let's forget about the key business, which isn't very interesting anyway. M. Blanchonnet sent me. My name is Ravanini.
ELMIRE *(has risen from the deck-chair).* Do you know—
RAVANINI. M. Blanchonnet from Paris? I've known him by name for a long time—and I made his acquaintance in person ten minutes ago in the vestibule. A splended figure—and the first impression is what counts: he's the right man for the presidential chair!
ELMIRE. Were you sent by—
RAVANINI. In any case it's only a trifling matter, and there's no need to hold up the president with it. He has more important things on his

mind. I agreed to his suggestion—and came up here myself. Whereabouts are the cards?

ELMIRE. Cards?

RAVANINI. Admission passes for the delegates to the congress. Don't you know?

ELMIRE. I—know nothing—about it.

RAVANINI *(breaking off)*. The cards really should have been sent to us. But there wasn't a sign of them in the letter. Only the agenda came fluttering out. We started off just the same. Mrs. Brown and I—as delegates from the Argentine. And certainly no South American state ought to be without its representatives at the congress—for we are at the very centre of interest. Will M. Blanchonnet be out for long?

ELMIRE. He's gone to see the Prefect.

RAVANINI. Oh, well, that'll keep him quite a time. Confound. Without the passes neither Mrs. Brown nor I can get on with our work. And every minute is precious. Perhaps we could look for them? Our passes must be about somewhere.

ELMIRE. When my—

RAVANINI. Hours will have passed by the time your employer gets back. A Prefect always has his breakfast. Meanwhile the end of the world may come—and we shall bear some of the blame. Doesn't that trouble your conscience?

ELMIRE. My employer?

RAVANINI. Will surely have given his secretary enough authority to permit her to look through all the files. The cards are somewhere about—but where?

ELMIRE. His secretary?

RAVANINI. Or does he take such a charming young lady with him on his travels for the pleasure of it? That would be in the most absurd conflict with the aims of the congress.

ELMIRE. I'm not—

RAVANINI. Forgive me. It was only a joke—no more than a joke to laugh at. Let's both have a good laugh. Nothing I like better than having a good laugh with someone. Mrs. Brown's always enjoying a laugh. On the trip across we sometimes laughed so much that the boat rocked with it. Laughing is good for sea-sickness—and for all the troubles on the continent. *(He laughs.* ELMIRE *is unable to laugh.* RAVANINI *falls silent. Then in a businesslike way)* Will the congress have anything fresh to offer us? *(He sits down in an armchair.)*

ELMIRE. *(takes her seat in the other).* This evening the Prefect's giving a garden-party.

RAVANINI. Are you going to be there too?

ELMIRE *(quickly).* No, I shan't—I certainly shan't.

RAVANINI. Only your employer. And where will you spend the evening?

ELMIRE. I shall stay in the hotel!

RAVANINI. It's miserable sitting here all alone, while the others are enjoying themselves.

ELMIRE. I always stay in the hotel.

RAVANINI. I'll send Mrs. Brown in to see you—she'll take you out. You'll have a wonderful time. There's a good variety show on. I can particularly recommend a couple of dancers to you. Fabulous body— the man's an Adonis in his nakedness. Mrs. Brown and I were delighted yesterday. When does the garden-party begin?

ELMIRE *(confused)*. At nine—

RAVANINI. Then Mrs. Brown will knock at nine—and off you'll go!

ELMIRE. No, no—it's quite impossible!

RAVANINI. Nothing's impossible if you want it enough. *(He regards her narrowly.)* You will want to—and not offend Mrs. Brown.

ELMIRE. You're completely mistaken. *(She gets up—makes for the desk.)*

RAVANINI. What are you wishing to do?

ELMIRE. I want to telephone—

RAVANINI *(anticipates her—rests his hand on the instrument)*. You won't telephone.

ELMIRE. Why shouldn't I telephone?

RAVANINI. Well, why do you want to telephone?

ELMIRE *(smiles timidly)*. Now I don't want to telephone any more.

RAVANINI. You do change your mind quickly. So perhaps you'll go to the variety show with Mrs. Brown this evening after all?

ELMIRE. Definitely not!

RAVANINI. Everything for the congress? If everyone took their duties as seriously as you do, the world would soon be freed of the scourge.

ELMIRE. But I have nothing to do with—

RAVANINI. With your watch by day and night—over the documents?

ELMIRE. I don't know anything—

RAVANINI. M. Blanchonnet can congratulate himself on this Cerberus, who doesn't even betray where the valuables are by barking. As for me, as far as you're concerned I'm not even a member of the International Action League until I can present my credentials.

ELMIRE *(in her chair–looking up at him in perplexity)*. Are you a member?

RAVANINI. Veteran of a hundred battles. Not one who sets the world to rights from his desk—but one who takes an active part. Sometimes pistol shots have cracked out behind me. Have you ever heard of the Calle Junin in Buenos Aires? House upon house—and the toughest men of all the oceans. Blood and love—they belong together for that rabble. If you call that love. For the world has been defiled for all time. Would you be capable of going on living, if you'd witnessed the actions which people of your own sex had been forced to go through under threat of death?

ELMIRE *(hesitant)*. What sort—of actions?

RAVANINI *(looks at her searchingly).* What sort of actions?

ELMIRE. —were people of my own sex forced to go through under threat of death?

RAVANINI. To give their love to a man who pays for it.

ELMIRE. Love?

RAVANINI. Wasn't I at pains not to insult the word? Let's leave the word love out of it—it's a traffic with the body that is carried on by the most repulsive of creatures. I don't mean the girls who have to sell themselves—and for a pittance at that—only the traders are vile, who supply the material that is brutally abused by anyone at any time! *(ELMIRE listens.)* Occasionally they can be saved—but it's a venture in which you risk your life. Their mistresses keep them shut up behind bars like animals. Inhuman and unworthy—but it exists, for life admits of everything. One often wonders where God can be living. It's certain that he's mostly not at home, otherwise he'd never tolerate the witches' sabbath on his own doorstep. Don't you agree? *(ELMIRE crosses herself weakly.)* It will interest you to hear that we had two of these pitiable creatures on board. Girls snatched away from Europe—whom we were bringing back home. Daughters of good families—who knows how they had found their way overseas. Perhaps the police will get the secret out of them. We suspect it was white slave traders—and it's to be hoped that the congress will well and truly put paid to their activities. Does that establish my good faith? Haven't I a thorough command of the subject?

ELMIRE *(stammering).* The—congress—

RAVANINI. —of the International Action League against the White Slave Trade!

ELMIRE. The International Action League against the White Salve Trade—

RAVANINI. Convened under the chairmanship of M. Blanchonnet!

ELMIRE. —under the chairmanship—

RAVANINI. And I'm a member. Carlos Ravanini from Buenos Aires. Have you no recollection of reading my name in the list of members?

ELMIRE *(with difficulty, pushes herself to her feet).* I'll—have—a look —*(swaying, she reaches the door back left, which she leaves half open behind her.)*

RAVANINI *stands up. At the same moment there is a knock at the door right. He goes across right—opens—admits* MRS BROWN. *She is an elderly, stout woman dressed in silk—carries a Pekinese in her arms.*

RAVANINI *(very loud).* We're in luck, Mrs. Brown. The passes weren't on the desk. I should never have been successful by myself. Naturally, my sense of priority would have stopped me going into the other room. But now the secretary is helping us.

MRS BROWN *(also loud).* A secretary?

RAVANINI. We've had a most interesting talk about the aims of the congress. She has the whole thing at her finger-tips. One can't tell whether she's keeping quiet or whether she knows nothing. At all events, she gave me such an examination that the sweat poured down my face. No unauthorized person is going to get past her. Without our passes, we simply don't exist for her!

MRS BROWN. Is she looking for the passes in there?

RAVANINI. First she's checking the lists. To see if our names are on them. Ravanini and Mrs. Brown from Buenos Aires, who have had an invitation to the congress, but no passes!

MRS BROWN. I don't see why we should suffer because of such slackness!

RAVANINI. Complain about the president, but not about his secretary. She does her job—and one doesn't criticize subordinates!

MRS BROWN. I'm quite determined to leave, if the slightest difficulties are put in our way!

RAVANINI. That's what I feel, too. I'm just waiting to hear that our names don't appear on the lists either!

MRS BROWN. That would be the limit!

RAVANINI. Our protest will be sent to the organisers fo the congress in writing!

MRS BROWN. It certainly won't be a verbal one!

RAVANINI. To forestall any attempt to make us change our minds!

MRS BROWN. As we shall already be on our way home—

RAVANINI. —to the Argentine! *(ELMIRE enters down left. RAVANINI adopts a pleasant tone.)* Well—did you find us on the lists? Mrs. Brown and myself?

ELMIRE *(with a forced smile).* Yes—

RAVANINI *(looks at MRS BROWN with a start; then to ELMIRE).* Or have you been making a telephone call?

ELMIRE. How could I make a telephone call *(indicating the desk)* without a telephone?

RAVANINI. Isn't there a telephone in every room?

ELMIRE. Not—in my room.

RAVANINI *(laughing).* It really is a hotel from the back of beyond. Terrific prices and the amenities of a country inn. *(To MRS BROWN).* You see, I was criticizing the miserable state of the locks when the young lady was with me just now. I had to work at it like a locksmith to get the door open with the key M. Blanchonnet entrusted to me. In any case, I know as much about locks as a baboon does about growing cucumbers!

MRS BROWN. Aren't you going to introduce me, my dear friend?

RAVANINI *(to ELMIRE).* This is Mrs. Brown—I was telling you about her. *(To MRS BROWN)* I was describing our trip over here, when we were laughing so much, so as not to get seasick. It's a remedy I shall recommend!

MRS BROWN. Now the young lady knows me—but whose acquaintance have I the pleasure of making?

RAVANINI. Allow me to introduce you to the best secretary in the world, whose possession we may well envy M. Blanchonnet. As silent as the grave—and as respectable as the madonna! *(ELMIRE raises a startled hand towards him—crosses herself with the other.)* And modest into the bargain, like all people of real genius!

MRS BROWN *(goes quickly to* ELMIRE—*takes her hand).* At last he's come out with what I want to know. *(To* RAVANINI*)* Do be quiet now—you're making the dear child quite embarrassed with your massive compliments. *(To* ELMIRE*)* He does talk so, but he's really a good sort. My over-zealous equerry. Now he's been moving heaven and earth over the passes—and he's even launched an attack on M. Blanchonnet. Is the president of the congress to bother himself even about admission tickets? He has other things to think about. But my friend can't stop to think when it's something for me. *(To* RAVANINI*)* Why didn't you come back down to the vestibule? Instead I have to come looking for you—and I catch you in the most charming company. Of course, I'm too old for you-

RAVANINI. My dear lady—

MRS BROWN. My dearest friend, you won't shock me. Anyone who doesn't concede the victory to such youthful freshness can't ever have been young. *(To* ELMIRE*)* Isn't that right?

ELMIRE. I'm—still very young—

MRS BROWN. I'd put my name to that, just from one look at your pretty little face. Cheeks like almond-blossom and eyes like violets. No man could help falling in love—at first sight. *(To* RAVANINI*)* Could he, Ravanini—on your honour?

RAVANINI. That's what kept me!

MRS BROWN. Honesty is the best policy. *(To* ELMIRE*)* Just look at your victim—he's reduced to a sentimental jelly! That doesn't often happen to him—and I'll be in for a bad time of it! *(To* RAVANINI*)* Don't neglect me too much, my friend, when your mind is taken up with this angel of a secretary, whom even M. Blanchonnet keeps shut up behind lock and bolt like a treasure.

ELMIRE. He does that because I—

MRS BROWN. You have no need to blush on my account. It's not only the documents that are locked away! You have to look after your bird too, so that doves from the wrong dovecote don't come paying her flying visits. Or the savage hawk, hunting its prey in the clouds. He'd gobble her up bones and all. Has he already pecked you?

ELMIRE. It's all quite different—from what you're saying—

RAVANINI *claps his hands together.*

MRS BROWN. He's reminding me that it's time to go. Our labours call us. May I kiss you goodbye on the forehead? You'll allow an old woman to do that. The touch of youth makes us young again ourselves! *(She does it.)* I've quite taken to you. *(To* RAVANINI*)* It was the nicest possible beginning the congress could have had for me. Off we go, then, quickly.

They both go off. ELMIRE *walks slowly over to an armchair, leans on its back. She gazes into space. Outside a key is inserted into the lock—which rattles as repeated attempts are made to turn it.* ELMIRE *is only able to pay slight attention to what is happening. Suddenly the door flies open, and* BLANCHONNET *comes flying in.*

BLANCHONNET *(at a loss).* It's unlocked! While I was afraid a bit had broken off the key, the door was unlocked all the time! Did you get them to open it? *(*ELMIRE *is motionless.)* I locked it. The key clicked twice—and I didn't go until I had tried the door. But now I didn't need to unlock it. How do you explain that? *(*ELMIRE *is silent.)* I can't be mistaken—and yet I must be labouring under a delusion. A hotel is far too much of an everyday affair to sport a ghost. One would sooner expect to find apparitions and mysteriously open doors within the walls of your convent. This is a modern building with lifts and central heating. As unromantic as ourselves! Well, then, Blanchonnet was mistaken. The matter's closed—and let's close the door as well. Abracadabra—that'll lay the ghosts—and now we're back to reality again! *(He slams the door, puts his top-hat down on the desk and tosses his gloves into it.)* Well, that's that. The Lord was good to me. I had some wonderful moments. I could feel how I was making a deeper and deeper impression. My improvisation was a little masterpiece. The way he registered astonishment at my appearance was plain to see. The Prefect hadn't expected that. Instead of a crank—Mormon or Salvation Army style, long white beard, scruffy coat—a gentleman from head to foot. The ice was broken in a moment—and we knew right away where we stood, Paris became our main topic. We discovered mutual acquaintances in every nook and cranny of the metropolis. Important names were bandied about. We even took a quick look into the Elysée. A fantastic panorama! *(He presses his temples.* ELMIRE *watches him.)* When wine was served, the conversation flowed freely. Some political dirty-linen got a bit of a washing. There were intimate peeps at ministers. The unwritten records of secret sessions were hawked for my private benefit. We roared over delightful interludes which never reach the ears of the man in the street. Suddenly one finds oneself on terms of familiarity with these gods of public life! *(*ELMIRE *says nothing.* BLANCHONNET *goes to her—takes her face between his hands.)* You don't understand a word of what I'm saying. And how should you? You're still more affected by convent bells than by signals resounding from the great world outside. But wait—wait just a little longer: they'll penetrate to you—this very noon—to offer you their greeting. What will that be like? *(*ELMIRE *tries to free herself from* BLANCHONNET'S *hands.)* Guess—and don't shy away. Those who guess right may stand in the sunlight. And as its full glare will fall on you, I'll help you—the Prefect is paying me a return visit! *(ELMIRE frees herself.)* Am I alone here? Who is the enchanting young lady? *Voilà*–my daughter. Well, sir, and what do you think of her? He'll kiss your hand and pay you daring compliments. You'll be a lady—one to whom a prefect has paid homage! Doesn't that make your heart beat faster? *(ELMIRE looks at him searchingly.* BLANCHONNET, *taking her hand)* Feel mine. It's beating fast enough to sweep you along with it. Notice the rhythm—we shall be marching in time to it. I shall be at the front—leading my assembled forces into the field. You, too, have your part in the plan of battle. And battles there will be. The prefect is only the beginning—but what will be the end of it?

He stands there with legs planted apart—gazing upwards and still gripping ELMIRE'S *hand. She stares at the door on the right—and shakes her head vehemently.*

ACT TWO

BLANCHONNET *is sitting behind the desk: he is having his photograph taken. The* PHOTOGRAPHER *is standing beside his camera in the middle of the room.*

BLANCHONNET *(suddenly).* Stop. Stop. Leave off. Close your shutter!
PHOTOGRAPHER *(covering his lens).* Oh Lord! Right in the middle of the exposure!
BLANCHONNET. I moved.
PHOTOGRAPHER. You hadn't moved a muscle!
BLANCHONNET. At the end I did.
PHOTOGRAPHER. I should have noticed it.
BLANCHONNET. I twitched—it made me jerk over from the right to the left. Everything moved. My blood rebelled against an unnatural repression and surged with a faster pulse-beat. We must have a respite, during which I can again force my whole body into obedience.
PHOTOGRAPHER. In the meantime I'll put in another plate.
BLANCHONNET. Strange, how one gets up after ten seconds of that, stiff in every limb. I'll have to do some gymnastics to loosen up my joints. Shall I keep still any better the second time?
PHOTOGRAPHER. I did recommend an instantaneous exposure.
BLANCHONNET. On the balcony. With tree-tops as a background. Having a wonderful holiday here, love and best wishes. Photos like that are two a penny. No, my dear fellow, that sort of thing is no use to us—it's quite essential for me to be sitting at the desk. That's the only way I want to be seen.
PHOTOGRAPHER. Then it'll take another ten seconds.

BLANCHONNET. And that requires terrific concentration from me. But my will-power can rise to the demands made on it. The first time the attempt failed—perhaps imperceptibly. My mind went on working—I had not achieved inner stillness. That would have shown up on the plate. After all, it's not only the surface that gets photographed.

PHOTOGRAPHER. I wish there was enough light for it in the room.

BLANCHONNET. We'll get the picture that has to be taken even in spite of the light. In twelve—or even twenty seconds—if the technical possibilities can't be bought more cheaply. I guarantee to remain still to the point of rigidity. Now I have myself under control—with unswerving gaze directed towards the star that shines over me. Seize your chance—quick! *(He has sat down in the chair at the desk—rests his arm on the papers which are strewn over it—and freezes in a rigid pose.)*

PHOTOGRAPHER *(gesticulates—photographs).* That's it. Thank you.

BLANCHONNET. Did I promise too much?

PHOTOGRAPHER. Dead still. Amazing.

BLANCHONNET. A test for myself, to see if I have the reins firmly in my hands. On the road to my goal. Past all the side-tracks of Scylla and Charybdis. The picture will provide the proof. I'll keep it before my eyes if ever I feel myself weakening. When can I see a print?

PHOTOGRAPHER. By this evening.

BLANCHONNET. Quick work. When will it be in the papers?

PHOTOGRAPHER. I'll send it off right away.

BLANCHONNET. Are you certain it'll get to Paris?

PHOTOGRAPHER. We have our regular customers.

BLANCHONNET. Draft a text with plenty of punch. Words like 'the new President' and 'reception at the prefecture' must stand out. You won't forget anything?

PHOTOGRAPHER. Our office is very reliable.

BLANCHONNET. Then that's how I'll expect it to be!

He holds out his hand to the PHOTOGRAPHER *and escorts him to the door—opens it. At the door is the hotel* PAGEBOY.

BLANCHONNET *picks up a card from the tray—reads. The* PHOTOGRPAHER *leaves.*

BLANCHONNET *(looks up in surprise).* For me?

PAGEBOY. The gentleman is in the hall.

BLANCHONNET. Let him come up. That's most convenient—the photographer has only just left. Ask him to come up! *(The* PAGEBOY *leaves.* BLANCHONNET *closes the door—takes up his stance in the centre of the room. There is a knock.)* Come in! *(The* GENTLEMAN *comes in.)*

BLANCHONNET *(emphatically).* An emissary of the spheres?

GENTLEMAN. A flattering title for a representative of the broadcasting organisation.

BLANCHONNET. The obeisance of modern man to the global empire of the microphone!

GENTLEMAN. You give me hope that my request will be granted.

BLANCHONNET. Let's sit down. *(Both sit in armchairs.)* How can I be of service to you?

GENTLEMAN. Would you be prepared to give a talk on the radio?

BLANCHONNET. When?

GENTLEMAN. When would be suitable for you?

BLANCHONNET *(indicating the desk)*. I'm pretty busy.

GENTLEMAN. I can see that. And people making all sorts of requests. I collided with the photographer by the lift.

BLANCHONNET. The Prefect will be paying me a visit.

GENTLEMAN. We know about that. The press keeps us informed. And come to think of it, we might be said to be the newspaper of the air, mightn't we? May I make a suggestion?

BLANCHONNET. Please do.

GENTLEMAN. Well then: at once.

BLANCHONNET. Now?

GENTLEMAN. The car's waiting outside the hotel. I'll take you along —you give a twenty-minute talk—the car brings you back: the whole business would take up only half-an-hour of your time.

BLANCHONNET. I could manage that, of course.

GENTLEMAN *(takes out a sheet of paper from his pocket)*. We'll cancel the talk on 'Soot Formation in Bent Chimneys'—that won't be missed! —and instead we'll put in *(looking up)* 'My Personal Experiences in the Struggle against the White Slavers'.

BLANCHONNET *(startled)*. Personal experiences?

GENTLEMAN. The way you snatch these girls from the clutches of these brutes'll shake the oldest of the old out of their wheel-chairs.

BLANCHONNET. What do you imagine it's like?

GENTLEMAN. Exciting enough to take your breath away!

BLANCHONNET *(collecting himself)*. Certainly—

GENTLEMAN. Will you choose particularly shocking episodes?

BLANCHONNET. Well, you know, there's a lot that isn't suitable for broadcasting to the public.

GENTLEMAN. Even the lot won't be enough!

BLANCHONNET. On the contrary: I have to guard the records very carefully. Our—struggles against the white slave traders are subject to a vow of silence—we are bound by our oath!

GENTLEMAN. It's true enough that one has never yet heard anything about these struggles.

BLANCHONNET. There, you see! We should be surrendering our best weapon if we betrayed our methods to our opponents! We act silently— but rely upon it, we are at work. And our silent labours are bearing fruit!

GENTLEMAN. Could you at least give the statistics of the number of females you liberate each year, and the number of kidnappers you hand over to the police each year for their well-merited punishment?

BLANCHONNET. That—will be in the records, and I'll have to look it up. But that will hold us up—and the time you've allowed me is running out. Oughtn't I to come to the microphone straight away?

GENTLEMAN. Yes—but what do you propose to talk about?

BLANCHONNET. About—the organization of our international league.

GENTLEMAN. It wouldn't be long before they switched off. Tomorrow there'd be a flood of letters from the public: a great song and dance—and all about nothing. Protests. Licences dropping off!

BLANCHONNET. There won't be any protests. I'll give an inspired talk—inspired by my own oratory. My address will conclude with a universal appeal to the conscience of all the peoples of the world to join with this league of ours, which I intend to build up into one of the most powerful of corporate organisations—comparable to the omnipotent church, which looks to its pope as its highest represenative—then this congress will be taken seriously—as it is a prefect who holds a reception for it in his garden. That argument cannot fail to silence even the most sceptical!

GENTLEMAN *(rising—shrugging his shoulders)*. Let's go.

BLANCHONNET. You go on ahead. I'll come down to the car. I shall have to take some papers I'll need. *(He digs about among the papers on the desk. The* GENTLEMAN *leaves.* BLANCHONNET *desists immediately—rushes to the door left back—pulls it open.)* Say goodbye to me! I'm just going off on an air-journey. Among the waves of the ether. Would you like to see the magic coach whose wheels are to carry me to the place of departure? (ELMIRE *appears hesitantly in the doorway.* BLANCHONNET *takes her by the arm.)* From the balcony everything will present itself to your gaze. Step out there with me. *(He leads her on to the balcony.)* Peep through the foliage. Can you glimpse the fairy coach? To you it looks like an ordinary taxi-cab. Its occupant appears to be no cavalier, up to his ears in braid. All in all, an everyday affair. And yet a miracle. Do you understand how?

ELMIRE *(softly)*. No.

BLANCHONNET *(coming back into the room)*. Not much to look at, like most of the marvels of this world. Just look at me! A father talking to his daughter. Here the words are trapped in the room. A thin door holds them fast. Now. In ten minutes they will be winging across the heavens—and no barricade of forest or mountain will hold them back. This tongue between my gums—this little flap of red flesh—will send its sounds across distances of miles. I'm going to talk on the wireless!

ELMIRE *(as before)*. Yes.

BLANCHONNET. To a hundred thousand ears. To two, three, five thousand ears. They say there is a huge number of sets. I've never bothered myself about the figure before. Possibly the million has been reached. Directly after my talk I'll buy everything that's been written about it. I must know how many listeners I had. Was there a set in your convent?

ELMIRE. No.

BLANCHONNET. Of course there wouldn't be. The strictness of the rule would forbid it. You live on an island, to which no little ship from our continent plies. Doesn't it set your blood tingling to find yourself thrust into the midst of stupendous events here?

ELMIRE *(with an effort)*. What–are these events?

BLANCHONNET. You may well ask. I can't help laughing. All morning you've been observing this sequence of apparitions passing on their way: the Prefect's secretary—a journalist—a photographer—a man from the radio. Doesn't it make your head spin?

ELMIRE. Why are all these people coming to you?

BLANCHONNET. A photographer, for example? What does a photographer want with Blanchonnet? To trim his beard? He wants a picture of him–beard and all! To capture the complete, genuine Blanchonnet on his photo, so as to bring him to the eyes of millions— yes, it's millions again! Your magazine will soon be carrying me across the seas.

ELMIRE. To—the Argentine?

BLANCHONNET. One little corner of the world that occurs to you. Whatever makes you think of that in particular? *(ELMIRE looks at him helplessly.)* What about the Argentine? Does it spring to your mind because it was one of the last things you learnt about at the convent?

ELMIRE *(quickly)*. It wasn't in the convent.

BLANCHONNET. Where else, that you should pick on the Argentine of all the countries in the world?

ELMIRE *(hesitant)*. From Buenos Aires—there are–

BLANCHONNET. The capital of the Argentine. Quite a busy trading port. The chief export is frozen meat or tinned meat. But that's enough geography. I must get ready to give my talk. *(He rummages among the papers on his desk.)*

ELMIRE *(making a fresh start)*. What are you going to talk about?

BLANCHONNET *(looks up in astonishment)*. Just as if that wireless fellow had left his echo behind. Are you trying to pull my leg?

ELMIRE *(goes closer to the desk)*. What—is your talk to be about?

BLANCHONNET. I shan't know that myself until I'm standing in front of the microphone, and there's no escape. Anyway, I can't find anything interesting among these papers. Away into the drawer with them! *(He locks them all away.)* Perhaps there's something more worthwhile in the case. *(He dashes into his room down left and returns with a yellow case, which he sets down on the desk and opens. First of all he takes out a bundle of money.)* Ahah–that's lying right at the top for anyone to take. *(Thumbing over the notes)* Quite a bit of money. It's silly to keep all that much in a hotel room. It ought to be in a safe. Why didn't I deposit it when I was talking to the manager about it? I was side-tracked –and I hope we hadn't spoken about it too loud. Did you notice if anyone in the hall showed any special interest when I was saying that this case had a lot of money in it? No? But I'm still not too happy about it. Up here you are the custodian of the treasure! *(He puts the bundle of notes aside and takes out some papers.)* Useless–useless–none of it'll satisfy their hunger for the sensational. Statutes–programmes– programmes–statutes—*(looking up)* it's true enough, as soon as you get your hands on something, it runs through your fingers like water. Where's some action??

ELMIRE *(exclaiming almost joyfully).* There isn't any—you say so yourself.

BLANCHONNET. What have you been hearing?

ELMIRE. That there–isn't any–in—

BLANCHONNET. In?

ELMIRE. —in the Argentine either!!

BLANCHONNET *(shaking his head).* The Argentine seems to be the land of your dreams. *(The sound of a motor-horn outside.)* That's a signal blaring out for me. Into the universe. I must obey its call. Even without a script. I'll conquer the cosmos off the cuff. The spur of the moment shall be my blessing—or my undoing! *(He shuts and locks the case.)* Don't let it out of your sight, the yellow case. It contains money— a lot of money! *(Takes the case into the room down left—returns with hat and gloves. Kissing* ELMIRE *on the brow.)* Stay by yourself for just half-an-hour–I won't be longer, or I'll miss the Prefect's visit. This time I won't lock you in—you keep the key and lock the door from the inside. I might get it all muddled up again! *(He leaves–right.)*

ELMIRE *(stands still, ponders—until with an effort she cuts short her indecision by lifting the telephone).* I want to speak to Mrs Brown– Mrs Brown–Brown–In the hotel—Not in the hotel? *(Puts down the telephone—stares in front of her. Then she decides to make her way to the door—hesitates at the door—opens it—leaves.* ELMIRE *returns with* MRS BROWN—*in an overcoat, the dog in her arms.)*

MRS BROWN *(panting).* My dear child, what methods you use! Veritably falling upon me in the vestibule—dragging me to the lift—my poor heart feels as if it'll burst! What's it all about?

ELMIRE. You're just leaving?

MRS BROWN. Who's just—

ELMIRE. That's what you said to the manager.

MRS BROWN. Did you hear that?

ELMIRE. When I came up, before I spoke to you.

MRS BROWN. Certainly, I asked for my bill. But that doesn't necessarily mean I'm going away. We're simply moving to another hotel in the town.

ELMIRE. And you shouldn't have gone away—before I'd talked to you.

MRS BROWN. Couldn't you have let me know what you wanted downstairs, in a rather less aggresive fashion?

ELMIRE. When I tried, I couldn't reach you on the telephone, Mrs Brown.

MRS BROWN. Did you telephone?

ELMIRE. The porter didn't know you.

MRS BROWN. Because—we'd already cancelled our booking. The names are already crossed out in the register—and in his head. To make room for new arrivals. The porter is quite blameless—I'm defending the man myself.

ELMIRE. What the porter said is of no importance.

MRS BROWN. You know, the room I had was directly above this one, on the second floor. Balcony and view as alike as two peas in a pod. Hasn't Fifi's barking sometimes disturbed you, when I took him out on to the balcony on certain little errands? He has such a funny, sharp bark. Like an angry turkey-cock.

ELMIRE. Shall we sit down, Mrs Brown?

MRS BROWN. But why? Everything's quite in order now, you know. I've got my pass. *(Searching in her handbag)* Here it—Fifi, get out of the way. Fifi's perpetually in the way. Fifi won't let me look for the pass. *(She shuts her bag again)* Mr Ravanini is also in possession of a pass. Surely nothing else can be wrong?

ELMIRE. It's—It's about Mr Ravanini.

MRS BROWN. About—has he behaved badly to you? You were alone with him earlier on. He does get carried away so easily. A terrible failing of his. Did he make suggestions to you?

ELMIRE. He—told me lies.

MRS BROWN. What? What lies? *(ELMIRE nods.)* Why should he tell lies-that you see through afterwards? *(ELMIRE looks at MRS BROWN.)* What in the world was he trying to make you believe then?

ELMIRE. I-told a lie too.

MRS BROWN. My dear girl-you'll really have to speak more plainly to an old woman like me!

ELMIRE. I hadn't found your names on the list, when I was looking for them in the other room.

MRS BROWN. Well why did you say you'd found us then?

ELMIRE. Because I was so utterly confused—by what Mr Ravanini had been saying-that I couldn't have read if I'd tried!

MRS BROWN. I don't know what Mr Ravanini told you, but judging by the effect, he must have served you up some hair-raising stories. You actually make me curious—and I'm used to his juicy tales. Well?

ELMIRE. It got me into such a state that when you were here before with Mr Ravanini-I couldn't even tell you who I am.

MRS BROWN. And who are you?

ELMIRE. I'm-not the secretary. I'm the daughter-whose father fetched her only yesterday from the convent. This evening my mother's coming

-with Gaston-this evening I'm to be engaged!! *(Covers her face in her hands.)*

MRS BROWN *(watches her, then lays her hand on* ELMIRE'S *arm).* What's your name?

ELMIRE. Elmire.

MRS BROWN. Daddy's little girl, whom he leaves sitting here all alone.

ELMIRE. Yes.

MRS BROWN. And what's become of daddy meanwhile?

ELMIRE. Gone off to give a talk—they came for him with a car.

MRS BROWN. A cruel papa!

ELMIRE. Father isn't cruel—

MRS BROWN. Or poor fiancé, who's not arriving until the evening. Do you love him so much?

ELMIRE. I don't know him—and I don't want to know him—until everything Mr Ravanini said turns out to be—lies.

MRS BROWN. Has Mr Ravanini been saying things about your intended?

ELMIRE. Not about him-not about individuals. He spread darkness over the whole of God's creation.

MRS BROWN. Only the devil himself can do that. And Ravanini has never appeared to me in that shape!

ELMIRE. It can't be true—because my father's every look, every word contradicts it!

MRS BROWN. Did you inform him about us?

ELMIRE. Could I have brought out a single word—without falling senseless with shame?!

MRS BROWN. You didn't mention our visit to M Blanchonnet?

ELMIRE. No—I couldn't do it!

MRS BROWN. Then-why are you calling me back?

ELMIRE. Is there anyone but you I can talk to? You have taken to me- you kissed me on the forehead. So I tried to telephone you and then took you by surprise in the hall. Forgive me. Will you forgive me?

MRS BROWN. My dear, I've long since forgotten all about it.

ELMIRE *(kisses her hand).* How kind you are! Like a mother. I can ask you things one would ask a mother. Will you tell me the truth?

MRS BROWN. If I know it—

ELMIRE. By the sacred heart of Jesus?

MRS BROWN. Agreed!

ELMIRE. Then I'll tell you: the congress isn't like you think—like Mr Ravanini believes. You are all terribly mistaken. That sort of thing has never happened-it isn't happening. Not in the Argentine-or any other corner of the world-that girls are sold-into houses-where seamen come-and sail away again in their ships-after being in the houses with the girls-girls they don't know and don't love-and yet they take them- for money they hand over-just as they do for everything else they buy!! How can such a house stand in a street that runs through the centre of a

town? Wouldn't the screams of the girls, who are forced to endure that,
rouse the whole town?! You'd hear their cries for help from the moon–
and do you mean to say they're not heard down here?! Nothing is heard
–because there is nothing to hear–because the streets–houses–screams
and girls don't exist!!! *(She fixes her gaze on* MRS BROWN'S *face.
MRS BROWN smiles.)* Would my father let himself be photographed?
Would he go visiting the Prefect? Would he go running here and there
with a radiant face!? Didn't he search through the papers–and find
nothing? So there is nothing in it–and all the talk is so much empty
words–*(unsure of herself)* Why don't you say something?
MRS BROWN. When did they fetch you away from the convent?
ELMIRE. Yesterday. But why do you ask?
MRS BROWN. It would have been better—to leave you in the convent.
ELMIRE. I wanted to become a nun.
MRS BROWN. Then you've been greatly sinned against.
ELMIRE. Why?
MRS BROWN. Because angels lose their wings among mortals.
ELMIRE. What–do you mean by that?
MRS BROWN. That Mr Ravanini's account is unhappily true.
ELMIRE. What—is true?
MRS BROWN. What sounded so dreadful in your terrified ears when
    you first heard it. You got over your terror later on. Man is weak.
ELMIRE. I'm not weak–I want to know everything.
MRS BROWN *(sighing).* You're giving me a hard task—
ELMIRE. Don't refuse me. On my knees I beg you—
MRS BROWN. I'll do it—but don't start screaming in here!
ELMIRE. I'll sit here on my chair and not make a sound.
MRS BROWN *(pausing).* Don't you remember a friend—as young and
    as pretty as yourself–who suddenly disappeared one day–and no-one
    ever discovered where to?
ELMIRE *(pressing).* What would have happened to her?
MRS BROWN. This girl would have fallen into the hands of the white
    slave traders. A lightning attack in the open street–a car is waiting–
    quickly the victim is drugged–and when she wakes up again . . . the
    worst is already over.
ELMIRE. What is—the worst??
MRS BROWN. Her first client in one of the houses.
ELMIRE. In—
MRS BROWN. Or brothel, so as not to avoid the technical terms.
ELMIRE. Does the victim—kill herself after that?
MRS BROWN. Why should she kill herself?
ELMIRE. She'd have to kill herself!
MRS BROWN. Because a man was there? There are more to come. You
    don't die of that. Life can take many forms. You don't willingly
    separate yourself from your heart-beat. In the end you pay for it in any
    coin: in this case, with love. *(*ELMIRE *stares at her.)* Do you find it

very painful? A wrinkled brow? Real furrows in your white skin? What's going on in that little head?

ELMIRE *(expressionless).* Father has his photograph taken—

MRS BROWN. Does he do that?

ELMIRE. He talks on the air—

MRS BROWN. Oh?

ELMIRE. He visits the Prefect—

MRS BROWN. That too?

ELMIRE. He goes off to the reception in the gardens—

MRS BROWN. That's to be this evening.

ELMIRE *(looking at* MRS BROWN *in astonishment-shrinking from her).* Don't you see—the glaring contradiction-between this-and that??

MRS BROWN. Why, Elmire, whatever's the matter?

ELMIRE. You ask me that—me, who has no power—

MRS BROWN. Do at least moderate your voice!

ELMIRE. –to prevent your president for ever wasting his time??!!

MRS BROWN *(observes her narrowly-then gets up and goes to* ELMIRE*).* I understood you long ago. Only you had to think of it for yourself. It was not for me to set a daughter against her father. Now sit down, and hear my confession. For I haven't told the truth, either! *(She leads* ELMIRE *back to her chair, and sits down herself.)* It was not true that we-Ravanini and I-were moving to another hotel. In fact, we are going away. We're leaving the congress, which is incapable of achieving anything. Even the will to do so is lacking. It began with the slackness over the missing passes. And that remains typical of the attitude prevailing here. Not a trace of real seriousness. It's just a fair-ground for vainglory that's been opened. We shuddered to observe these things—and then to have them confirmed out of your mouth. The president sets the tone, and all the members of the congress follow his lead. They have no thought any more for the task they set themselves. Photograph-radio-prefect-Jack's no better than his master. All but two accepted a programme like that. But two didn't—and those two are Ravanini and myself. We are not prepared to play their game-we're washing our hands of the whole business!

ELMIRE *(hesitant).* If you leave the congress—

MRS BROWN. What difference will it make? Will it be any loss? We shall book a profit. We've learned—that it is we who must work-and ten times as energetically, to make up for the sins of omission here. The few get most done-believe me, there's never yet been a league-however many heads it could put together-which so much as scared a sparrow off a roof. But a single individual hits the mark every time with a gun that's as straight as a die. Over in the Argentine we shan't have a congress with president, photograph, and prefect-but we shall have time and have a purpose: to wage war on the houses of ill fame or brothels, until not a stone is left standing and all their victims are liberated from their gloomy walls!

ELMIRE. What wonderful things you say!

MRS BROWN. We mustn't let ourselves be carried away by words, my dear. That would be committing the very fault we are condemning. We must act–deeds, not words! There is no-one so humble that his services would not be welcome. You, too, can help. Soon you will be the first to join with us!

ELMIRE. How can I help?

MRS BROWN. Did I not speak of services–which you, and you alone, can render?

ELMIRE. What services do you mean?

MRS BROWN. The president has the documents that contain valuable pieces of evidence. Tomorrow he'll read them out to the congress—and then file them away again. They'll pass without having any effect. But it would be a great help to us if we knew about them. Do you see what I mean?

ELMIRE. The documents are in my father's possession–

MRS BROWN. And of course he shall keep them, my dear child–not a single precious page shall be removed. All I want to do is to make a few notes. I'll find what I want if I look through the papers. Are they in the desk?

ELMIRE. Yes.

MRS BROWN. Is the desk locked?

ELMIRE. My father locked it before he left.

MRS BROWN. Silly. Naturally we must respect the lock. But didn't you say something about a case that had documents in it?

ELMIRE. That's the yellow case.

MRS BROWN. Those will be the most important documents. They're the ones we ought to get hold of.

ELMIRE. The case is locked too.

MRS BROWN. That's no very great misfortune. I have a lot of keys, and one of them is sure to fit. Anyway, it's worth a try. Would you like to bring me the case?

ELMIRE. Shall I bring it in here from the other room?

MRS BROWN. I'll come with you, if it's too much trouble.

ELMIRE. It's not the trouble I mind–

MRS BROWN. Because we're doing it behind your father's back?

ELMIRE. It's not that—

MRS BROWN. But there is something that makes you hesitate to do this trifling service in the cause of chastity, isn't there?

ELMIRE. If—you wish—

MRS BROWN. Because it's necessary!

ELMIRE. I'll bring the case. *(She goes into the room left, leaving the door half open.)*

MRS BROWN *(rises, opens the door right and speaks to someone outside).* Is that you, Ravanini? I can recognize your step even through doors. It shows how accustomed one can get to someone's company.

Come on in! *(Ravanini enters.* MRS BROWN *continues very loud.)*
Were you looking for me, to set out on our journey home?

RAVANINI *(also loud).* Of course I was looking for you. Our train'll
be leaving without us. What's to become of us—without rooms? I don't
understand you any more, my dear friend!

MRS BROWN. I expected that. But all sorts of things have been
happening since I saw you—and they justify the highest hopes!

RAVANINI. You're not exaggerating simply to comfort me after my
long separation from you? You know it would be the death of me not to
see you!

MRS BROWN. I've found an invaluable helper in the charming person
of the president's daughter!

RAVANINI. Where is there a daughter here?

MRS BROWN. The one you took for the secretary is Mlle Elmire
Blanchonnet—brought yesterday from the convent and destined to
meet her future husband this evening!

RAVANINI. My congratulations!

MRS BROWN. Which are not called for, Ravanini. The innocent girl
from the convent is protesting against the way the most burning
question facing mankind is to be treated at the congress. That is,
frivolously. And as you know that is the reason we are withdrawing
from its deliberations. We can then carry on the work in the Argentine
at our own expense—with the material the young lady is going to let me
glance through. Meanwhile you can take Elmire over to the window
and entertain her in your charming way.

RAVANINI. I can hardly wait for the pleasure!

MRS BROWN. —so that I can look over the contents of the case at the
desk without being disturbed!

RAVANINI. Is she bringing the case in here?

MRS BROWN. It would be polite if you were to give the young lady a
hand with it!

RAVANINI. Wouldn't she think me presumptuous?

MRS BROWN. It seems to be desirable—she's taking a long time
coming back!

RAVANINI. Already too late—here she is!

ELMIRE *comes back into the room without the case.* MRS BROWN
looks at her.

RAVANINI *(to* MRS BROWN*).* Here she is—but without the aforesaid
case!

MRS BROWN. Isn't the case there?

ELMIRE. Yes, it is.

MRS BROWN. Why didn't you bring it? You can hear how my friend is
making fun of me, because I trusted you to help us. What makes you
disappoint me?

ELMIRE. I'm not going to disappoint you—

MRS BROWN. And yet you come out of the other room empty-handed?

ELMIRE. That doesn't alter my decision—to show you the case—this evening.

MRS BROWN. This evening? By this evening we shall be travelling through another part of the countryside. You can't have considered that properly!

ELMIRE. I want to see you again this evening, Mrs. Brown!

MRS BROWN. Why not before the evening? What's going to happen in the meantime? (ELMIRE *cannot speak.*)

RAVANINI *(to* MRS BROWN*).* You can see the young lady doesn't wish to talk about it at the moment. She wants to wait till this evening. We owe it to the cause to stay until the evening. Though not in the hotel, where we no longer have rooms. I'll be in the hotel garden during the evening—and when the young lady waves her handkerchief from the balcony, we shall know that we can come up here and make up for what we are missing now. Does that arrangement suit you?

ELMIRE. I'll wave my handkerchief from the balcony!

RAVANINI. What do you think, Mrs Brown?

MRS BROWN. I think of Romeo and Juliet.

RAVANINI. Because of the balcony scene?

MRS BROWN. And two very young people to play it!

RAVANINI *gestures to her to be quiet—bows to* ELMIRE *and leads* MRS BROWN *quickly out of the room with him.* ELMIRE *goes over and shuts the door to the balcony. The door on the right is thrown open—* BLANCHONNET *comes in—pushes the door shut behind him.*

BLANCHONNET. Well, that's the ether conquered, too. The intrepid spirit of conquest—the legacy of generations—came into its own and subdued the oceans of the air—with its winging birds and its howling winds. Could you hear it rushing past the window? It was I who caused it! *(He goes up to* ELMIRE, *pats her cheek.)* Of course, it's technically impossible for radio to raise the wind. Words leap from aerial to aerial in complete stillness. It comes to life only in the receiver. So you can't have heard anything! *(Laying aside hat and gloves)* You can't—but a thousand and ten thousand besides: they were listening to me. And I didn't disappoint them. I have done what was required. I fulfilled every demand. Even in the car I still found myself confronting the void—in vain I cast about in the emptiness. But in front of the microphone the wall collapsed. I was filled with burgeoning fancies. Sentence upon sentence poured from my lips. I scarcely recognized my own voice. It took on a resonant tone that surprised me. Finally I was speaking simply for the sake of this resonance. It lent me wings—I sketched the most striking pictures in the most vivid colours. Details leapt to my mind. I showed corsairs being hunted down on the raging seas—I stood on the bridge myself. I arranged struggles in the dingy dockside streets in which blood was flowing. I didn't even omit the aeroplane from which we came floating down by parachute. I commanded an army of agents, every one of them fevered with desire to lay down his life for my standard. A sublime vision! I have seized the moment that will not come again—or will it return? A yet greater moment beckoning to Blanchonnet? What will it hold for me?! *(He stands gazing heavenward.)*

ELMIRE *(forcing herself to speak calmly)*. You—must let them know you can't attend the reception this evening.

BLANCHONNET *(alarmed)*. Has the Prefect sent a message? Can't he manage it? Already gone back to Paris?

ELMIRE. Because—you can't manage it.

BLANCHONNET. Has something happened to Gaston? Have you had a telegram from your mother? Where's the telegram?

ELMIRE. None of them will go to the reception. Not one.

BLANCHONNET. Who are 'they'?

ELMIRE. You and the others—who have gathered for the congress.

BLANCHONNET *(jokingly)*. Have the prefecture gardens been struck by a hurricane, so that he can't receive any guests?

ELMIRE. The reception must not take place.

BLANCHONNET. In heaven's name—whoever is protesting about it?

ELMIRE. The victims, who are living in the brothels. *(*BLANCHONNET *stares at her speechless.)* The girls in the houses of ill fame who are waiting to be liberated!

BLANCHONNET *(stuttering)*. Who was—Where did you—*(*ELMIRE *resolutely withstands his searching scrutiny.)* Is there a radio in the hotel? Did you hear my talk? Is there a loud-speaker going in the neighbourhood? *(*ELMIRE *makes no reply.)* Desk and case are locked—are they locked? *(Goes towards the desk.)*

ELMIRE. Yes, they are.

BLANCHONNET. Then I can't understand how you—

ELMIRE. That's the least of your worries!

BLANCHONNET *(disconcerted)*. Elmire—have you taken leave of your senses? Using words that one never mentions—that a young girl like you shouldn't even know!

ELMIRE. I do know them now—and I'll never forget them again!

BLANCHONNET. I couldn't be more surprised if I were struck by lightning—Was it only yesterday you left the convent?

ELMIRE. Just in time—to remind you of your duty!

BLANCHONNET. Have I neglected anything? Was the Prefect here on his return visit? Has he been explaining things to you?

ELMIRE. The Prefect doesn't come into it.

BLANCHONNET. I should have to make my apologies at once, and let him know the reasons for my absence. I could telephone—or to nip any disagreeableness in the bud—see him personally. Has the Prefect called?

ELMIRE. No.

BLANCHONNET *(with a sigh of relief)*. Otherwise it would cause me to regret this interlude with the wireless—however valuable it is as propaganda.

ELMIRE. The only important thing is—for you to set an example for all to see.

BLANCHONNET. In what connection?

ELMIRE. To act—and not merely talk!

BLANCHONNET *(puzzled)*. What are you talking about?

ELMIRE. So far about nothing. So far your whole interest has been absorbed by photographs and the wireless and the Prefect!

BLANCHONNET. When have I been left any time for you?

ELMIRE. I don't need it. I am not in danger. I live in the protection of the convent or of my home. But—my sisters are crying out for help!

BLANCHONNET. Where have you any sisters?

ELMIRE. In the ports of the world—where seamen come from their ships—and go to the girls in the houses!

BLANCHONNET. That doesn't exist!

ELMIRE. Don't the dark streets run through the centre of sunny cities?

BLANCHONNET. Not as far as you are concerned!

ELMIRE. Have you obliterated them from the town-plans? Between morning and noon? With the photographer or the Prefect? Will their liberation be celebrated in his garden this evening?

BLANCHONNET *(disconcerted)*. I must be dreaming—the voice—can it be Elmire's voice?

ELMIRE. The voice is mine—but its cry reaches you from all those you have abandoned in their suffering! Will you hear them?

BLANCHONNET. I can hear nothing!

ELMIRE. You're busy. You've no time. You forget who you gave the key of your room to—and are surprised by open doors!

BLANCHONNET. Who did I give the key to?

ELMIRE. You've forgotten. It's of no consequence. Passes are missing —and anyone watching the way you waste your energies on showy trivialities—packs up and goes home!

BLANCHONNET. Whose passes are missing?

ELMIRE. You play the part of president—as if the president were more important than the congress. You have your photo taken and your picture appears in the papers. It'll be seen everywhere, won't it? Everywhere!! In the brothels, where the girls will look at it—and heap curses on it, because the president, in spite of all his power, has failed to save them! He failed to save them—because he thought to win greater glory by visiting the Prefect and receiving his visit!!! *(The telephone on the desk rings.)*

BLANCHONNET *(goes to it and lifts the receiver)*. Personally—Yes, certainly—Yes, please ask him to come. *(Replacing the receiver—to* ELMIRE*)* The Prefect is on his way to see me!

ELMIRE. You shan't receive him!!

BLANCHONNET. Am I to send the Prefect away?

ELMIRE. With the plain statement that your time belongs to the poor violated creatures—and not to the Prefect! Telephone through that you can't see him!!

BLANCHONNET. It's too late. He's already in the lift.

ELMIRE. Lock the door!

BLANCHONNET *(in amazement).* With the Prefect coming??

ELMIRE. It will be the clearest indication of your transformation!!

BLANCHONNET. Into a fool. *(ELMIRE backs away from him.)* Are you going? I want to introduce you to the Prefect! *(ELMIRE reaches the door back left—turns the handle. BLANCHONNET shrugs.)* All right then—some other time! *(There is a knock. BLANCHONNET gets himself into position.)* Come in!

The door on the right is opened by two PAGEBOYS. ELMIRE leaves, back left. BLANCHONNET is already bowing towards the door on the right.

ACT THREE

BLANCHONNET *comes out of his room: he is wearing a braided smoking-jacket. After considerable stretching and yawning, he goes over to the door back left.*

BLANCHONNET. Elmire, it's time we went to the station. How would it be if we walked? That would give us some fresh air after the long afternoon in our rooms. At least, it would do me good to get an airing. I slept like a log—my head felt like a lump of lead. I must get that blown away. Get yourself ready!

He saunters to the balcony and looks through the panes. ELMIRE enters. The costume of the convent schoolgirl shrouds her in black—the large crucifix shines silver on her breast.

BLANCHONNET *(does not hear ELMIRE coming).* Splendid weather —might be made to order. It'll be the work of the devil if everyone isn't in an exalted frame of mind. I certainly won't be found wanting! *(He turns round—sees ELMIRE. Taken aback)* Are you going to meet mama and Gaston dressed like that? *(ELMIRE shakes her head.)* Why have you put on your convent clothes?

ELMIRE. I've been praying.

BLANCHONNET. Praying?

ELMIRE. For you!

BLANCHONNET. You desire the success of the functions for which I am responsible. With the aid of heaven, to which you have appealed on my behalf. Thank you for that! *(He goes to her.)*

ELMIRE. That was not what I was praying for.

BLANCHONNET. Well then, you had some other motive. Tell me about it on the way. We are walking to the station. We can talk as we go. Go and get dressed now. I'm going to change my jacket, too. *(He makes to go into his room.)*

ELMIRE. I'm—not going!

'BLANCHONNET. On foot? Do you want to go by car?

ELMIRE. I'm staying here—and wearing no other clothes but my convent uniform!

BLANCHONNET. What's the meaning of that?

ELMIRE. That I don't want to be guilty of forgetting for a single moment to pray that your darkness may be lightened!

BLANCHONNET *(uncertainly)*. Does that refer to the business with the Prefect, whom I was supposed to send away?

ELMIRE. To everything that is not connected with the salvation of those most pitiable of creatures!

BLANCHONNET. Are you repeating—what I thought I was merely dreaming?!

ELMIRE. So long as the reality exists, I'll speak of it—to you—to everyone!

BLANCHONNET. Not to Gaston!

ELMIRE. I shall call upon everyone to help!

BLANCHONNET. Elmire—you don't know what you're doing. The very fact that you aren't there to meet Gaston from the train will upset him. I shall make excuses for your absence, of course. But to proclaim to your fiancé even before your first kiss a knowledge of matters—in a young girl who came out of the convent yesterday and is getting engaged today—it'll lead to catastrophe . . . Don't you see the grave you're digging?

ELMIRE. Whose grave?

BLANCHONNET. Whose? Your own!

ELMIRE. No—I don't see it.

BLANCHONNET. You'll fall blindly into it—if I don't hold you back. Elmire, pray that I may be given grace to open both your eyes. Your charm lies in your innocence. For Gaston. For men in general. There you have a capital asset that no dowry could make good. You are a Croesus in your innocence. Don't squander this one asset—with thoughtless words. Say nothing in front of Gaston. Not now—not soon —after years you can talk about everything. It can't do any further damage then!

ELMIRE. I won't tell lies—by concealing what I know!

BLANCHONNET. Why, you know nothing at all. You've picked up a few odd words. Wisps of hints floating on the breeze. I don't know their origin.

ELMIRE. Nothing was kept from me!

BLANCHONNET. All right, then: you know all about it. You're thoroughly informed about everything that goes on in the world. There are dens of depravity—just as there is nothing that does not exist on earth. But leave it to me to worry about getting rid of these disturbing things. Leave it all to me—the man who brought together this congress!

ELMIRE. You have your photo taken—

BLANCHONNET. I'm doing my best to meet the demands made on me. Can I be reproached if I gain some personal advantage at the same time? It's simply added unto me—am I to try subtracting it? You don't realize—my sweat and my money are both flowing!

ELMIRE. Your money?

BLANCHONNET. My money—with which I'm financing the congress. I'm meeting the cost from my own pocket. I've turned everything I possess into cash, down to the last penny. Don't you believe it? Open the yellow case—and the notes'll flutter out at you. With their loss I should be poor—but made for life if I spend them properly!

ELMIRE. On the congress?

BLANCHONNET. On this International Action League against the White Slave Trade, which has mouldered for years among the files of a deceased client, whose papers I had to sort out. I brought it back to life —I mobilized the surviving members and invited them to the conference—at my expense. That's how I became president! One has to be president—of something or other—that opens the way ahead. To any heights. I have every intention of forging ahead—and I'm already picking the first fruits from the tree of fulfilments: our union with the Sillon-Dudet family. The way leads to the palace of another president —the President of the Republic! Is a whim of my daughter's to stand between me and my brightest prospects?!

ELMIRE (trembling). I'll never get engaged to—

BLANCHONNET. Don't I speak convincingly?

ELMIRE. I shall tell Gaston—

BLANCHONNET. What will you tell him?

ELMIRE. Why you've arranged the congress!

BLANCHONNET. What sort of effect do you promise yourself from that? It'll do nothing to alter the fact of my presidency! In any case, your mother will forbid you to pass any remarks of a dubious character.

ELMIRE. Mother will understand me, if—

BLANCHONNET. If you use these terrible expressions?—I don't dare even to remember having heard them from your lips!

ELMIRE. But she's my mother!

BLANCHONNET. And you can thank your creator that she is! Otherwise we'd all be lost. She won't tolerate the breath of a syllable of what you're preparing to say. Or would you defy your mother's orders? We should be surprised.

ELMIRE. Then who am I to talk to?

BLANCHONNET. You won't find anyone among our acquaintants to listen to you. And who else is there?

ELMIRE (hesitant). None of you—

BLANCHONNET. Here you are watched over between these four walls!

ELMIRE. Who–else–is there? *(Turns her head towards the balcony door.)*

BLANCHONNET. What are you thinking of? What are you looking at? What do you find so interesting out there?

ELMIRE *(grips his arm)*. Pray with me!—Down on your knees!—We must pray—pray—pray! *(She kneels.)*

BLANCHONNET. What does this sudden outburst mean?

ELMIRE *(pressing the crucifix to her lips)*. I want to pray—that I may not do it—and I kiss the holy cross—from which comes the power—and the strength—

BLANCHONNET. What do you need the strength not to do?

ELMIRE *(reaches out a hand to him)*. Help me in my prayer—for which I am too weak alone—to raise my supplication—to the throne of the Virgin—

BLANCHONNET. Moderate your incomprehensible transports!

ELMIRE *(almost touching the floor with her forehead)*. I beseech you—unsullied maiden of heaven—for your grace—and for forgiveness for all the things—that I shall do!

BLANCHONNET. That's enough, Elmire. It's high time we were going. You've still got to get changed. I'll hurry, too. We'll scarcely get there in time by car now! *(He goes into his room. ELMIRE remains kneeling. BLANCHONNET returns with hat and gloves.)* Aren't you getting ready to come to the station with me? *(ELMIRE makes no move.)* Apparently not. I don't want to force you to. You don't feel like it. We'll overlook it, as it's you. In everyone's interest. So your first meeting with your fiancé will be arranged here in the hotel. But we won't have any of your antics. You know what's at stake. I'm relying on my daughter. Sort out your ideas. All honour to the cross—but the honours of this world have their glories too. A true Blanchonnet doesn't start crying when glimpses of the future open up before her to the accompaniment of thunder and lightning. Wait for Gaston, as we described you to him: a radiant girl, ripe for love—and not a penitent with cross and rosary and veil. He wouldn't look twice at that. See to the necessary transformation while I'm away. I'm going now! *(Leaves right.)*

ELMIRE *realizes that she has been left by herself. With a plaintive gesture she stretches out her arm. She rises from her knees—gravitates to the balcony door—opens it—steps out on to it—peers over the balustrade—waves. Now she waits in the room—her gaze fixed on the door right. RAVANINI—with hat and coat—enters quickly.*

RAVANINI *(rapidly surveying the room)*. I—didn't knock. If one's expected, one can skip the formalities. At least in my humble opinion.

ELMIRE. Where's Mrs Brown?

RAVANINI. Mrs Brown will be here too—if it's worth her while.

ELMIRE. Why hasn't she come yet?

RAVANINI. You can't expect an elderly lady to walk all that way again, when she's already done it twice in one day.

ELMIRE. Walk where?

RAVANINI. Up here. In the morning—in the afternoon—and both times without any tangible success. Now her confidence is a bit shaken, I can assure you.

ELMIRE. But I am prepared—to do anything!

RAVANINI. You said that once before, and came back from the other room—without the case.

ELMIRE. I'll explain that to Mrs Brown once she's here. I can speak only in Mrs Brown's presence!

RAVANINI. There are difficulties about that—

ELMIRE *(alarmed)*. Has she left?

RAVANINI. Supposing she has left?

ELMIRE. I should have to—kill myself!

RAVANINI. Whatever's the matter?

ELMIRE. If Mrs Brown doesn't come—I'll kill myself!

RAVANINI *(businesslike)*. Shall we be alone here? Mrs Brown, you, and I? Mrs Brown refuses to meet any member of the congress—including the president. Absolutely!

ELMIRE. We are alone.

RAVANINI. Nobody else in the other rooms—either there or there?

ELMIRE. My father has gone to the station.

RAVANINI. No-one else?

ELMIRE. Only myself.

RAVANINI. Will you bring us the case?

ELMIRE. I'll bring Mrs Brown the case.

RAVANINI. Is that a promise?

ELMIRE. I waved, didn't I?

RAVANINI *gives her a quick, searching look—then he goes out on to the balcony and waves his hat. He comes back into the room!*

ELMIRE. Where is Mrs Brown?

RAVANINI. She's been sitting for hours in the café over there. And I had a hard enough time keeping her there—until you could bring yourself to give the signal. In the end I was counting the leaves on the flowers down there. Four million of them. Would you believe that?

ELMIRE. Yes—I believe you.

RAVANINI. That is charming of you. As a matter of fact, it was five million. What do you say to that for honesty?

ELMIRE. I think you're telling the truth.

RAVANINI. How have I come to enjoy your blind faith in me?

ELMIRE. Because Mrs Brown wouldn't have brought you with her on this trip otherwise!

RAVANINI *(laughing).* You must tell that to Mrs Brown yourself!— Here she is. *(He goes to the door left and opens it.* MRS BROWN *enters –in hat and coat, without the dog.)*

MRS BROWN *(to* ELMIRE*).* What's happened? In black? Has there been a death in your family?

ELMIRE. I'm wearing my convent clothes again.

MRS BROWN. To welcome your intended? Is that what he wanted?

ELMIRE. To help me concentrate better in my prayers.

MRS BROWN *(to* RAVANINI*).* She's been saying her prayers! *(Taking* ELMIRE'S *hands)* Have they all been answered? Surely. When angels pray, God cannot but give them his blessing. That's right, isn't it?

ELMIRE *(shakes her head).* They just faded away—into emptiness.

MRS BROWN. Oh surely not. Why, that's blasphemy. Then we should all have to remain silent and despair of God's goodness. He will show himself in his own good time!

ELMIRE. Never!

MRS BROWN. You sound as if you were utterly without hope. Who is standing in the way of your begging and praying?

ELMIRE. My—father.

MRS BROWN. Has he left you all by yourself again?

ELMIRE. I refused to go to the station with him.

MRS BROWN. Are they arriving now?

ELMIRE. My mother—and my fiancé—whom I shan't marry!

MRS BROWN. Whom you won't— These are just fairy-tales you're telling me, to scare me.

ELMIRE. Can I marry him, while these terrible things are going on in the world?

MRS BROWN. What sort of terrible things?

ELMIRE. That men—in those houses—buy girls!!

MRS BROWN. My dear child, if that's the nightmare which is tormenting you, then take my advice—get married as soon as possible. That'll set your mind at rest!

ELMIRE. You talk like that because you mean to be kind to me. And it's only you I can talk to, because you are disgusted with the congress and prefer to run away rather than have anything to do with this deadly sin of omission that will be on the conscience of all of them—my father and the others!

MRS BROWN. That can be mitigated—

ELMIRE. By no excuse before God or man!

MRS BROWN. —by doing what the others failed to do: by working. We were prepared to do it—but you withheld from us the papers we must look into, if we are to work effectively. So who is it you're accusing?

RAVANINI. Once the case had almost got as far as making its appearance, but you gibbed at the last moment, my dear young lady!

MRS BROWN. So who is to blame now?

ELMIRE. I'm quite ready to admit my weakness, and to reveal why I came back from the other room without the case. Before I produced it, I wanted to beg my father to give up the reception—to forget the Prefect—to have nothing on his mind except the rescuing of God's creatures from the most hideous mistreatment!

MRS BROWN. Well?

ELMIRE. The answer he gave me, Mrs Brown, plucked out my heart, that beat with a child's affection, bit by bit. Mrs Brown, my father is lying when he seeks the help of others. He doesn't want to help. He wants to be president. That serves his purpose—his own purpose! It's to his advantage—even my marriage to Gaston from the ancient Sillon-Dudet family!!

MRS BROWN. What do you think of our president, Ravanini?

RAVANINI. Consideration for his daughter's presence prevents me offering any criticism.

MRS BROWN. A sentiment that does you credit, Ravanini.

RAVANINI. Did you expect anything else of me, Mrs Brown?

MRS BROWN. Poor Elmire! After that, how could I help understanding how difficult it is for you to marry.

ELMIRE. Father intends to force me—mother is going to make me—they demand my silent acceptance, when Gaston comes asking for me. Mrs Brown, I have no mother if you don't listen to me—I shall die a thousand deaths if you don't protect me!

MRS BROWN. You are getting yourself worked up into a state!

ELMIRE. Save me—save me—from—

MRS BROWN. From whom?

ELMIRE. From Gaston!!

MRS BROWN. Am I to take you back to the convent and the everlasting nuns?

ELMIRE (calmly). I'll fetch you the case—

MRS BROWN. At last!

ELMIRE. —on one condition.

MRS BROWN. Any condition—provided the case gets here.

ELMIRE. You must—take me with you!

MRS BROWN (in consternation). But where to?

ELMIRE. Where you are going. To the Argentine.

MRS BROWN. Whatever do you want to go to the Argentine for?

ELMIRE. You come from the Argentine—you are returning to the Argentine. You told me that yourself. You mustn't deny it now—simply to shake me off! (MRS BROWN looks at RAVANINI.)

RAVANINI. Of course we're going back to the Argentine—just as we came from the Argentine. Why shouldn't that still be the case, Mrs Brown?

ELMIRE (close to him). Thank you, Mr Ravanini, for supporting me in my request to Mrs Brown! (To MRS BROWN) And it isn't just a single individual who is involved. You'll be gaining a helper in your task. I want to work at your side—to devote myself to the cause with such dedication as no-one has ever shown before. I'll do exactly as you tell me—and count myself happy to win a smile of satisfaction from you. Don't thrust me away from you!! *(She bends over* MRS BROWN'S *hands.)*

MRS BROWN. My dear child—you put me in a situation—*(looks over her head at* RAVANINI, *who smiles.)*

ELMIRE. Which will surely favour the fulfilment of all your wishes? You wanted to make some hurried notes from the documents—I'll take them and hand them over to you for good!

MRS BROWN. The documents?

ELMIRE. My father has no use for them. He'll let them moulder again. You mustn't hesitate when I offer you my help!

MRS BROWN. I'm not underestimating the value of your efforts, but—

ELMIRE. I might be a nuisance to you on the journey?

MRS BROWN. You'll understand—

ELMIRE. Because travelling costs money? I can pay my own fare—and when we get there I can live on my own money, Mrs Brown—for a long time!

MRS BROWN. Can you lay your hands on such a large sum?

ELMIRE. There's money in the case. Everything my father possesses. He turned it all into cash—for the congress!

MRS BROWN. Are you proposing to relieve him of it?

ELMIRE. To be without it will jog his soul. God intends to chasten his spirit—through me, when he finds it gone. I feel myself to be the instruments of the divine dispensation. Should I hesitate to take father's case?

MRS BROWN. Now you've completely demolished my doubts. Anyone who has this unshakable determination, and—the world being what it is—money, is welcome to travel with me. Come to my arms, Elmire—let me be another mother to you!

ELMIRE *(throws her arms round her)*. And I'll love you and respect you like a mother! *(They kiss each other.)*

MRS BROWN *(to* RAVANINI*)*. You've no need to laugh, Ravanini—because it brings tears to my eyes.

RAVANINI. I'm just congratulating us—on a travelling-companion who is as resolute as she is charming.

MRS BROWN *(to* ELMIRE—*indicating* RAVANINI*)*. You've broken someone's heart, Elmire.

ELMIRE *(laying a hand on* RAVANINI'S *arm)*. I'm sure we shall become good friends, Mr Ravanini.

RAVANINI *(drawing her close to him)*. I am your friend, Elmire! *(*ELMIRE *steps away from him in confusion.)*

MRS BROWN. Well now, let's get moving if we're going to leave. Every minute is precious. Get ready, Elmire!

ELMIRE. I shall hurry now! *(Goes off quickly back left.)*

MRS BROWN *(watching her go and shaking her head)*. Anyone who still didn't believe in miracles must have a heart of stone in his breast!

RAVANINI. Or else learn not to be surprised at miracles, if she actually carries out her intention!

MRS BROWN. Do you doubt that she will?

ELMIRE *(returns—in overcoat and hat)*. I'm only taking my hat and coat. I'll buy what I need on the way.

MRS BROWN. The prettiest things!

ELMIRE. No—I shall dress simply.

MRS BROWN. Thrift is a virtue too!

ELMIRE. Because I want to learn self-denial.

MRS BROWN. That you shall!

ELMIRE. I'll fetch the case! *(Goes off into the room up left.)*

MRS BROWN *(after a short pause)*. We must get hold of a car.

RAVANINI. Why a car?

MRS BROWN. We must get out of the town by car. Or do you want her father to bring her back from the station with a hue and cry?

RAVANINI. It won't come to that.

MRS BROWN. He won't chase after his daughter?

RAVANINI. Because she won't go with us. What's keeping her now?

MRS BROWN *(glancing towards the door)*. Yes, what's keeping her?

RAVANINI. Weren't my doubts justified? The last moment before the final departure is a mountain at which the foot flags. And here it is the delicate foot of a girl about to take a step—

ELMIRE *enters with the yellow case.*

MRS BROWN. Here she is!! Ravanini was doubting whether you'd really come.

ELMIRE. I've just written a note to tell my father that I'm going away from it all. That's what delayed me.

MRS BROWN. That's right, my child, You must let them know where you are, when you aren't there any more.

ELMIRE: I'll put it on the desk. *(She does so.)*

MRS BROWN. The white envelope will flash at him—like a gun going off in his face!

ELMIRE *(to RAVANINI)*. Here—you can take the case.

MRS BROWN. No-one can take it from you now. You must bring it along yourself. Can we walk out of the hotel carrying someone else's luggage? The manager and the porter both know the yellow case. We shouldn't get across the threshold with it—and out into the wide world, which is what you want. You see that, don't you, my angel?

ELMIRE. I'll have to carry it myself?

MRS BROWN. Only out into the street. Then you'll join us in the car —and away we'll go for a fine fast ride through the countryside, and get as far as we can.

RAVANINI. At forty miles an hour!

MRS BROWN. Where to go will occur to us on the way. First we must make a successful start. We can do that if Ravanini and I go on ahead, and you, Elmire, follow us in a little while. Those are our marching orders—and they must be observed whatever happens. Otherwise I can guarantee nothing. Do you hear, Elmire?

ELMIRE. I'll do just as you say.

MRS BROWN. Come along then!

MRS BROWN and RAVANINI *leave, right.*

ELMIRE *waits a while—surveys the room once more—goes to the door. She leaves.* BLANCHONNET *enters. He rapidly crosses the room— knocks on the door at the back left.*

BLANCHONNET. They're here—that is, they're not here yet, but we can expect them to appear at any minute. I dropped a hint to your mother to take Gaston a roundabout way—he's buying you some flowers—because I wanted to find out what state of mind you were in before your fiancé arrives. Incidentally, he looks wonderful! Have you calmed down? Have you changed your dress? All these things are immensely important at the moment—Gaston is expecting something really stunning! Mother has prepared him splendidly on the journey. He's all ready to marry you without stopping to think! We're right on top of the world, Elmire—mother and I. So don't you go putting a spanner in the works! Now you can laugh for sheer happiness. *(He listens.)* You might at least deign to give me some sort of answer. How far have you got with your toilet? Do you need some help? I'll send for the maid. Shall I send her in to you? *(He listens again—knocks.)* Elmire, don't overstrain my affection—and the confidence I have in my daughter. You're not saying a word—and the words are wrung from my agonized heart. That's no exaggeration. Keep faith with me. The thread on which the fame and fortune of the house of Blanchonnet hangs is a silken one. The touch of a finger will sever it. Don't touch it! Come out— and stand resplendent at my side! *(He listens.)* The wood of the door seems to make me unintelligible to you. You ignore my knocking. So you compel me to take less polite measures. Don't attempt any resistance from the inside with the key—with all the strength of desperation I shall break in the—*(He turns the door-handle—and the door opens easily. In astonishment he looks into the room)* Elmire— *(He goes to the door up left—opens it.)* Can you be in my room? *(He returns after glancing into the room; then he inspects the empty balcony —muttering)* No Elmire— *(He goes over to the desk—lifts the telephone)* Porter—is my daughter down in the hall— *(He has already caught sight of the letter. He puts down the telephone—tears open the envelope—and reads. He re-reads it, bending close over the letter, which he presses flat on the top of the desk. Puts his hand to his brow in bewilderment.)* It can't be true—*(Sits erect)* It would be true if— *(He dashes into his room down left—staggers back again.)* The case is missing—*(Now he hurls his hoarse voice into the telephone)* The manager—the manager—I must see the manager—he must come at once!! *(The telephone falls from his hand. He stares at the door right. There is a knock.* BLANCHONNET *gasps out only a gurgling sound. The* MANAGER *enters.)*

MANAGER. Yes, sir, you wanted—

BLANCHONNET *(gestures him to silence. With rasping voice).* Who are—Mrs Brown and Mr Ravanini??

MANAGER. The names are not known to me.

BLANCHONNET *(incensed).* Don't you know the names of your own guests? Don't you have the names of everybody staying in your hotel at your finger-tips? Not Mrs Brown? Mr Ravanini?

MANAGER. The people you mention are not living in the hotel.

BLANCHONNET. They were living in the hotel—but now they've left— and taken with them—prop yourself against the wall for a firm support —*(shouting)* my daughter!!!!

MANAGER *(perplexed).* You'll have to explain it to me more clearly—

BLANCHONNET. Perhaps reading this letter will do that—I can recommend it! *(Hands him the letter.)* Read out what it says—I'm quite muddled up by its contents for a start!

MANAGER *(reads).* 'Father—I am going to devote my life to the work that you have no time for. I am leaving for the Argentine with Mrs Brown and Mr Ravanini. The case with the documents and the money I have taken with me. I shall put it all to its proper use. May God give you enlightenment, Elmire. P.S. It will mean my death if you search for me. *(Looking up)* Who are Mrs Brown and Mr Ravanini?

BLANCHONNET. —who steal my case and my daughter and disappear to the Argentine?

MANAGER. What are the documents that are referred to?

BLANCHONNET. All the important papers concerning the congress are contained in that case. Irreplaceable records. Top secret documents dealing with the organization and methods of the league. The most powerful weapons in the battle against the white slave trade.

MANAGER *(attentive).* Is that what has been stolen?

BLANCHONNET. By the bundle. Not a single scrap remains in our hands. Without records, we are face to face with the void!

MANAGER. Who can have an interest in these papers, M. Blanchonnet?

BLANCHONNET. Have you any idea?

MANAGER. Your adversaries. The enemy you're fighting. The white slave trading fraternity! They took her by surprise—here, in your very headquarters—and these two who call themselves Mrs Brown and Ravanini in this letter, and who sneaked into the hotel under other names—which we'll soon find out—are spies belonging to the gang— they're white slave traders!

BLANCHONNET *(stuttering).* White—slave—traders?

MANAGER. That's perfectly clear to me. A carefully laid plan has been carried out here—and with a degree of boldness that is characteristic of these desperadoes of human society—that is, of these white slavers!

BLANCHONNET. My daughter—in the hands of—white slave traders—

MANAGER. It's certainly the height of impudence: to abduct the daughter of the president of the Action League against White Slave Traders at his own congress!

BLANCHONNET *(wide eyed)*. To the Argentine—she talked about it —I could never understand why—and suddenly knew words—at first their origin was a mystery—now it's lit up by fiery rockets—when it's too late—Elmire is going—unprotected—to her ruin—that will be the downfall of us all!!

MANAGER. The only thing that worries me now is that it happened under my roof. There'll be an awful scandal. The name of my hotel will be linked with it. Its reputation will suffer. I shall be relieved of these evil consequences by your assurance that this matter will be dealt with, as it were, behind closed doors. Can I rely on your scrupulous compliance with my request?

BLANCHONNET *(losing his temper)*. Am I to sacrifice my daughter—for the sake of your wretched guesthouse? Are you out of your mind, man?!

MANAGER. I must ask you to consider—

BLANCHONNET. —your other guests, who haven't got a daughter on her way into the unknown?! I'll stir things up! I'll raise the alarm in every corridor—I'm not giving up! They can't have gone far—their departure can't have been more than half an hour ago—now the pursuit is on—Flying Squad, Vice Squad, the lot! Now the exchange will set telephones jangling in all the police-stations, which will be on the alert. I shall give the cue! *(He makes to telephone.)*

MANAGER. Let me telephone—experience has made me a past-master at it. *(Unhurriedly telephoning)* Porter—get the police up here right away—What's that? The police are here already?—Send the inspector up! *(To* BLANCHONNET*)* Couldn't have worked out more smoothly!

BLANCHONNET. Will they bring my daughter back to me?? *(There is a knock on the door right.)*

MANAGER. Come in!

An INSPECTOR *and two* DETECTIVES *enter—one of them is carrying the Pekinese in his arms.*

INSPECTOR *(to* BLANCHONNET*)*. Are you the victim?

BLANCHONNET. What—do you know about it?

INSPECTOR. About the bandits who slipped through our fingers five minutes too soon.

BLANCHONNET. These—white slavers—

INSPECTOR *(looks at him uncomprehendingly. Then continues)*. Two of the slickest hotel thieves in the whole continent that we'd had information about. Unfortunately a bit too late. The birds had already flown. Apart from a few worthless suitcases, all they left behind was this dog. Brutes, abandoning such a little animal like that! What have you found missing? Money? Valuables? Can you give us a list?

BLANCHONNET *(confused)*. A case of mine is missing—

INSPECTOR. What did it look like?

BLANCHONNET. Yellow—with brass fittings—

INSPECTOR. What was in it?

BLANCHONNET. My money—all my money—a fortune—

INSPECTOR. You mean to say you didn't deposit it in the safe?

BLANCHONNET. That was my intention—I discussed it with the manager down in the hall—

INSPECTOR. And was anyone listening to this conversation in the hall?

MANAGER. To be sure, the president was talking in a loud voice.

INSPECTOR. It came to the ears of the scoundrels—just the sort of opportunity they're waiting for! *(To the MANAGER)* As the case is fairly conspicuous and known to you, didn't it seem queer to you—or your porter—to see strangers carrying it out of the hotel?

MANAGER. M. Blanchonnet's daughter walked out with the case.

INSPECTOR *(to BLANCHONNET)*. Where is your daughter now?

BLANCHONNET. The thieves inveigled her into— *(breaks off.)* Are they thieves, who are only after the money—and are not going off to the Argentine with her—with my Elmire?!

INSPECTOR. Why to the Argentine? Your daughter's little excursion won't last very long. Then the two thieves'll leave her and the emptied case behind somewhere.

BLANCHONNET. When will that be? In an hour?? In three hours??

INSPECTOR. You can't count on it being before tomorrow. You'll have to reckon it taking that long.

BLANCHONNET *(tonelessly)*. A night will pass—when she is away from home— *(Holds his head in his hands.)*

INSPECTOR *(after a pause, to the MANAGER)*. Is she pretty? *(The MANAGER nods. The INSPECTOR shrugs. To the DETECTIVES)* We'll get on doing what we can. *(Leaves with the two DETECTIVES. The telephone rings.)*

MANAGER *(picks up the telephone and listens. To BLANCHONNET)*. Mme Blanchonnet and M. Gaston have arrived. *(BLANCHONNET regards him with lack-lustre gaze.)* Shall I have the lady and gentleman shown up here?

BLANCHONNET *nods weakly.*
The MANAGER *leaves.*

BLANCHONNET *(sinking into a chair)*. Gaston won't want any more to do with—*(with failing voice)* I abdicate—before my coronation—

bury me—*(There is a knock right. The hotel* PAGEBOY *throws open the door.)*

PAGEBOY *(announcing the new arrivals).* Mme Blanchonnet and M. Gaston Sillon-Dudet!

BLANCHONNET *does not stir.*

THE FLIGHT TO VENICE

Play in Four Acts

Translated by B. J. Kenworthy

Characters

SAND
MUSSET
BROTHER
THE ITALIAN DOCTOR
THE ENGLISHMAN
THE ENGLISHMAN'S YOUNG WIFE
THE GERMAN GIRL
DOCTOR'S SERVANT

Venice. The space of a large room, the time of one night.

ACT ONE

MUSSET *and his brother in an open loggia.*

MUSSET *(reading a paper).* A sworn mortal enemy writes a criticism that a man out of his mind for love could not have made more emphatic. As the others always follow where success leads–the easiest way to edit a journal–this is the only one that counts: the triumph of the evening was complete. *(He puts it with the other papers.)*

BROTHER. The rare event: stalls, boxes, circle and gallery all agreed in their applause.

MUSSET. And after the performance?

BROTHER. At Balzac's.

MUSSET. Did he praise the play?

BROTHER. He didn't find the time to. He swamped the dinner-table with the torrent of his literary plans.

MUSSET. Then he was enthusiastic about it. When his heart is full of other things, his mouth overflows with new ideas of his own. Perhaps the only defence against artistic violation.

BROTHER. His speech addressed to the one unoccupied chair was superb. Worth putting into one of his books.

MUSSET. Hadn't he arranged for it to be taken down? If not, he's an incompetent writer. Who was missing from the empty seat?

BROTHER. Beside—

MUSSET *(quickly).* Beside?

BROTHER. –Balzac's speech was about you.

MUSSET. What about the special chair?

BROTHER. For you!

MUSSET. –I live in Venice.

BROTHER. For a long while your hiding-place was not to be discovered!

MUSSET. How was it found?

BROTHER. Musset the poet cannot keep himself hidden away!

MUSSET. Have you come with a definite message from someone?

BROTHER. A request from our mother–friends–literary Paris–

MUSSET. Musset the man is dead–Musset the poet has risen and is breathing again.

BROTHER. You are working again?

MUSSET. Not a plan that is left unformed. All my projects pass through my mind in a steady procession–without jostling one another–and immediately assume their final form. No creation can be less laborious or more pleasurable.

BROTHER. Your publisher burned into my soul his wish for a manuscript from you.

MUSSET. Fill your pockets–everything is at his service!

BROTHER. Do you find that your stay here is inspiring you to creative work?

MUSSET. Strike out life–and you live for yourself alone.

BROTHER. Just as Venice is dead–and yet is there.

MUSSET. Didn't I construct the most genuine setting for myself?

BROTHER *(pauses)*. Have you had any more of your attacks?

MUSSET. The least significant chapter in the story of my life.

BROTHER. The worry about your health–for which we have every justification–the unaccustomed climate for you, who are more susceptible to a change of zone than anyone else–must always be with us.

MUSSET. Do you not see me healthy–obviously stronger–almost robust?

BROTHER. So your flight has benefited you in every way. Now turn to account what you have gained, in the only place where you can use it— back in Paris!

MUSSET. You call flight the undertaking of a journey made necessary for the sake of works—

BROTHER. Headlong–out of the house by night–your leave-taking a note for us—

MUSSET. Under the spell of fresh inspiration—

BROTHER. With every sign of flight–like someone fleeing from surroundings aflame–who is to return when the blaze has died down–and has been frightened by the mere semblance of a fire!

MUSSET. Did I rush away like a rabbit running across the fields?

BROTHER. From the phantom of your own imagining!

MUSSET. How sure of it you sound.

BROTHER. With the pledge of proof in my hands! *(Takes out a small, flat box.)* Key and casket are for you.

MUSSET. Mysterious riddles. *(Unlocks and opens it.)* What is it?

BROTHER. Don't you recognize it?

MUSSET. Soft, fleecy–russet-coloured–a scent of—*(Looks up.)* What does that prove?

BROTHER. Love–for you alone!

MUSSET. Is that how she explained it to you?

BROTHER. Without reserve–overflowing in emotion that truly loves with every breath!

MUSSET. Does she look disfigured without her full head of hair?

BROTHER. She loves you!

MUSSET. That will hardly compensate for the loss of an allurement which lies twisted at the bottom of the casket–in the eyes of her new friends.

BROTHER. If you had reason for jealousy then–today—

MUSSET. I am not jealous.

BROTHER. Your headlong departure from her house—

MUSSET. Because she was love-making with Dumas or Mallarmé in the next room?

BROTHER *(shaken)*. It must have been terrible for you!

MUSSET. The part of the cuckold? I didn't play it tragically. Neither I nor anyone else. No-one approaches that woman with exclusive claims. Every marvel of a unique phenomenon is within the reach of the generality. That is George Sand.

BROTHER. George Sand herself—

MUSSET. —is petty in putting the blame on me. She should not decide to make me the hero of such a farce. This time I should have to protest publicly.

BROTHER. How seriously she is taking the quarrel that has broken out between you *(points to the casket)*—nothing could testify more conclusively!

MUSSET. It shows that she loves me.

BROTHER. You are convinced—

MUSSET. As in the past and for the future.

BROTHER. -and with the extent of your all-encompassing understanding you can accept the particular temperament of this woman?

MUSSET. What she does commands admiration.

BROTHER. Now I no longer understand your flight–your refusal.

MUSSET *(Takes a single sheet from among the newspapers.)* This?

BROTHER. The theatre programme.

MUSSET. Who figures as author?

BROTHER. George Sand.

MUSSET. A falsification!

BROTHER. On the part of Sand?

MUSSET. In suppressing the name of her collaborator.

BROTHER. Is the play not by her alone?

MUSSET. No.

BROTHER. You know who else?

MUSSET. Precisely.

BROTHER. Who?

MUSSET. Myself.

BROTHER. How did you collaborate?

MUSSET. She wrote it down–I supplied the material.

BROTHER. She asked you? This request–your claims waived–her craving for the sole glory–the crude, boundless vanity–that?

MUSSET. That would be petty-minded–and George Sand is always magnanimous.

BROTHER. It will create a tremendous stir in Paris!

MUSSET. Didn't they guess straight away?

BROTHER. Not a word—

MUSSET. —that was not fed with my blood—pumped by pulses that draw life from the fulness of life—from such savouring of life as falls mute in the savouring! That was how I lived–and George Sand wrote it all down! And so I fled . . . so I had slept with death in the shape of a woman–and such a woman!

BROTHER. Nothing in my memory catches an echo of the reality!

MUSSET. Because the event is without parallel–life with George Sand!–to others it will be something alien until the end of the world–a play by George Sand!–literature covers everything with its shifting sands!

BROTHER. Are you certain that the reflection you see is of you?

MUSSET. Of me–and of another man–and another–and another! Open any book of hers, and I'll name the man who served as model for the hero, who fell victim to her. A vampire sucks at our arteries, we yield up our heart's blood–and are left bloodless phantoms!

BROTHER. Is she not merely obeying the great artistic law?

MUSSET. Terrible, when it possesses a woman. Then yes and no are conjoined in a single syllable. Chaos or the ideal is created. Plato's eros walks among men. Divided humanity–half man and half woman–is united. The yearning of the sexes is stilled–frost chills the waters to ice!–George Sand is the perfect being. Seductively beautiful as no other woman–a man with her creative genius. Fatal for those of us still divided, who still desire–and are strangled like sparrows by the man in her.

BROTHER. As a writer she uses a man's name, too–George Sand.

MUSSET. So sure is her instinct about herself!

BROTHER. Is there no bridge to unite you and her in the future?

MUSSET. I have made my escape. I have taken the leap with my last remaining strength. The ground is hardening beneath me. Only one who had abandoned hope would abandon the gain–*(ironically)*–and anyone who will accept something less can find his satisfaction more cheaply.

BROTHER. And yours?

MUSSET *(laughing)*. I–am working!

BROTHER. I myself no longer ask you to come back.

MUSSET *(looking up)*. The last gondola is leaving the canal. Every evening this is the last one. A stickler for time. There–it's turning away. My night has begun.

BROTHER. Do you like the utter silence?

MUSSET. Noise, light disturb me–until the minimum of disturbance is reached–there is always some disturbance–*(He takes the casket.)* It might distract the poet Musset from his task–Musset the poet has come into his own again–Musset the man consigns to the sea the most glorious hair in the world, and charges the canals of Venice to bear it, past all the pomp of the palaces, to the boundless ocean. From that there is no return! *(He drops the hair lock by lock. At last he looks up.)* How did you travel?

BROTHER. Overland.

MUSSET. So tedious a way?

BROTHER. In Geneva I had to arrange–the sale of our property. Now considerable means are at your disposal. I'll give you—

MUSSET. Tomorrow. When are you leaving for Paris?

BROTHER. To make my report about you presses me to hurry.

MUSSET. By sea?

BROTHER. Through Marseilles.

MUSSET. That makes the journey three times shorter. For me it turned into a dream–the coach clattering out of Paris–storm and high seas as far as Genoa–a coach full of chattering people crawling through the gorges of the Apennines–the gliding gondola here–*(He leans far out over the parapet and stares down. With hollow voice)* There!

BROTHER. What are you looking at?

MUSSET. The gondola!

BROTHER. Heading this way.

MUSSET *(horrified)*. Visible to you––

BROTHER. A gondola plying.

MUSSET. ––what I am dreaming?

BROTHER *(in great anxiety)*. Don't excite yourself!

MUSSET. Tell me: am I here?–am I down there?

BROTHER. A late gondola–

MUSSET. There never is one at this hour!

BROTHER. –heading this way–

MUSSET. The boat in my dreams—

BROTHER. —and putting in!

MUSSET *(with a cry)*. —stranded!

A woman's voice from below: Landed!

MUSSET *(straightening up–coldly)*. In collusion with her?

BROTHER. I knew nothing. In Paris she breathed no syllable of any such plan. She must have made up her mind afterwards–she had time enough–she came by the other route—

MUSSET *(calmly)*. Go and show in Mme George Sand.

The BROTHER *leaves.*

MUSSET *in complete command of himself–arranges the newspapers, places the casket on top of the pile.*

GERMAN GIRL *(enters; young, fair–in travelling clothes. Kisses* MUSSET'S *hand)*. These hands–loved by her–now adorable to—

MUSSET. And you are?

GERMAN GIRL. With George. Friend, sister, maid. A German. I come to study in Paris–see George–abandon everything–break with my family–touch George to the heart–and love with George where she loves!

MUSSET. You are misdirecting a wealth of feeling—

GERMAN GIRL. No mistake in this sudden passion. Never a comparable effect where a man was concerned. She is more than the creature of outward form that she seems. One must love George–or obliterate oneself.

MUSSET. Don't recite that catechism too often.

GERMAN GIRL. Fervently–every second without her holds only this for me. That speeds the time.

MUSSET. You are German?

GERMAN GIRL. Your reason for doubting?

MUSSET. I thought such transports affected only–

GERMAN GIRL. Every friend close to George! *(BROTHER enters.)* Where is my George?

BROTHER. Help her with a suitcase she is opening.

GERMAN GIRL. George must not–*(She leaves.)*

MUSSET. Is the big scene being prepared?

BROTHER. She's making the most of her good fortune in catching me before I left. She carried out an undertaking to report on her trip in letters to the *Revue des deux mondes.* She is giving me the manuscript that she is now putting in order.

MUSSET. A bolder illustration of my text couldn't be imagined!

BROTHER. She recommends me to take the opportunity offered by her carriage—

MUSSET. The gondola down below–your despatches press! Just one more note: I close the first stage of my sentimental expedition writing in the hallway of this palazzo, where–

SAND *(enters; dressed in men's clothes).* I thought your brother was back in Paris long since. His journey here was tiresome, the return trip will be all the quicker. Paris awaits news of you. *(To the BROTHER)* I'll let you have a few lines for the journal. *(Goes to the loggia–calls down.)* Don't leave–a passenger requires the gondola!

MUSSET. I fear you and your companion will find little comfort. I keep no servants.

SAND. Who could sleep tonight? Tomorrow we will open up all the rooms. We are two women who are yours to command.

MUSSET. But that suit? Have you?

SAND. Diverted all suspicion–*(putting her hand up to her hair).*–and, disfigured, no target for strangers' glances. *(MUSSET looks at her.)*

GERMAN GIRL *(appears in the doorway. Indicating a tied package).* George–the manuscripts.

SAND. More writing-paper! *(She leaves with the* GERMAN GIRL. *The* BROTHER *comes in–wearing his overcoat.)*

BROTHER. The obligation to calm our mother's fears—

MUSSET. —urgently demands your departure after the fleeting hours of your visit.

BROTHER. Reproaches enervate honesty—

MUSSET. ... with which I too answer you. You must vouch for me to our mother–to a Paris pressing its claims upon its poet–just as I will not avail myself of subterfuge to evade the high demands on me.

BROTHER. I can take your publisher—

MUSSET. By special messenger. You are overburdened with commissions. *(The* BROTHER *shrugs his shoulders.)* I shall not make a hasty selection. Much needs revision.

BROTHER. You feel sure of—

MUSSET. —overrating myself. I lack perspective. I became obsessed with myself.

BROTHER. Let me have it.

MUSSET *(almost wearily).* That is now–very unimportant.

BROTHER *(breaking off).* The notification for the bank. Watch for the change to a favourable rate of exchange. Get a Lombard to act as your agent. *(He hands over the paper.)*

SAND *(enters; gives the* BROTHER *the packet and a letter).* This is for the *Revue*–this for the *Journal.* In a week there will be a sensation. Tolerable only because this time we shall not have to parade about exhibiting ourselves in drawing-rooms. Make no secret of our aversion to it.

BROTHER. With the promise that this exile will be a short one.

SAND. Like Balzac's Chinese dressing-gown trailing behind him.

MUSSET *(exaggerating).* With that fanfare your message will be wittily authenticated for the whole of Paris.

GERMAN GIRL *(enters, swinging a small bunch of keys).* The keys– *(runs over to* SAND *and whispers busily with her.)*

The BROTHER *takes silent leave of* MUSSET–*refuses with a gesture to be seen out. Then takes leave of* SAND, *who casually shakes his hand– while listening to the* GERMAN GIRL'S *whispering. He leaves.*

SAND *(freeing herself).* Yes–tyrant! *(The* GERMAN GIRL *leaves.)* She is locking my bags, so that I can't change my clothes. The girl has fallen head over heels for the pseudo-man. In the end they took us for a honeymoon couple. That Venice was our destination was the final confirmation of their mistake. Men looked daggers at me because their wives were giving me sly glances. I enoyed playing up to them–and the trip nearly ended in a duel.

MUSSET. A strange adventure.

SAND. Is it material for comedy or tragedy?

MUSSET *(calmly)*. You will decide whether to humiliate or glorify the child. Either outcome means disillusionment for her.

SAND *(Looks at him quickly)*. Am I to send her away?

MUSSET. If every possibility has been exhausted you no longer need her.

SAND. You don't like it–that decides me. No-one shall be near you any longer–

MUSSET. Am I terrified of a girl?

SAND. I–want to be alone with you. Never again to suffer so–because everything can be fatally falsified. In Paris appearances gave you just cause–but only appearances. Nothing more! The theatre captivates me–it has the hundred heads of the hydra and ensnares with its every fair word. You have to adjust yourself: to show greater interest than the half that is aroused–to shake hands with this or that person ten times more often than you want to–to untangle intrigues whose significance is ridiculously out of proportion to the time devoted to them! Reserves of energy are consumed–and you float along with the stream that carried you along with it!

MUSSET. The success proves you were utterly devoted.

SAND. To what I had undertaken. It is not a matter of personalities. All the buzz of chatter is idle. You heard rumours–which a single piece of evidence refutes!

MUSSET. Something really vital?

SAND. Because it was for you, it was easy for me: giving up an adornment that in verses is adjudged my crowning glory!

MUSSET. I still have the casket.

SAND. Open it if you have the slightest doubt again.

MUSSET. I scattered the contents on the waters. You glided in your gondola through your own hair, as it floated to meet you.

SAND. —Will nothing prove—

MUSSET. —since I am not jealous.

SAND. —my love to you?

MUSSET. It is not love—

SAND. More!

MUSSET. —or less. You don't know how to love. I am sorry for you.

SAND *(pauses)*. What stands between me and you?

MUSSET. At that time I was reading your play in the night. Who appears in it? You and I. What is portrayed to perfection there corresponds exactly with the intimate facts of our experiences together–properly hidden from the audience by the external form. In that you succeeded flawlessly.

SAND. Did I overestimate my powers when I used our—

MUSSET. You admit it straight away?

SAND. What I believe to be the value of my play!

MUSSET. Poor George–I tried to go on believing in a coincidence, but now my regret turns to pain.

SAND. Are you rebuking me for betrayal you say—

MUSSET. I–who am overwhelmed by your appalling self-deception.

SAND. Don't confuse me, my friend!

MUSSET. You are so dead in life–and so alive in death. Landing on green shores–and emerging from the waters only as far as your waist. Half here–half there, a sad creature of the seas.

SAND. And you so cold with your words.

MUSSET. Are you not frozen beneath your skin, that breathes warmth? Touch it with your fingers: it burns–underneath ice is forming. In the mould of your body life and death is fashioned. Compassion kneels before you.

SAND. Not more ardent in my existence than ever the life of a woman?

MUSSET. A shop-keeper's wife fills her daily round more intensely. You don't know how to live. You are immediately set outside yourself–and weigh up the scene in which you appear as actor and audience. The eternal chastity of living and feeling is shattered–you become the harlot of your true awakening to life.

SAND. Do you feel injured that no material meant more to me than your ecstasy and mine?

MUSSET. The discovery drove me away. I shrank in alarm from the very possibility: to let yourself go–and to hold yourself back. To speak and to keep silent with a single mouth. To talk and to listen to yourself. To register the extremities of emotion. To languish–and to arrive in the bottomless depths–with a jotting for the writer's note-book!

SAND. With you–I died a thousand blissful deaths!

MUSSET. And each one duly recorded in your dramatic chronicle. The sigh with which I sank in raptures–lost to me for ever!–written down by you. Hawked on the open stage: you–me. For this the screens were torn from souls as never before from the knowledge of two people one of the other. What rendered me silent in rapture and struck the pen from my hand like a poisoned knife–that was for you the object of careful polishing for a play! The author drew upon experience and opened up new regions of the soul!

SAND (slowly). I was alive–yet I did not live–

MUSSET. Can you call that alive?

SAND. What does it mean: to speak–and to listen to yourself?

MUSSET. Deceiver and deceived in one!

SAND. Actor and audience at the same time–am I that?

MUSSET. Cold in the heat of passion–warm in coldness!

SAND. –dead . . . yet living–

MUSSET. A corpse that walks–and loves!

SAND. I shall go now.

MUSSET. Where?

SAND. I am going to send the German girl back home.

MUSSET. On what grounds?

SAND. I might be tempted to prolong my encounter with her so as to find the ending for a short story as well. I must not destroy her illusions.

MUSSET. Let her stay happy in her love.

SAND. To the bitter end?

MUSSET. Right down to the poisonous dregs.

SAND. You say that?

MUSSET. Poison for her . . . and for me!

SAND *(looking at him)*. No!

MUSSET. Who gives away an hour in which he can live?! Who obliterates himself–and then in ecstasy solicits fresh pulse-beats? Even the deluding statue of life offers allurements a hundred times more seductive than dark death! Laugh–and lie: we shall not escape you–resist your scourge as we will! Call down your Gorgon's blessing on us, so that you can kill us–Medusa!

SAND. I am no murderess!

MUSSET. You are everything–you are nothing–in origin and advent perfection–not yes, not no–a word as yet uncreated that you will coin–attempt it with me–I surrender myself–I stammer inspired syllables in your lap–you note them down directly–you will not lose them–a priceless possession will be preserved–a warning voice cries out–a hazard is cordoned off–genius is a curse–the monster stands in the pillory–stone–stone–the woman–the woman–the woman I love! *(He falls.)*

SAND *stands stiffly–runs to the door–claps her hands.*

ACT TWO

SAND–*in women's clothes–and the* GERMAN GIRL *sitting close together.*

GERMAN GIRL *(holding* SAND'S *hands)*. Cold–cold– freezing–lifeless—*(*SAND *stares before her.)* Now I'll bed them between my hands–covered over–I'll melt the icy fish–magically–in my encasing warmth—

SAND *draws her hand away–gets up–goes to a curtained doorway–opens it slightly–looks out–returns. The* GERMAN GIRL *takes her hands again.*

SAND. I want you to leave tomorrow.

GERMAN GIRL. George—

SAND. Yes.

GERMAN GIRL. What—

SAND. To prevent your lying one day as he is lying in the next room.

GERMAN GIRL. I love you–without jealousy.

SAND. He feels none either.

GERMAN GIRL. He is a man.

SAND. That means nothing in this case.

GERMAN GIRL. You are a woman—

SAND. Not to him.

GERMAN GIRL. How does he love you?

SAND. No longer.

GERMAN GIRL. Have you doubts?

SAND. His confused state a quarter of an hour ago.

GERMAN GIRL *(calmly)*. It will be the death of him.

SAND. What are you saying?

GERMAN GIRL. Just as I shall die when I no longer love you.

SAND. When will your love cease?

GERMAN GIRL *(smiling at her)*. Yes, George-when?

SAND. You come to Paris-brush aside the resistance of a family indignant to your trip abroad-you study with determination grim enough to enforce success-at home they are starting to speak of you with pride—

GERMAN GIRL. The next instalment?

SAND. Chance leads you to me-which turns out to be your fate-the change is complete-you forget the purpose of your stay in Paris-loose family ties in Germany-lavish more of your affection on me than I make claim on—

GERMAN GIRL. An exciting story!

SAND. You accompany me to see my friend in Venice-I travel disguised as a man-you in the part of the young wife-we arrive here one rainy evening—

GERMAN GIRL. The conclusion?

SAND. Your leap into the canal, when you read all the exciting things that have happened to you-in my short story.

GERMAN GIRL. All this merely material for—

SAND *(with a short laugh)*. Not exciting enough?

GERMAN GIRL *(pauses)*. Is that fatal?

SAND. Do you want an example? The curtain separates you from him-convincing as he lies there rigid.

GERMAN GIRL. Where did you write that up?

SAND. My so enthusiastically applauded play in the theatre!

GERMAN GIRL *(pauses)*. I will read nothing-and live.

SAND *(vehemently)*. You can protect yourself-you shut your eyes and see and realize nothing!

GERMAN GIRL. Protected like a blind man on the brink of a precipice.

SAND. Does that help me? Can I root out my own perplexity: am I my own shadow or a solid body?

GERMAN GIRL. George encompasses a whole great world.

SAND. That is my life-but I am not living! When events carry me away-when they fire my blood: like a white salamander I jump out of the

retort and stare into the glass at what is happening there–happening to
me, who am both outside and inside. Skeleton and flesh divorced. A
phantom apes me–I lie naked and shameless before a mirror and cannot
tell who is genuine in the double image!

GERMAN GIRL. No life ranges wider than yours.

SAND. Take it in exchange for an existence that begins with the morning
and forgets by evening. As narrow as days–and nothing but rounded
days between dawn and dark!

GERMAN GIRL. No fate for George.

SAND. It is how I would live. I have no wish to be shut out from the
teeming life that surges around me–fulfilling itself in joy or silent in
sorrow. That is truly life!

GERMAN GIRL. Never yours.

SAND. Mine too. My every resolve eager to seize it, wherever it may
offer. If it reaches out for me–then nothing shall matter but the
moment!

GERMAN GIRL. Why does George want to be rid of her own self?

SAND. For the sake of proof I need–so as not to kill myself!

GERMAN GIRL *(sits up)*. He is speaking! *(*SAND *quickly leaves
through the curtain. The* GERMAN GIRL *follows her half-way)* A
doctor?

SAND *(returning)*. He is convulsed–fingers clenching–breast heaving!
Where can we find a doctor here?

GERMAN GIRL. I'll raise the alarm among the neighbours across the
yards at the back–

SAND. Beg the people with a thousand entreaties to hurry—

GERMAN GIRL. George Sand in Venice and the poet Musset ill—

SAND. I will write a note—*(she does so.)*

GERMAN GIRL *(throwing on a shawl)*. Is it written?

SAND *(getting up)*. It must wrench the oldest of doctors from his sleep
merely to read the names!

The GERMAN GIRL *goes off.* SAND *stands deliberating. Then fetches
a small hand-case–opens it and takes out some sheets of paper. Goes out
on to the loggia and drops sheet after sheet over the parapet.*

GERMAN GIRL *(returns)*. Success! In the corner of the yard a lighted
window. I knock and knock. A man staggers and stumbles behind
shutters. I knock–the door is unbolted. A drunken beast bellows at me.
I shout back and tell him what I want. Foul obscenities from his mouth.
Then I call out who sent me. At once he is silent–takes a hold of
himself–sobers up–and recites the most marvellous lines of a poem of
yours. Now he is delivering the message without payment–for George
Sand!

SAND. Is it far to the doctor's?

GERMAN GIRL *(listens)*. His voice!

The GERMAN GIRL *leaves.* SAND *waits tensely.*

GERMAN GIRL *(returns).* He made a din outside the house and woke up the whole district until the doctor showed himself willing. He threatened to return with a worse uproar if he took more than five minutes. But he is asking for some reward for going. Let him have a line written by you.

SAND. No!

GERMAN GIRL. Quickly–a piece of paper.

SAND. Not one stroke!

GERMAN GIRL. You are quite determined?

SAND. George Sand is obliterated–who is living I do not yet know–

ITALIAN DOCTOR *(enters–formal and assured).* Is the patient here?

SAND *(to the* GERMAN GIRL*).* Keep him quiet down below. *(The* GERMAN GIRL *leaves.)* You received my note?

ITALIAN DOCTOR. The call was urgent.

SAND. My words were not.

ITALIAN DOCTOR. They are just two names.

SAND. What names?

ITALIAN DOCTOR. Unknown to me. Where is the patient?

SAND. Have you not been living in Europe up to now?

ITALIAN DOCTOR. In Venice and near Naples, where I have a country house.

SAND. Musset—

ITALIAN DOCTOR *(reading from the card).* George Sand–two gentlemen. Frenchmen?

SAND *(changes).* Attend to the patient.

The ITALIAN DOCTOR *leaves through the curtain.*

GERMAN GIRL *(enters).* You have that man on your conscience. He said he would never drink again if he had a talisman from you. Now he is drowning his disappointment in a flood of spirits. Is the doctor with him?

SAND. With the gentleman from France.

GERMAN GIRL. Who is that?

SAND. The poet Musset.

GERMAN GIRL. Does he dislike Musset?

SAND. He knows neither Musset nor George Sand. Your toper recited verses.

GERMAN GIRL. Is the man human?

SAND. Perhaps he is–*the* man.

GERMAN GIRL. He's coming.

SAND. No word of explanation about who we are! *(The* ITALIAN DOCTOR *enters.)* How is he?

ITALIAN DOCTOR. I must wait to see how he reacts. Your husband?

SAND. My–brother.

ITALIAN DOCTOR. Profession?
SAND. Businessman.
ITALIAN DOCTOR. Easily upset over losses?
SAND. He always feels he has been deceived.
ITALIAN DOCTOR. Has he suffered business reverses lately?
SAND. Verging on bankruptcy.

The GERMAN GIRL *goes off.*

ITALIAN DOCTOR. Keep him well away from business matters for the present. Put a good face on bad news. Paint everything in a rosy light. Invent facts that he will believe. Can you do that?
SAND. For the sake of his life.
ITALIAN DOCTOR. That may be his salvation.
SAND *(fetches a book).* It might help you to pass the time.
ITALIAN DOCTOR. No, thank you.
SAND. Do you never read?
ITALIAN DOCTOR. No.
SAND. Only a doctor?
ITALIAN DOCTOR. By inclination and without undue industry.
SAND. What appeals to you more strongly?
ITALIAN DOCTOR *(looks at her).* You are interrogating me?
SAND. And you are answering frankly.
ITALIAN DOCTOR. I have nothing to hide.
SAND. I shall find that boring.
ITALIAN DOCTOR. You are a woman.
SAND. Your argument is superficial.
ITALIAN DOCTOR. Because I am a man.
SAND. What rights does that give you?
ITALIAN DOCTOR. To act without hesitation. The commentary on it is provided by the weaker sex.
SAND. By us.
ITALIAN DOCTOR. One party is always defeated.
SAND. In your case–I am.
ITALIAN DOCTOR. In every case–the other person!
SAND. Are you certain that you are so vastly superior?
ITALIAN DOCTOR. The assessment is intended quite impersonally.
SAND. Your demon?
ITALIAN DOCTOR. Life knows neither demons nor divinities.
SAND. A third alternative?
ITALIAN DOCTOR. My existence. The patient is calling. *(Leaves through the curtain.)*
GERMAN GIRL *(enters).* George–a strange intruder on the stairs. With a flood of entreaties she prevents me turning her away!
SAND. A woman?
GERMAN GIRL. Muffled up–come in great haste on a vital matter.
SAND. She wants?

GERMAN GIRL. She ignores the question–demands to be let in—
SAND. Bring her!

The GERMAN GIRL *goes–returns with the* YOUNG WIFE *of the Englishman.*

YOUNG WIFE. I knew it!

SAND *gestures the* GERMAN GIRL *to leave. She does so.*

SAND. You know me?
YOUNG WIFE. Now I know–*(tears her veil aside)*–my rival!
SAND *(attentive).* For–*(She goes over and makes sure that the curtain is well closed.)* Now continue!
YOUNG WIFE. Further explanations? Perhaps you have a prior claim–
SAND. To?
YOUNG WIFE. Claim him later–when he has left me!
SAND. I never demand what is not willingly given me!
YOUNG WIFE. The note from you? *(SAND relaxes.)* Is that not a summons to him?! You don't deny it. We shall fight for this man, who cannot mean to you a fraction of what his presence means to me!
SAND *(smiling).* You find me prepared. We will compare our interests and with a minus give up our claim to the other's plus. What tells in your favour?
YOUNG WIFE. Defend your claim!
SAND. The challenger first.
YOUNG WIFE. Your very coldness concedes my victory.
SAND. If you have much to lose, you hold the last card cautiously.
YOUNG WIFE. I have lost–myself! What shall I be after this affair? A ghost will walk beside me–my husband!
SAND. You are married?
YOUNG WIFE. Does that mean nothing?!
SAND. A great deal.
YOUNG WIFE. We travel from England—
SAND. Are you English?
YOUNG WIFE. Scarcely weeks since we got up from the wedding-breakfast—
SAND. Did you not love your husband?
YOUNG WIFE. With all my affection.
SAND. And in spite of that?
YOUNG WIFE. A single glance that changed my fate.
SAND. Exchanged?
YOUNG WIFE. At midday. On the open piazza. We arranged a meeting secretly in the darkness of a church. After, the evening with him. Then your letter arrives–the moment is shattered and my heart broken!
SAND. What do you suspect?

YOUNG WIFE. Awake at once. His departure in crass confusion. Niggardly with his answers. I follow him secretly–and confirm my suspicions with the cruel reality.

SAND. Are you not afraid of misinterpreting these events?

YOUNG WIFE. No doubts shall obscure what is clear in my mind!

SAND. It is dangerous to fill the air with accusations.

YOUNG WIFE. When the crime has been discovered?!

SAND *(breaking off)*. It says much when an Englishwoman deceives her husband and slips away to a lover virtually on her wedding night.

YOUNG WIFE. Does that argument convince you?

SAND. Not yet.

YOUNG WIFE. What greater sacrifices have you made?

SAND. Where there are sacrifices, love is already blighted.

YOUNG WIFE. Yet it still blossoms!

SAND. —why do you love this man?

YOUNG WIFE. If I found an explanation, I should not love him! Search for a word that embraces everything: happiness–fear–delight–torment– but no regret!–it does not exist. It is a feeling that wells up without a yesterday or a tomorrow, and lifts a single day above all the passing days and years that follow!

SAND. You are lavish in your praise.

YOUNG WIFE. I see now that you are not in love. You are defeated. The breath of your passion is swept away by my tempest!

SAND. I was listening to you.

YOUNG WIFE. Too patiently. There is not a gleam of enmity in your eyes. You're amusing yourself–I'm in love!

SAND. You are passing sentence—

YOUNG WIFE. Which concedes my case!

SAND. —before the judgment?

YOUNG WIFE. Who should pass it?

SAND. The only judge in this women's dispute.

YOUNG WIFE. Do you propose to let him—

SAND. —determine where the needle of the balance rests.

YOUNG WIFE. In our presence?

SAND. You shall learn your fate here, or else—*(leading her to a side-door.)* Stay here until you are called.

The YOUNG WIFE *leaves.* SAND *is still holding the door-handle when the* ITALIAN DOCTOR *enters, does not notice her–stamps his feet in impatient annoyance.*

SAND *(advancing)*. Dissatisfied–with your patient?

ITALIAN DOCTOR *(controlling himself)*. He may be asleep, or he may be unconscious–perhaps he is sleeping.

SAND. Are you staying?

ITALIAN DOCTOR. The night.

SAND *(in surprised silence)*. What can I arrange for your comfort?

ITALIAN DOCTOR. I need nothing.

SAND *is silent. The* ITALIAN DOCTOR *looks into the loggia.*

SAND. Are you not making a great sacrifice by staying?

ITALIAN DOCTOR. I am doing what has to be done at the moment: a sick man is lying in there, and I am a doctor.

SAND. Forgive me for forcing you to come.

ITALIAN DOCTOR *(turns quickly)*. By what means?

SAND. The messenger roused the district with his shouting.

ITALIAN DOCTOR. The fool.

SAND. You agreed to come--and saved a situation.

ITALIAN DOCTOR *(asks in surprise)*. Where?

SAND *(smiling)*. Here--where I was left worrying about my brother.

ITALIAN DOCTOR. I hope--there will be no further complications.

SAND. Are developments getting more involved?

ITALIAN DOCTOR. It is a mystery how you see through the ramifications of the situation.

SAND. Are you anxious to know the solution?

ITALIAN DOCTOR. Your interest?

SAND. To ridicule the vaunted triumph of the male.

ITALIAN DOCTOR. You are right: I left a woman waiting for me. The siege of my house threatened to compromise us. I complied with the bawling demands of the fellow outside and put a stop to his din.

SAND. I am not asking for a confession.

ITALIAN DOCTOR. It has the value of disposing finally of the subject.

SAND. Where you are concerned.

ITALIAN DOCTOR. The other party could not have put her word in here.

SAND. Would she be satisfied with your exposition?

ITALIAN DOCTOR. Of?

SAND. The rankling of your flight from her embrace.

ITALIAN DOCTOR. Do you suspect there were scenes?

SAND. I know it.

ITALIAN DOCTOR. I shall not conceal this conversation.

SAND. Is that sufficient to ensure your absolution?

ITALIAN DOCTOR. Am I to bring further accusations against myself?

SAND. The only way.

ITALIAN DOCTOR. By inventing a tale—

SAND. Which includes another woman!

ITALIAN DOCTOR. You set me a task I shrink from undertaking.

SAND. But self-evident in view of your obligation not to offend a woman you love.

ITALIAN DOCTOR. Why should the true reasons--that you called me to your brother--not be acceptable?

SAND. Because you did not disclose it straight away.

ITALIAN DOCTOR. It seemed foolish to me to interrupt a lovers' meeting for such a cause.

SAND. By giving that impression you will only confirm the doubts of the lady you abandoned.

ITALIAN DOCTOR. With your constructions you create facts ultimately no less impassable than the campanile.

SAND. Then it is more sensible to go round it than to batter your head against it.

ITALIAN DOCTOR. I fear that can't serve me either.

SAND. Why?

ITALIAN DOCTOR. Because another wall stands at the end of the cul-de-sac.

SAND. Is that what you are going along?

ITALIAN DOCTOR. Like a boy who has lost his head completely and seeks wild excuses for a stupid prank.

SAND. Do you find that especially difficult?

ITALIAN DOCTOR. I am tormenting myself to no effect.

SAND. To think out some little fib?

ITALIAN DOCTOR. The greatest a man can tell: to boast of an amorous adventure he has not enjoyed.

SAND. You will have to bring yourself to tell some such story.

ITALIAN DOCTOR *(quickly)*. The note will be my evidence! *(He takes it out.)*

SAND. Was it seen?

ITALIAN DOCTOR. I was holding it when I went in.

SAND. Then there is even less hope of her being sympathetic.

ITALIAN DOCTOR. It is the names that carry conviction: Alfred de Musset–a man.

SAND. He won't carry any weight.

ITALIAN DOCTOR. And the second name–George Sand—

SAND. —is mine.

ITALIAN DOCTOR *(taken aback)*. Why do you hide behind a man's name?

SAND. It is usually accounted a revelation.

ITALIAN DOCTOR. She will never guess there is a woman behind this George Sand!

SAND. The attempt would be met with deadly laughter.

ITALIAN DOCTOR. Would I encounter doubts?

SAND. I swear to you that in your credulity you will not find your double in the whole of Europe!

ITALIAN DOCTOR. Do you know women so well?

SAND. I know women–who mistrust!

ITALIAN DOCTOR. The cul-de-sac closes in–I surrender.

SAND. Your resistance so soon over?

ITALIAN DOCTOR. I capitulate to myself. I am condemned to be the fool of my own fate. I blurt out the first lie and become a charlatan–a coxcomb flaunting his amours-an impudent scoundrel who is forbidden in future ever to possess a woman.

SAND. You judge yourself harshly.

ITALIAN DOCTOR. I no longer distinguish fact from fantasy-the pose becomes a habit and the occasional lover ends as a cheap, contemptible creature. And that is despicable!

SAND. What are you going to do now?

ITALIAN DOCTOR. To lie-and afterwards dismiss the woman from my life!

SAND. Can I regret that?

ITALIAN DOCTOR. In face of what accusation?

SAND. Have I not done everything to prevent the woman waiting for you from being disappointed?

ITALIAN DOCTOR. You pleaded her cause most valiantly—at my expense.

SAND. You admit that?

ITALIAN DOCTOR. Your triumph is great—complete: I seem ridiculous to myself in my defeat!

SAND. And am I to regret that? *(She looks at him, smiling.)*

ITALIAN DOCTOR. The success of a victor without scruples is understandable.

SAND. When the victor is a man.

ITALIAN DOCTOR. As distinct from the woman's point of view?

SAND. A woman forgives herself only when a victory carries with it a conquest as well.

The ITALIAN DOCTOR *looks at her searchingly.*
SAND *returns his look.*
The ITALIAN DOCTOR *shakes his head.*

SAND *(changed).* The patient!

The ITALIAN DOCTOR *leaves through the curtains.*
SAND *goes to the door, lets in the* YOUNG WIFE.

YOUNG WIFE *(looking about her).* Not here? Where is-
SAND. Still here.
YOUNG WIFE. Lost?!
SAND. Suffer a short postponement of yes.
YOUNG WIFE. To me? To you?
SAND. Three or four words will decide that.
YOUNG WIFE. Where shall I see him?
SAND. Stay in the hall. I'll send him to you.
YOUNG WIFE. At once?
SAND. I assure you.
YOUNG WIFE. Don't plan trickery: if wronged, I am capable of blind revenge.

SAND *leads her to the door.*

The YOUNG WIFE *leaves.* SAND *writes rapidly on the back of the note. The* ITALIAN DOCTOR *enters and* SAND *looks at him.*

ITALIAN DOCTOR. The patient is sleeping and no longer needs me. He will wake up well and arise and walk. My task is discharged.

SAND. How shall I repay my debt?

ITALIAN DOCTOR. Reckon it to the reparations borne by the vanquished.

SAND. Your outlay was too great for me not to bear some part of it.

ITALIAN DOCTOR. Its very extent rules out compensation.

SAND. If the debtor excludes no possibility?

ITALIAN DOCTOR. In that case even a spendthrift could not but turn miser!

SAND *(close to him).* What exceeds my powers to wipe out the debt?

ITALIAN DOCTOR. The stake I put up.

SAND. So valuable?

ITALIAN DOCTOR. In my own person.

SAND. Is there nothing to set against it?

ITALIAN DOCTOR. Only one thing compares.

SAND. What can mean so much to you?

The ITALIAN DOCTOR *looks at her.* SAND *veritably drinks in his gaze. In control of himself, he holds out his hand to her.*

ITALIAN DOCTOR. Tomorrow I leave Venice–with a beautiful dream in my head. *(*SAND *presses the note into his hand.)* What are you giving me?

SAND *(smiling).* A promissory note. Read it on the way downstairs! *(The* ITALIAN DOCTOR *leaves.* SAND *waits.)*

ITALIAN DOCTOR *(returns, tottering, stammering, speaking).* Four words–and a paradise opened!

SAND *spreads her arms wide. The* ITALIAN DOCTOR *takes her in his arms.* MUSSET *comes out through the curtains. Sees–steps back, his face contorted. He disappears.*

SAND *(in complete surrender).* I love you–love you—

ACT THREE

The GERMAN GIRL *and the old* SERVANT *of the Italian Doctor enter.*

GERMAN GIRL *(sleepy).* Has the day begun already?

SERVANT. And begun dangerously!

GERMAN GIRL. What's threatening us?

SERVANT. Nothing threatens you–we are the ones who have the devil on our heels. *(Looks round)* Where is he?

GERMAN GIRL. With the patient. Not you!

She leaves through the curtains. The SERVANT *goes out on to the loggia– makes gestures to calm someone below. The* GERMAN GIRL *comes back through the curtains.*

SERVANT *(goes to her).* Is he coming?

GERMAN GIRL. The patient is asleep—

SERVANT. The doctor—

GERMAN GIRL. —is not with him.

SERVANT. Has he left the house?

GERMAN GIRL. I went to sleep—

SERVANT. Do you live here alone?

GERMAN GIRL. I am the maid.

SERVANT. Wake your employers. I must have some reliable information. I've given my word on his behalf. Life and honour are at stake!

GERMAN GIRL. I don't know where I—

SERVANT. There is the door. Since he left it must be exactly—

GERMAN GIRL *(tries the latch of the side-door).* Locked.

SERVANT. Try knocking!

GERMAN GIRL. Keep quiet! *(She knocks-presses her ear against the door. Alternately speaking and listening.)* George–George–yes, me–while I was sound asleep–the doctor's servant–the doctor's!– what?–I can't hear–did you say something?

SAND *(in loose night-gown—enters. To the* SERVANT*).* Tell me the message you have for the doctor!

SERVANT. Is he in the house?

SAND. That–is not what I am asking about. Who wants the doctor?

SERVANT. Someone–is looking for him.

SAND. What for?

SERVANT. —a duel!

SAND. How long until—

SERVANT. He has come with me–a foreigner.

SAND. Tell the gentleman his opponent will be with him inside ten minutes! *(The* SERVANT *leaves.)*

GERMAN GIRL *(worried).* George–have I done something wrong?

SAND. Wait! *(Pushes open the door. The* ITALIAN DOCTOR *comes in.)*

SAND. You must get away!

ITALIAN DOCTOR. From this dream?!

SAND. It might mean your death if you stay. Preserve it for us both.

ITALIAN DOCTOR. Whose hand is raised against me?

SAND. Your pursuer is down below.

ITALIAN DOCTOR. Is it the—

SAND. Someone or other. A man who is risking his life and putting yours—and mine!—at the mercy of chance.

ITALIAN DOCTOR. I will inscribe the law of finality above his heart.

SAND. There will be no fight for you to lose.

ITALIAN DOCTOR. The outcome decided even before the first thrust?

SAND. If you survive, you'll be handed over to the authorities. In either event separation will part our ways. The outcome is always fatal!

ITALIAN DOCTOR. Can there be no other?

SAND. Flight—to your country house.

ITALIAN DOCTOR. That is too far from—

SAND. We will get there with all speed.

ITALIAN DOCTOR. To Naples with you?!

SAND. To the ultimate oblivion!

ITALIAN DOCTOR *(draws her close to him)*. Who are you?

SAND. Call me by a new name.

ITALIAN DOCTOR. Who until yesterday?

SAND. I can no longer remember.

ITALIAN DOCTOR. If you do not come, how can I seek you out?

SAND. Shall you try to find me?

ITALIAN DOCTOR. The whole world over for the whole of my life!

SAND. I shall come! *(freeing herself.)* You leave Venice now—I in a few hours. Wait for me on the mainland.

ITALIAN DOCTOR. With a carriage and provisions.

SAND. She will take you into backyards—*(to the* GERMAN GIRL.*)* Press your drunkard into service again—promise him the impossible —let him run as if to save his own skin, and then he can drink himself senseless!

ITALIAN DOCTOR. The irate swordsman outside the door?

SAND. I'll keep him back!

ITALIAN DOCTOR *(seizing her in his arms)*. In a few hours then!

SAND. For all time!

The ITALIAN DOCTOR *goes off with the* GERMAN GIRL. SAND *listens for a moment—quickly leaves through the side-door. The* ENGLISHMAN *and the* SERVANT *enter.*

SERVANT. He promised to be here.

ENGLISHMAN. The gentleman is unpunctual. He must be reminded.

SERVANT. There is no-one here-

ENGLISHMAN. My own eyes tell me that.

SERVANT. I am in someone else's house-

ENGLISHMAN. The room is very suitable, we can settle the matter here and now.

SERVANT. I was told a sick man is lying in that room there—

ENGLISHMAN. Soon he won't be the only one here.

SERVANT. That is as much as I know.

ENGLISHMAN. That is enough. This is the right place. Fetch up the swords.

The SERVANT *leaves. The* ENGLISHMAN *waits, his arms crossed.* SAND *enters—in men's clothes. The* ENGLISHMAN *looks at her— remains in the same position.* SAND *keeps in the half-light near the side-door.*

ENGLISHMAN. There is no need to tell you the name of your adversary. You know who is suddenly stepping out of your little adventure and demanding satisfaction. *(*SAND *makes no reply.)* I learn of your existence. That discharges the formalities, which in this case have no personal appeal for me. *(*SAND *is silent.)* Your silent recognition of the wrong done me hastens the business that will occupy us jointly for a few minutes. You will be in no doubt about the magnitude of your offence, as it is a double one: against my wife and myself. You attacked me by seducing my wife—and my wife by bringing upon her disgrace which words fail me to describe. *(*SAND *makes no move.)* Because of my shame that others should learn of it, I forgo my second. I make no objection to a second on your part. *(*SAND *shakes her head.)* The choice of weapons is mine—and the decision to fight to the death. *(*SAND *nods.)* We can begin. *(The* SERVANT *enters with two rapiers.)* As I have brought the weapons, it is for you to select one. *(*SAND *takes a rapier. The* ENGLISHMAN *takes his. To the* SERVANT*)* You are dismissed on the orders of your master. *(The* SERVANT *leaves.)* Into the middle—only here is there enough light for our blades. *(Stands ready to fight.* SAND *comes forward—raises her rapier. The* ENGLISHMAN *lowers his.)* You are—a woman. *(*SAND *lowers her rapier.)* A degree darker shadow—and you would have exposed me to the danger of committing manslaughter. *(Takes the rapier from her hand.)* Forgive me for raising my sword against you. Is the cavalier evading his responsibility by your proxy?

SAND. He is no longer in Venice.

ENGLISHMAN. That will compel me to allow the fugitive to determine my travelling plans for the time being.

SAND. Are you going to follow him?

ENGLISHMAN. I shall be able to avail myself of the invaluable support of my countrymen in every continent and so shall not waste too much time.

SAND. Are you certain of success?

ENGLISHMAN. As the quarry perishes in the closed circle of huntsmen.

SAND *(picks up the rapier).* I prefer to be killed outright—rather than to suffocate slowly. Defend yourself!

ENGLISHMAN *(drops his rapier. In surprise).* Are you quite unmoved by all I have told you?

SAND. How does it concern me?

ENGLISHMAN. We have both been wronged. You too have been betrayed. Your true passion requited with deception.

SAND. I don't understand you.

ENGLISHMAN. Did he not come to you—from the arms of another woman?

SAND. Why do you repeat it?

ENGLISHMAN. To let you know—

SAND. What I knew already! *(The* ENGLISHMAN *steps back—silently.)* To explain or to hide anything of this has become senseless. In the tempest of the night's events any attempt at thought is wrecked. We two are drifting helplessly with our destiny—I and your wife. Not the event—only the figures are different. Hear from me the confession your wife withheld: a man is there—I have never seen him before. Until yesterday he did not exist–today he is life itself to me. How can that happen? Through light-years a star advances towards our planet–suddenly its light burns down on us. Destiny aimed from out of the darkness–now we are hit. No escape–no evasion: in offering ourselves up to it we act with honesty and purity such as no action of ours showed before!

ENGLISHMAN. You are creating a new law.

SAND. Law is preparation for the special case. There its validity ceases. If atonement is demanded, it is as a quip tagged on to the sublime. It is mediocrity lusting for petty revenge!

ENGLISHMAN. Are you putting these offensive ideas into the mouth of my wife?

SAND. If you can respond with intensity of feeling, your taking up a weapon becomes a crime!

ENGLISHMAN. Am I, wronged, to be castigated too?

SAND. Did you love your wife?

ENGLISHMAN. We married!

SAND. And that showed the extent of your esteem.

ENGLISHMAN. That it was complete.

SAND. Can your wife lose her worth overnight?

ENGLISHMAN. She deceived me.

SAND. Had she deliberately planned it?

ENGLISHMAN. That I cannot believe.

SAND. How overwhelming must her feelings have been, that she abandoned herself to them?

ENGLISHMAN. Inordinately so.

SAND. Do you want to diminish the happiness of the woman you love?

ENGLISHMAN. A confusing question—

SAND. What do you gain from this act you are putting on for your own benefit—the duel?

ENGLISHMAN. I wipe out an intolerable disgrace.

SAND. And thereby thrust your own person into the foreground.

ENGLISHMAN. Am I not the one wronged?

SAND. Not in this case. In what she did, she had no thought of you–you faded into the distance. Deception could not touch you.

ENGLISHMAN. Because she forgot me!

SAND. She is raised above guilt and freed of it. There was no double-dealing–with half an eye here and half peeping furtively there. A single emotion filled the moment. You existed far away across oceans!

ENGLISHMAN. Now I have returned!

SAND. And no poorer for the loss of anything you possessed. You find the house lit by new lamps. If you ask about the price, no treasure on earth can pay for its value. Thus you have grown richer in your absence.

ENGLISHMAN. Where does the advantage come from?

SAND. From a person who has experienced what it is to be herself!

ENGLISHMAN. I have reason not to overrate that experience: my wife betrayed her seducer and levelled the reproaches against him.

MUSSET *appears in the doorway and listens to the rest of the conversation.*

SAND. Does that disprove the heat of my own passion? I do not shrink from the profanation of confessing—it is engulfed in heightened ardour. No part of my being remains untouched. With every pore I am still breathing unlived day. Now the light seethes. I resound quivering in the flood of air. Yesterday a name–today a human being! What can mar the exchange? I am in love! Who would wish to escape the spell? A harlot with her itching palm–not a woman!

ENGLISHMAN. You are bridging an infinite abyss.

SAND. One leap will take you across it–on the wings of love. Hesitation robs the miracle of its power. I love–and no longer know who lives and who dies beside me. What significance have the faces of yesterday? Things of the past! Whispering once precious to the ear– leaves no echo. I am in love!

ENGLISHMAN. You were not afraid of death.

SAND. When we love, does much remain alive? The dying beat of the heart is its strongest. Is there a difference between dying and loving?

ENGLISHMAN. I could not have expected such a depth of feeling.

SAND. It is unbounded. It surges in and drowns me in ecstasy. A sleep-walker led by a will not my own. Who can call so loud as to shake me from my sleep?

ENGLISHMAN. The awakening had to come for my wife, too.

SAND. She buried herself in her fall. I snatched the man from her–first out of curiosity–then deliberately–at the last passionately. She allowed him to be taken from her through this betrayal to you–her husband!

ENGLISHMAN. Can you imagine any other way of behaving?

SAND. I should have kept silent. It would have cracked my lips to decry him. I have savoured what gives life to the living: dissolution in emotion that possesses the whole being in a single experience. Who would stamp out this torch which scatters sparks until the end of time and casts its light into the grey gloom of death?!

ENGLISHMAN. What do you advise me to do?

SAND. Leave Venice. At your back the city will be swallowed up by the sea. Scarcely the recollection of any such reality will remain. You will count it among the fables that have no foundation of truth.

ENGLISHMAN. Do you believe it possible?

SAND. Just as I know that your wife could not help loving the man-whom I now love!

ENGLISHMAN *(goes to her, takes her hand).* When the sounds of Venice have died away from my ears, I shall hear the start of a new sound.

SAND. What is it?

ENGLISHMAN *(kissing her hand).* The legend of the greater love! *(He leaves.* SAND *watches him go).*

MUSSET *(huskily).* Who-keeps running in and out of here? *(*SAND *turns to him.)* Such a coming and going. The lagoon overflows and casts up creatures. I lie in leaden sleep *(suddenly laughing)-*and in the next room the human beast is making love! *(*SAND *stares at him.)* Where have you got another lover hidden? Behind the curtain-it's bulging!-under the sofa-it's swaying!-Have you got rope-ladders hanging down to the canal? *(Clapping his hands)* Time to get up! Time to give up your love-making! Daylight shows up vice! If you don't look sharp, you'll be caught! *(*SAND *remains motionless.)* You-persaude him to come out-he is afraid-he's stuck in the wardrobe-suffocating in the chest!-he needn't be frightened!-what can I do to him: the patient to the doctor?! *(Falls into a chair.)*

SAND *(with a loud cry).* I love—

MUSSET *(sitting up).* A confession for all to hear?! Importunate in confessing-tiresome in repetition: I was listening in the wings and learned the whole text as you rehearsed it. Not a cue missed-the scene is effective. Is the scoundrel loitering somewhere?

SAND. I am in love!

MUSSET. The role assigned me is a powerful one: I close the performance with a corpse at my feet! On with the play-it is rushing to its end. My adversary?! *(Pulls open the side-door)* Empty!

SAND. No-one is with me!

MUSSET. That is no ending-there must be a body. There are rules which cannot be ignored. Props ready to hand: rapiers on the carpet. One each. Let's begin! *(He has seized one and takes up his position opposite* SAND.*)*

SAND *(with arms thrown wide).* Kill me!

MUSSET *(drops the rapier)*. That would be selling too cheaply! Revenge clumsily squandered! You have to know the way to kill! I know one that works—*(with a sudden roar of laughter)* that will work – must work! *(Stumbles out, still laughing.* SAND *stands perplexed.)*

ACT FOUR

MUSSET *asleep in the armchair—a rug over his knees.* SAND-*in women's clothes—watching him intently.*

GERMAN GIRL *(enters)*. Safe! Out of the yard and along alleys-the drunkard swore sacred oaths by the Madonna that he would see him safe-you must reward him in the only way he wants! No danger as far as the lagoon-then his luck must help him across!

SAND *(calmly)*. He is travelling without pursuers.

GERMAN GIRL. The Englishman?

SAND. On his northward journey home.

GERMAN GIRL *(pleased)*. You are staying in Venice?

SAND. Perhaps.

GERMAN GIRL. George—with me?

SAND. I have not yet found the answer to that.

GERMAN GIRL. When will you be sure?

MUSSET *moves. The* GERMAN GIRL *notices him-gives* SAND *a look.*

SAND. He came in-and heard too much.

GERMAN GIRL. He is awake.

SAND. Go. *(The* GERMAN GIRL *leaves.)*

MUSSET *(raises his head and looks at* SAND*)*. Who went out?

SAND. I sent the German girl away.

MUSSET. Do we have to be alone?

SAND. Just for an hour-it cannot be put off.

MUSSET. Better to keep nothing secret-that may protect you from being taken by surprise.

SAND. Do you despise me?

MUSSET. I love you-George Sand.

SAND. With what convulsion of love?!

MUSSET. Love is love. Am I not as gentle as an eternal lover?

SAND. I-love you-and I loved you to distraction in Paris!

MUSSET *(smiling-towards the door)*. Is there no uninvited listener?

SAND. Would I have kept from you what happened here?!

MUSSET. Neither from me nor from anyone.

SAND. From whom besides you?

MUSSET. The audience at the L'Oeuvre theatre or the readers of the *Revue des deux mondes.*

SAND *(slowly)*. What happened to me last night was for your sake.

MUSSET. George Sand is deceiving herself.

SAND. Or for myself. The one cannot be without the other. You must be aware of yourself before you can give yourself. I know now that I am not cheating.

MUSSET. There's never an episode missing.

SAND. You fled from me in Paris, when you discovered yourself in the manuscript. Here it was I who was horrified by your explanation of my nature, divided as with a sword into a yes and a no to life.

MUSSET. You experience only as much as you are able to describe.

SAND. Is there any art which enables you to give the whole of yourself?!

MUSSET. You must rest content with being a genius.

SAND. Who brings death to you–to everyone–*(she breaks off)*.

MUSSET. We shan't die of it.

SAND. —saps my blood?!

MUSSET. You're standing there breathing.

SAND. In the midst of life. Its waves foam at my feet and close over my head. All I've been through here! You fall ill. You need a doctor. One is found. He refuses to come because there is a woman with him. My messenger–a prattling fellow who drinks–but recites my poetry–keeps on making a din under the doctor's window until he agrees, simply to avoid scandal. He comes. His self-esteem, which is genuine and yet not arrogant in its absorption with the present, excites me. He does not discover who I am. It is a meeting of complete strangers–who fascinate each other. That is the prologue.

MUSSET. Enough to arouse one's curiosity!

SAND. While he is with you, the young woman bursts in on me–takes me for a rival and demands that I give him up. This woman is recently married, comes from England and is on a honeymoon trip. Her meeting with the doctor has something exalted about it, in which chance and destiny can no longer be separated. She tells me quite frankly about what happened on the piazza and in the church. A volcano of passion. I feel sorry for her–and get her to hide in the room there.

MUSSET. The development is brilliant!

SAND. The doctor returns from seeing you. He is saturated with the English woman's effusions, so that it is doubly easy for me to take her place. I skilfully get rid of the woman, and the doctor stays the night in the house.

MUSSET. It's packed with action.

SAND. In the morning the doctor's servant bursts in on us. The woman has confessed everything to her husband–the Englishman challenges her seducer to a duel. I prevent the fighting by persuading the doctor to run away and myself–in my men's clothing–confronting the Englishman.

MUSSET. Is he going to recognize you?

SAND. I step into the light–he lowers his rapier. His amazement grows into admiration as he begins to realize the full extent of my feeling for the doctor, that his wife must also have shared. He goes away conciliated.

MUSSET. A climax!

SAND. Now you are drawn into the stream of events. You overhear—

MUSSET. Twice.

SAND. When did you before?

MUSSET. When you were kissing the doctor.

SAND. At that time you were—

MUSSET. A detail. Not important, but entertaining. But go on–we can scarcely wait for the continuation!

SAND. You pick up the rapier from the ground and point it at me. I have no intention of defending myself–for I have done nothing wrong to you. What did I do against you? For you I embarked on the adventure. I had to lay the ghost you saw–that stripped me of my flesh and laid bare a skeleton. You were suffering–I wanted to love: so as to prove to you the genuineness of my emotions. What was a stranger's today belonged to you before and will remain for the future an experience I went through for your sake!

MUSSET. A profound idea.

SAND. With a clear beginning and an evident objective!

MUSSET. Worthy of a George Sand. How does it end?

SAND. The doctor has gone on ahead to his country-house–I am following him today. We shall have a time of separation.

MUSSET. Where is his house?

SAND. Near Naples.

MUSSET. It will go down in history: George Sand will write one of her finest books there. I've just been hearing its contents.

SAND. I shall not set pen to paper there!

MUSSET. No—

SAND. Do you believe me now?

MUSSET. Because you will turn back half way if the end of the story has written itself.

SAND. It will never be a story!

MUSSET. Didn't it turn into a novel, even as you were telling it to me?

SAND. My life is in it!

MUSSET. You don't know the end. That will keep you afloat a little longer—then you'll be washed up at your writing-desk.

SAND. I swear to you!

MUSSET. George Sand must hold nothing back. She has to live for many people—and one life is always less important than a multitude. Doesn't that console me? You were the star above my world–should one reach out and desire it for oneself alone? The sky has room enough for everyone's gaze. What I achieved on a small scale, you will do on a large scale. There is an echo of bliss in that. It is no total indemnity–but it is a compensation.

SAND. You drain the strength from my blood.

MUSSET. Did I not want to have my revenge? Had I not devised a terrible plot? More deadly than a sword-thrust? Am I not a cunning devil? Didn't I poison you with ink? But I am not proud of my success-which would have come in any case. *(SAND stares in front of her.)* How is my rival holding his own now? He has soon given all he had to offer and has become a character in your next immortal work. I can bury my jealousy. *(SAND does not move.)* Are you mourning over him?

SAND. He is waiting—

MUSSET. Are you going to let him down already?

SAND. He seemed to me to be changed—

MUSSET. No figure retains its own features when taken over into literature.

SAND. It would trouble me—

MUSSET. You need him for the ending. Go to him.

SAND. Is not this already-the end?

ITALIAN DOCTOR *(wearing his overcoat-enters; without noticing* MUSSET-*loud)*. No flight from Venice! The strangest encounter makes caution superfluous. Through alleyways and backyards I reach the canal-call a passing gondola-the gondolier answers with my name-comes into the side: then a gentleman gets up from under the canopy and greets me-it is the Englishman with his wife!

SAND *(quickly)*. No longer angry?

ITALIAN DOCTOR. Perfectly polite. His deferential gestures couldn't be surpassed!

SAND. His wife's expression?

ITALIAN DOCTOR. Seeking forgiveness with a flood of tears!

SAND. Did you see it all clearly? *(The* ITALIAN DOCTOR *stops short.)* Tell me. Everything that happened is important. I shouldn't be able to invent that! *(The* ITALIAN DOCTOR *looks at her with growing surprise.)* And what were your reactions? *(The* ITALIAN DOCTOR *remains silent.)* As silent as you are now?

ITALIAN DOCTOR. I instructed my servant to get my house ready-for you.

SAND. The country house near Naples?

ITALIAN DOCTOR. We are staying-in Venice.

SAND. Who?

ITALIAN DOCTOR. You-with me.

SAND. You are not going to your country-house?

ITALIAN DOCTOR. I saw the danger disappear-as the gondola left the canal.

SAND. You are not afraid of anything now?

ITALIAN DOCTOR. Now-my fears are just beginning!

MUSSET *(claps his hands weakly)*. Impossible to think of a happier end: the lover arranging a discreet dinner and the lady doesn't arrive. She is busy elsewhere with a rival.

ITALIAN DOCTOR. Are you–her brother?

MUSSET *(to* SAND*).* Is that what you told him?

SAND *(to the* ITALIAN DOCTOR*).* I left you under a false impression. Now you have the explanation.

ITALIAN DOCTOR. Who are you?

MUSSET. Don't ask–it will be to your advantage not to yield to petty curiosity.

GERMAN GIRL *(enters).* George–a letter for you from Paris!

SAND. I must read it! *(She leaves with the* GERMAN GIRL *through the side-door.)*

MUSSET. Did you love that woman? *(The* ITALIAN DOCTOR *takes his hand and bends low over the chair.)* Who does not love her? It need be no cause for shame to have succumbed to such ardent feelings. You were thrown unsuspecting into her path. You will have no reason to regret it. What can I tell you about this person? It turns out to be the myth of the eternal suffering of longing and renunciation. To whom does life belong? Not to you–not to me. We know only the phantasm that we wrest from it. Its essential part works in darkness. What we call love remains but a cry in the night. We compose a gentle elegy and are happy if we hit upon a tolerable rhyme.

ITALIAN DOCTOR. Who is–this woman?

MUSSET. Who am I? Who are you? Who are we all? Scurrying also-rans of life–not heroes. We are not creating the statue of mankind. It would tear us apart. We can worship, but not celebrate mass. The cold finger of the demon would surely kill us.

ITALIAN DOCTOR. Is she—

MUSSET. The inhuman human! The second that glides away over our lives. Frigid and fertile, so that eternity becomes time. A falling leaf in autumn–the cry of a bird calling at dawn. We shudder–and exult in the same instant. The summation: life and death incarnate!

ITALIAN DOCTOR. Even the end is impossible!

MUSSET. Did I not survive? Be reassured by the example. Just as you were necessary to me, so I can find help for you. You are not the first or the last. My torment is now your horror. Tomorrow it will be shared by new arrivals. That soothes. It is petty–but one person needs another person to defend himself against genius!

SAND *(enters–in travelling clothes).* Flaubert is in Paris! From Egypt. He begs me urgently to return. He is making plans which only I can realize. A new magazine. My contribution first and foremost. His letter is a masterpiece of persuasion and style!

MUSSET. What are you going to write?

SAND. His request takes me by surprise. He isn't leaving me time to get an idea of any significance.

MUSSET. There has never been a time when you need be less embarrassed for material.

SAND. Where can I find it?

MUSSET. Has not the circle of the novel closed as we are here together without recrimination? Down below the gondola is carrying a strange couple out of Venice. *(*SAND *looks at them–hesitates.)* Am I not in good hands?

SAND. I could not leave you with reproaches.

MUSSET. No leave-taking was ever more amicable.

SAND. Are you as calm as that?

MUSSET. Am I not sharing half the pain with someone else?

SAND *(to the* ITALIAN DOCTOR*)*. Shall we see you in Paris?

ITALIAN DOCTOR. If my duties here permit—

SAND *(laughs)*. Ask for George Sand! *(The* GERMAN GIRL *enters from the side-door with a travelling-bag.)* Take this sheet of paper for the good fellow down in the backyard.

MUSSET. What have you written? *(*SAND *hands it to him. He reads it.)* Leave it with me.

SAND. It's nothing much.

MUSSET. Perhaps the truest thing you ever wrote.

SAND. Then for once I stand before you without any lie?

MUSSET *(shakes his head)*. You are sincere only in the greatest lie!

SAND *(kisses him on the forehead)*. You are alive–go on loving me. *(Holds out her hand to the* ITALIAN DOCTOR*)* Take good care of my friend. *(She leaves with the* GERMAN GIRL.*)*

MUSSET *(hands the paper to the* ITALIAN DOCTOR*)*. Read it. *(The* ITALIAN DOCTOR *takes it–reads.)* Aloud for us both.

ITALIAN DOCTOR. Words are the death of life.

ONE DAY IN OCTOBER

Play in Three Acts

Translated by B. J. Kenworthy

Characters

COSTE
CATHERINE, his niece
JEAN-MARC MARRIEN, the Lieutenant
MRS JATTEFAUX, the housekeeper
LEGUERCHE, the butcher's boy
SERVANT

The events of this drama of love have as their only setting the drawing-room of Coste's villa. At the back of the semi-circle of the room is the high French window leading on to the terrace above the park that lies further in the background. Two doors in the right-hand wall. The left wall has a single door.

ACT ONE

SERVANT *enters from the left-crosses to the right and knocks on the door further downstage.*

SERVANT *(opening the door).* Mrs Jattefaux's compliments, and she would like to know when Mr Coste wishes to speak to her. Right away? I'll inform Mrs Jattefaux. *(He shuts the door-goes off left. SERVANT admits MRS JATTEFAUX from the left-knocks once more on the door right, opens it.)*
SERVANT. Mrs Jattefaux is waiting.

Closes the door-leaves, left. MRS JATTEFAUX *looks intently at the door right.* COSTE *enters from the door right. He goes quickly up to* MRS JATTEFAUX *and greets her with a handshake-indicates an armchair and seats himself in a chair.*

COSTE. Did you have a good journey? Were all the connections I put in my letter correct?
MRS JATTEFAUX. I should have telegraphed, if it had been impossible to arrive punctually.
COSTE. I know that I can rely on you, Mrs Jattefaux.
MRS JATTEFAUX. I do my duty.
COSTE *(shaking his head).* Opinions may differ on that. I have made no agreement with you to give me your help in situations as painful as this one.
MRS JATTEFAUX. It is a very human one, and we must do all in our power to be of service.
COSTE. Does that imply that you are trying to make excuses for what has happened?
MRS JATTEFAUX. I have no wish to condemn, Mr Coste, until there is some light in our darkness.
COSTE. What still remains obscure? Catherine has named the father. It is Lieutenant Jean-Marc Marrien, and he exists. In Paris. In the Fifth Regiment of the line. Here is his address. *(He passes her a slip of paper.)* Are these things not realities?
MRS JATTEFAUX. Certainly they are the foremost considerations.
COSTE. The only one, Mrs Jattefaux. I reject any attempt at extenuation, from whatever side it may come!—Did it cost your sister

137

undue difficulty to put Catherine up during her confinement, without attracting public attention?

MRS JATTEFAUX. My sister lives a very secluded life. And in any case, Catherine was a relative whose husband was away on a trip to the colonies.

COSTE. Did she confide the name to your sister?

MRS JATTEFAUX. Yes.

COSTE. Not to you?

MRS JATTEFAUX. To me as well—without knowing it.

COSTE. How did that come about?

MRS JATTEFAUX. During the delivery. She bore the labour painlessly with a kind of rapture that increased as the birth progressed. In the midst of it all an almost other-worldly smile lit up her face, half-opening her mouth, which nonetheless said quite distinctly: Lieutenant Jean-Marc Marrien—our child! I made a note of the name and sent it to you.

COSTE. It served its purpose. It was not difficult to find an officer of this name in the army. And to my great surprise in one of the best regiments in France—and more: the son of the first family in the country. I had expected some fellow or other it would be impossible to check on. If it were not for the confession that I am carrying on me, written by your hand, Mrs Jattefaux—I would never have believed that a man of this social standing and an officer could so far forget himself as to enter into a relationship and then run away from the consequences. A relationship with my niece, who bears the name of Coste, which has every reason to be spoken of with the greatest respect everywhere! Catherine has no suspicion that we now know the father of her child?

MRS JATTEFAUX. I kept it from her.

COSTE. I believed that to be right, and still believe so. At least until Lieutenant Marrien's confrontation with Catherine.

MRS JATTEFAUX. Is Lieutenant Marrien coming here?

COSTE. I had to request him to do so several times—it was only when I threatened to report him to his regiment that he agreed to come. He arrived almost at the same time as you. To achieve that, I arranged the timing of your journey with Catherine down to the last hour. I wish to see my niece here only to provide a father for her child. The marriage can take place quietly in Paris. I'll not have riff-raff under my roof!

MRS JATTEFAUX. Perhaps Catherine needs forbearance, Mr Coste.

COSTE *(incensed).* Did either of the two show me any forbearance when they sullied my name? Or was it forbearance that made the lieutenant hide himself away and forbid his lady-love to betray him? What is your opinion of that, Mrs Jattefaux? *(MRS JATTEFAUX is silent.)* You can find no answer to that. I couldn't either. Here the morals of a thoroughgoing blackguard are being displayed. Just imagine this Lieutenant Marrien cajoling the girl, reduced to defencelessness by her love, into giving herself to him, and then extorting a vow of silence from her when he has made her pregnant. Doesn't he deserve a horse-whipping?

MRS JATTEFAUX. Catherine didn't speak because she didn't want to speak. Before the birth of the child and after its birth. She never gave the impression of being oppressed by a secret. She went through the term of her pregnancy with calm cheerfulness.

COSTE. What made her remain silent, Mrs Jattefaux, when I asked her? She was as obstinate as a child sucking a sweet. She smiled—and my anger grew. What caused this stubborn defiance of hers?

MRS JATTEFAUX. You will find that out, Mr Coste, when Lieutenant Marrien and Catherine meet here—you will also find out where the two met previously.

COSTE. Mrs Jattefaux—I have capitulated in face of this riddle!

MRS JATTEFAUX. It fills my every thought. I would not be sitting here before you, Mr Coste, if I could think of any negligence on my part. It would have been the death of me. I speak in all seriousness, Mr Coste, and with God's judgment-throne in mind. I have watched over Catherine's every step-as her own shadow accompanies her. I was proud when you entrusted your niece to me-and very happy to devote all my energies to this most lovable of people. You could not lavish more care on your own daughter than the protection I have given Catherine. I am trying to discover the flaw in my attentiveness. Where did she meet someone I did not see as well? How did she strike up an acquaintance that escaped me? Where could she have got so far out of my sight that she could-surrender herself? However can it have happened?

COSTE. Mrs Jattefaux, no blame attaches to you. Had I ever had any doubts about your reliability, they must have been dispelled by the sacrifices you and your sister have made for me. You have kept dirt from my door that would have flooded into every corner of my house. Now not a soul knows of my niece's indiscretion. For that I have you to thank. *(He rises and kisses her hand.)* I owe you a great debt-how am I to repay it?

MRS JATTEFAUX. I would ask you never to withhold your trust from me, Mr Coste.

COSTE. What could shake it?

MRS JATTEFAUX. What you will now hear from Catherine's lips in the presence of Lieutenant Marrien.

The SERVANT enters, bringing a visiting-card on a tray. COSTE takes it—reads—nods. Exit SERVANT.

COSTE *(to MRS JATTEFAUX).* Stay with Catherine until I call. *(Referring to the visiting-card)* Not a word about the visit!

MRS JATTEFAUX leaves back right.
COSTE crushes the visiting-card in his clenched fist-lets the screw of paper fall to the floor. The SERVANT admits LIEUTENANT

MARRIEN. *Exit* SERVANT.
MARRIEN *eyes* COSTE—*makes a slight bow.*

COSTE *(responds barely perceptibly).* You put off taking up invitations I sent you in Paris. Were you not staying in Paris?

MARRIEN. I received letters from you in Paris.

COSTE. To which you paid so little heed that you omitted to answer them.

MARRIEN. I thought that I might spare myself the trouble.

COSTE. Subsequently you changed your mind?

MARRIEN. When a threat was contained in the last letter.

COSTE. That made you feel uncomfortable?

MARRIEN. No.

COSTE. Nevertheless you have presented yourself here.

MARRIEN. After I had happened to show the letter to another person, who enlightened me as to its sender. The name Coste was described to me as one of the foremost in France. I could no longer assume that it was personal harassment, but was forced to conclude that a matter of some seriousness had occassioned the letters to me.

COSTE. Have you never heard the name Coste before?

MARRIEN. Not that I recollect.

COSTE. Are you suggesting that you didn't know who it was you— *(He breaks off.* MARRIEN *waits.* COSTE *continues calmly.)* I shall have gained a clearer idea as to the degree of your credibility—

MARRIEN. What right have you—

COSTE. —as soon as a matter has been settled in the only possible way. When do you intend to get married? *(MARRIEN stares at him.)* Perhaps you are insufficiently informed as to the most recent developments, after you broke off your connections with my niece when the consequences became evident. A short while ago Catherine gave birth to a child in a remote provincial town at the home of my house-keeper's sister, and named Jean-Marc Marrien as the father of the child. Since, as it was possible to establish, there is only one Lieutenant Jean-Marc Marrien in the whole wide world, there can be no doubt that the father of Catherine's child is standing before me.

MARRIEN *(faltering).* I—do not—know your niece—

COSTE. Are you saying that Catherine was not known to you as my niece? Did she conceal the name Coste? Out of consideration for me? Was there just a girl called Catherine lying in your arms?

MARRIEN. Catherine is also unknown to me—

COSTE. Did she keep even her first name secret? What name did she use when she was with you? *(MARRIEN shrugs his shoulders.)* Don't attempt to seek refuge in meaningless gestures. You will have to do some remembering, Lieutenant. Now you are trying to make this affair look like an adventure that you have when you pick someone up off the street and no questions asked. You approached my niece in the full knowledge of her identity, just as Catherine knows your name and situation. Even now I am still trying to ward off an affront to my niece, whom you are labelling a whore!

MARRIEN *(collecting himself)*. Where are our meetings supposed to have taken place?

COSTE. Here in the town. Where else? Catherine has not been out of the town for a year.

MARRIEN. I have never set foot in the town.

COSTE. You must be mistaken.

MARRIEN. That is, I have set foot in it—

COSTE. Lieutenant Marrien!

MARRIEN. —for the first time today, to clear myself of a suspicion that has inexplicably fallen on me. No action of mine has involved me in the events you describe. There is a misunderstanding, and it must be left to you alone to remove it!

COSTE. I ask your help, Lieutenant Marrien. You deny any acquaintance with my niece. How is it that Catherine knows you?

MARRIEN. I do not understand your niece.

COSTE. Was she to remain silent? She did remain silent–and she forgot herself only once: when the child arrived. A woman does not lie when she is giving birth. Then–involuntarily–she uttered a name–the one you bear. You alone. Lieutenant Jean-Marc Marrien. Are you Lieutenant Jean-Marc Marrien?

MARRIEN. I am not the father of the child of Catherine Coste, your niece!

COSTE *presses a bell. The* SERVANT *enters left.*

COSTE. Mrs Jattefaux! *(The* SERVANT *goes towards the back right.* COSTE *calls after him.)* Mrs Jattefaux alone!

The SERVANT *leaves back right.* MRS JATTEFAUX *enters.*

COSTE *(with introductory gestures)*. Mrs Jattefaux—my housekeeper and Catherine's companion. Tell Lieutenant Marrien what took place in your sister's house. I was not present myself—I must depend on the statements of witnesses whose reliability is beyond all doubt. Even as regards their hearing, which plays a decisive part in this matter. Did Catherine speak during her delivery?

MRS JATTEFAUX. Very little.

COSTE. Was her voice impaired by loud moaning?

MRS JATTEFAUX. She made no sound.

COSTE. Apart from certain words?

MRS JATTEFAUX. Those she spoke distinctly.

COSTE. What were they?

MRS JATTEFAUX. Lieutenant Jean-Marc Marrien—our child!

COSTE. You heard that clearly?

MRS JATTEFAUX. Together with my sister.

COSTE *(calmly)*. Lieutenant Jean-Marc Marrien denies paternity. *(MRS JATTEFAUX regards MARRIEN in astonishment. MARRIEN makes no move.)* Lieutenant Marrien has never seen Catherine. And yet she mentions every detail of his name. It will be necessary to question Catherine closely. It may well be that she will have to apologize to Lieutenant Marrien. *(To MRS JATTEFAUX)* Bring Catherine in. *(MRS JATTEFAUX goes off right. To MARRIEN)* Your presence might upset my niece. Perhaps you would wait in my room. You will find reading-matter, so that you won't get bored.

He shows MARRIEN *into the room down-stage right.* MARRIEN *leaves.* COSTE *takes a few paces up and down—stands still.* CATHERINE *enters—behind her* MRS JATTEFAUX, *who remains for a short time and then withdraws silently. Without hesitation* CATHERINE *goes slowly up to* COSTE. *Still similing, she regards him with clear-eyed gaze.* COSTE *looks at her closely, holds out his hand to her.*

CATHERINE. My hands are caught up in my shawl. Now the left one is free. Do you want the other one?

COSTE. Whichever one you give me.

CATHERINE. Is it really all the same to you?

COSTE. As I said.

CATHERINE. There, the right hand has freed itself. Now I can offer you the proper hand!

COSTE *(presses it)*. I take it as a token of the good-will with which you return to my house.

CATHERINE. Am I not always obedient—whether you send me away or summon me to you?

COSTE *(pulls up a chair for her)*. Sit down. *(CATHERINE sits down on her chair,* COSTE *on another.)* Are you very tired from the journey?

CATHERINE. Nothing tires me.

COSTE. You have come through the difficult time that is now behind you very well. Mrs Jattefaux wrote to me about it.

CATHERINE. I have been through no difficult time.

COSTE. It is the expression normally used of someone who has become a mother.

CATHERINE. But it isn't correct.

COSTE. Not always, perhaps—and in your particular case it fills me with confidence that our talk will not suffer because of your condition, which according to your own words is of the strongest. So it will not overtax your strength to follow what I have to say. Would you care for some refreshment?

CATHERINE. Nothing.

COSTE. I should like to ensure that all disturbances are avoided.

CATHERINE. I shall cause none.

COSTE. I might remind you that you have already caused such turmoil that to call it a disturbance would be putting it very mildly. But I don't wish to conjure up shades of the past. Neither need you concern yourself with the degree of understanding I have for the things that have happened. I am quite resolved to approve retrospectively your right to decide for yourself about actions such as yours have been. You are your own mistress—and we shall take care not to set up as judges over our neighbours. Do you understand that from now on it is my wish to suppress any reproaches?

CATHERINE. Have you already rebuked me?

COSTE *(looks at her)*. No, Catherine, not if you have no recollection of it. So things which are over are buried. It is no longer a question of you and your secret relationships—it is a question of the child!

CATHERINE. Yes.

COSTE. It has been born, and with its birth it announces its claim to legitimation. It must not be disregarded. It borders on murder to curtail its most natural right—to bear the name of its father. I am not the one to ask what reasons moved you to answer me before–I don't wish to probe with my clumsy hands into your innermost being–forgive me, if I ever did pry!–only for the child, who needs my help, do I ask you for an admission. Who is the father? *(CATHERINE shakes her head— silent.)* Open your lips for these few syllables. You are a mother and your responsibility is a fearful one. Do not forget the child because of the interest you have in your secret. I don't know what it is, and I don't want to know. But the child demands the naming of its father! *(CATHERINE remains in the same unaltered attitude. COSTE waits a short time. Now almost matter-of-fact.)* Then I must tell you that I know it: Lieutenant Jean-Marc Marrien.

CATHERINE *(as calmly as ever)*. Then why did you ask me?

COSTE *(taken aback)*. It is true—that Lieutenant Marrien?

CATHERINE. You say that you know.

COSTE. You stand by this admission—that names Lieutenant Marrien?

CATHERINE. Did he not tell you his name?

COSTE. Catherine—you must bear in mind everything you have said. Or you can't remember. Your consciousness had left you—that was why you spoke. In the hearing of Mrs Jattefaux and her sister. The name was spoken by you–and by you alone!

CATHERINE. By me–when our child was being born!

COSTE. Now you must repeat it to me. Now you are fully aware. Now that you can hear your own voice. Weigh it carefully. The honour and the fate of a man are at stake. Is Lieutenant Marrien the father of your child?

CATHERINE. Yes.

COSTE. Lieutenant Marrien denies it! *(CATHERINE smiles, nods her head.)* You are not angered by his denial. You accept it as though you were expecting it. Why does one deny it after the other has admitted it?

CATHERINE. He will not want to say it, just as I did not say it.

COSTE. So I have chance to thank, which made you speak beyond the reach of your own will. For the sake of the child who drew the statement from you. Would the truth never have been revealed otherwise?

CATHERINE. Oh yes. Sometime.

COSTE. Had you reached an understanding which laid down the time the secrecy was to be maintained?

CATHERINE. Until I had given birth to our child.

COSTE. Now he heard about it—and is refusing to acknowledge the child?

CATHERINE. He has not yet heard about it.

COSTE. What?

CATHERINE. That he is the father.

COSTE. It is difficult for me to follow your train of thought closely enough to obtain a clear picture of this relationship between two people, the developments of which are so heavily veiled. But the consequences cannot be overlooked. The child is there. This is the only fact I can take into account in my desire to bring about the outcome that the situation demands. I must ask you to leave me alone now. *(He rises and goes over to the door back right; opens it.)* Mrs Jattefaux! *(*MRS JATTEFAUX *enters.)* Catherine will remain near at hand— *(*CATHERINE *gets up. With steady step she reaches the door back right. She leaves.* COSTE *shuts the door after her. To* MRS JATTEFAUX*)* What is your opinion of Catherine's character? Does she tell lies? Did you ever catch her being deceitful?

MRS JATTEFAUX. Catherine is truthful with every breath of her body.

COSTE. Nothing about her indicates a defect of this sort, which might show itself later?

MRS JATTEFAUX. It would not have escaped me.

COSTE. You have not the slightest doubt as to Catherine's veracity?

MRS JATTEFAUX. Neither today nor previously.

COSTE. She is again declaring that Lieutenant Marrien is the father of her child!

MRS JATTEFAUX. Then it must be true, Mr Coste.

COSTE. That is the conviction which takes hold of my mind when I think of Catherine's reactions. She did not falter or change her expression at the mention of the name. Not a trace of a blush spread over her face when I told her that Lieutenant Marrien denied her statement. Only someone who had no fear of detection can smile like that. Catherine is too sure that— *(He hesitates and falls into silent thought.)*

MRS JATTEFAUX. That what?

COSTE. —that Lieutenant Marrien—*(again he falls silent.)*

MRS JATTEFAUX. What does she expect of Lieutenant Marrien?

COSTE *(collecing himself)*. Lieutenant Marrien will not be permitted to cast the whole affair aside like a glove! *(He gestures to* MRS

JATTEFAUX, *who goes out.* COSTE *goes over to the door down right —opens it.)* Lieutenant Marrien—we will complete our business. *(*MARRIEN *enters.)* I have no knowledge of what ways and byways brought you and my niece together. Neither do I have any inclination to pursue the matter further. I dispense with details. Time and place of the assignations sink into oblivion as mere trivialities. They took place *(*MARRIEN *starts.)* Don't interrupt me. You are defending a position which has become untenable. In spite of all the hazards of the retreat. As far as you are concerned, everything is at stake. Catherine has a child that was born before her legal union with you. To state this publicly would be the ruin of your career. You will have to disappear from Paris. Your regiment will be lost to you. These are consequences which you appreciate clearly enough to resist the revelation of the truth.

MARRIEN. These would be the consequences—

COSTE. —also of your resistance to the marriage. Without further delay I shall go to the commanding officer of your regiment and tell him the facts. Within the hour you will be cashiered. On all fronts. Not even in the most remote colony will you get a command. Do you understand, Lieutenant Marrien?

MARRIEN. I understand that neither the one threat that you are uttering nor the other can touch me: up to now I have not had occasion to make your niece's acquaintance.

COSTE. And I have not had occasion to unmask my niece, who grew up in my care, as a liar!

MARRIEN. She has persisted in this accusation against me?

COSTE. With the frankness born of her conviction that you were only waiting for news of the baby's birth before coming forward!

MARRIEN. She overestimated my interest in matters–which have occurred in a world to which I have no access.

COSTE. Is this your final denial, that you couch in the form of contempt?

MARRIEN. I do not know your niece and deduce from the description of her personality you have given that, as the author of a tissue of inventions intended to label a total stranger as the father of her child, she is either ridiculous or-

COSTE. Or what?

MARRIEN. There is no or, when one's opponent is a woman.

COSTE *(ironically).* Do you feel you have been insulted, Lieutenant? I am ready to give you satisfaction.

MARRIEN. My involvement in this business does not extend that far. The attempt of your niece to appropriate my name to cover up adventures of a dubious nature-

COSTE. So she appropriated your name!

MARRIEN. -is infamous conduct, and deserves punishment. Administered by you, Mr Coste, in my presence. That is the satisfaction you owe me. I am Lieutenant Marrien, and I owe it to the army to seek retribution for every defilement of the uniform I wear. A most insolent attack has been made by your niece, who accuses me of dishonourable conduct. Give her the reprimand the matter merits—I am waiting!

COSTE *(goes to the door back right, opens it)*. Mrs Jattefaux—send Catherine in! *(He then stands with his back to the french window. CATHERINE enters and catches sight of MARRIEN who looks at her. For a while the eyes of both rest upon each other. At length, with a loud voice.)* Who is this, Catherine?

CATHERINE *(turning to Coste, smiling)*. Who?

COSTE. Do I have to introduce him to you, Catherine?

CATHERINE *(as before)*. Whom?

COSTE. My visitor here!

CATHERINE. Were you visited today by – Lieutenant Marrien?

COSTE *(advances a few paces-fixes his eyes on MARRIEN)*. You missed nothing, Lieutenant Marrien?

MARRIEN. Nothing—

COSTE *(to CATHERINE)*. Today is not the first time you have seen Lieutenant Marrien?

CATHERINE. Because he has come today he wants me to disclose our secret.

COSTE *(to MARRIEN)*. Do you not wish to anticipate what she has to say? I am warning you at the twelfth hour, Lieutenant Marrien!

MARRIEN. I have no secret to hide—

COSTE *(to CATHERINE)*. Why do you think Lieutenant Marrien has come today?

CATHERINE. Because I have come.

COSTE. Was it arranged between you?

CATHERINE. What has happened—is not arranged.

COSTE. What happened without being arranged?

CATHERINE. This—and the other thing.

COSTE. You deny there was any arrangement. Neither can chance have any part in it. The greatest pressure was necessary to persuade Lieutenant Marrien to make the journey here. I requested his presence to demand an explanation from him which he is not prepared to give. Will you ask him, Catherine, if today is the first time Lieutenant Marrien has seen you? *(CATHERINE turns her head towards MARRIEN—smiles.)* It is a tacit question, Lieutenant Marrien, that she is asking you. It is to make it doubly difficult for you to suppress the truth!

MARRIEN *(to CATHERINE, without agitation in his voice)*. Today in this room I have seen you for the first time. *(CATHERINE continues to smile at him.)* I am not mistaken. *(CATHERINE remains smiling at him.)* You must be making a mistake. I live in Paris, where you have not been for a year-I have never set foot in this town. *(CATHERINE slowly shakes her head.)*

COSTE. You are being contradicted, Lieutenant Marrien. You are doing violence to your memory. You will have to remember. *(To* CATHERINE*)* Has Lieutenant Marrien never been in the town? *(*CATHERINE *looks again at* MARRIEN.*)*

MARRIEN. Never.

COSTE *(to* CATHERINE*)*. Is that not the case?

CATHERINE. On the fourteenth of October you were.

COSTE. What date is that?

CATHERINE. When Lieutenant Marrien was in the town.

COSTE *(to* MARRIEN*)*. Where were you on the fourteenth of October?

CATHERINE *(to* MARRIEN*)*. In the town.

COSTE. How can Catherine state the day if there were any mistake?

MARRIEN *(pondering)*. On the fourteenth of October—the middle of October last year—I had orders—to take some documents to the south —on the return journey I had to change trains at midday—to catch the Paris express—which did not leave until late at night—it was in— *(looking up.)* Was it here that I waited for the train?

CATHERINE. You waited from midday until the night.

COSTE. Your statements contradict each other, Lieutenant Marrien. Your stay here is proved. How did you employ your time here, Lieutenant Marrien?

MARRIEN. For me it was just a town like any other that one passes through. Did I ever leave the station?

CATHERINE. At midday you looked at the display in a jeweller's window.

MARRIEN. Were you watching me?

CATHERINE. In the afternoon you knelt before the crucifix in church

MARRIEN. Did you see me again in the church?

CATHERINE. In the evening you sat in a box at the opera.

MARRIEN. Did you find me even at the opera?

CATHERINE *(bashfully)*. At night you were not travelling—

MARRIEN. Then where am I supposed to have stayed? *(*CATHERINE *looks at him.)*

COSTE. You did not leave the town then, Lieutenant Marrien?

MARRIEN. I had to be in Paris the next morning—on duty. It occurs to me that I left the opera before the end, so as not to miss my train. I caused a slight disturbance in the box. But I left on time. It can in no way be true that I spent the night anywhere but in the Paris express! *(To* CATHERINE*)* Even you will have to admit your mistake when I offer to verify the correctness of my arrival in the early morning through the entries in the regimental records! *(To* COSTE*)* Or better, yourself, if you accompany me to Paris to see the proof with your own eyes. I spent an afternoon and an evening here in the town—I was seen, but I saw no-one. The night, on which everything depends, I spent asleep on the cushions of my railway compartment!

COSTE *(to* CATHERINE*).* Lieutenant Marrien is offering proofs that can be checked. What have you to set against them?

CATHERINE *(in a whisper).* The child.

COSTE. With that assertion you could not survive in face of arguments whose credibility cannot be shaken. Lieutenant Marrien was travelling during the night that you claim to have spent with him. Was it Lieutenant Marrien who was with you that night?

CATHERINE. Lieutenant Jean-Marc Marrien.

MARRIEN. When did we arrange it? Outside the jeweller's? In church? At the opera?

CATHERINE. Outside the jeweller's—in church—at the opera.

MARRIEN. Three times—and I know nothing of any of them?

CATHERINE. But you do know.

MARRIEN *(simply).* How could I have forgotten?

COSTE. I will accompany you to Paris, Lieutenant Marrien. You will have to teach me that the truth can no longer be discovered by the living word, but that it requires dead print. What am I to believe? This is the behaviour of the gutter. A child comes into the world—and beside its cradle the quarrel rages: who is the father?

MRS JATTEFAUX *(enters from back left).* Leguerche, the butcher's man, wants to speak to you on an urgent matter, Mr Coste.

COSTE. Who?

MRS JATTEFAUX. Leguerche, the butcher's man who delivers the meat for the kitchen.

COSTE. You look after the housekeeping, Mrs Jattefaux, I don't order the meat.

MRS JATTEFAUX. He says he's come on a private matter.

COSTE. Send him away.

MRS JATTEFAUX. He won't be put off. It's essential for him to speak to you.

COSTE. A man who delivers meat?

MRS JATTEFAUX. Leguerche.

COSTE. Let him come in.

ACT TWO

COSTE *and* LEGUERCHE *sitting in armchairs.*

COSTE. Begin, Mr Leguerche. *(*LEGUERCHE *twists his straw-hat in embarrassed silence.)* The private interview that you asked for I have granted you—we are alone, as you see. *(*LEGUERCHE *remains in the same attitude.)* For my part, I have done everything to enable you to speak without interruption. If you now sit in silence, I must assume that you still have to consider what you want to say to me. In that case I must ask you to come and see me again later on. *(He rises.)*

LEGUERCHE *(remains seated)*. It is always the first word that starts things moving which is the most difficult.

COSTE. What matter does it concern?

LEGUERCHE. A number of things.

COSTE. That we have to discuss?

LEGUERCHE. Juliette, for a start.

COSTE. Who is Juliette?

LEGUERCHE. Once I was engaged to her—*(He breaks off.)*

COSTE. That must certainly be of great interest to you—

LEGUERCHE *(quickly)*. Don't you know Juliette any longer? *(*COSTE *shakes his head.)* She was in service with you as a chamber-maid—and then she left your service.

COSTE. Were there special reasons?

LEGUERCHE. That is what I'm referring to when I mention that Juliette gave up her job—so as to have time free for observations, which she naturally pursued with the appropriate discretion.

COSTE. Who was to be observed?

LEGUERCHE. The young lady.

COSTE. Which young lady?

LEGUERCHE. Miss Catherine.

COSTE. What's this? Your fiancée, a former maid in this house, devoting her attention to my niece after her dismissal? *(He sits down again.)*

LEGUERCHE. Even before that, Mr Coste, certain matters concerning Miss Catherine had not remained hidden from her. A woman soon knows what's what, when something isn't as it should be. They've got keen noses that smell out what's going on. You'd almost be surprised at what they find out. I say this about women in general, Mr Coste, for as far as certain facts regarding Miss Catherine were concerned, the discovery was in no way difficult. Quite the contrary, Mr Coste.

COSTE *(keeping cool with an effort)*. I am listening.

LEGUERCHE. Then Miss Catherine had to be packed off post-haste–to an unknown destination. Great importance was attached to secrecy.

COSTE. And your suspicions?

LEGUERCHE. We knew and we know. Juliette positively developed into a detective. Actually she enquired about the destination at the station. How did she manage it?

COSTE. How?

LEGUERCHE. She travelled on the same train, after asking Mrs Jattefaux for three days off when she was supposed to be visiting her mother in Normandy. But in reality she was travelling south—where the two ladies were going, without the faintest notion they were being pursued. She followed them like a shadow when they changed on to the branch line—followed their car in another. That's how carefully Juliette acted. She certainly has talents which not everyone of her sort possesses!

COSTE. What further use did she make of her special gifts?

LEGUERCHE. She discovered where Miss Catherine was staying–with Mrs Jattefaux's sister. That was enough to begin with. After that she came back here–went on working for a while–left, so as to return–for longer this time–to the place where Miss Catherine was staying. That's how it happened.

COSTE. I am not interrupting your story.

LEGUERCHE *(looking up with naive frankness)*. It's hard to put it in the way politeness demands. You grope around after the words that are on the tip of your tongue—but they won't get into formation. A butcher likę me is better at handling cleavers and knives!

COSTE. So far you have recounted the deeds of your Juliette with perfect lucidity.

LEGUERCHE. Juliette would be better at putting it all into words. Is she to present herself here? After all, I'm the one most involved.

COSTE. Juliette stayed for some considerable time–

LEGUERCHE. –in order to be certain about the birth of the child, which has in fact taken place.

COSTE. Who gave birth to a child?

LEGUERCHE. Miss Catherine.

COSTE. And your Juliette boarded the same train that brought the two ladies here, to let you, Mr Leguerche, know the exact time of arrival so that you shouldn't lose a minute in informing me about her observations.

LEGUERCHE *(eagerly)*. Juliette sent me a telegram on the journey, so that I could be ready and waiting to make my appearance here in a presentable state immediately on Miss Catherine's arrival.

COSTE *(after a pause)*. What is the purpose of your visit to me—in your presentable state, Mr Leguerche?

LEGUERCHE. We shall have to come to an agreement, Mr Coste.

COSTE. About what?

LEGUERCHE. Where money is not involved, any matter can be settled with money.

COSTE. What am I to pay for?

LEGUERCHE. For a promise I shall give you that it will remain between you and me.

COSTE. What you have nosed out about my niece with the assistance of your fiancée?

LEGUERCHE. If that's what you want to call it: nosed out–

COSTE. You will have to allow me to describe your conduct in even plainer terms. You are perpetrating an act of blackmail by suggesting that I should buy your silence in order to prevent matters becoming public that you recognize as being of a most painful nature. Your action is completely premeditated. A blackmailer is what you are, the police will take you in, so as to render people like you harmless. I am not afraid of you, Mr Leguerche–I shall call the police!

LEGUERCHE *(utterly taken aback)*. Am I to marry Catherine then?!
*(*COSTE *looks at him in astonishment.)* You call the police—you say
that I'm a blackmailer—you want to have me thrown into gaol: for
what–for what?? Because Miss Catherine pulled me into her room one
night and slept with me?! I wasn't pestering Miss Catherine with
proposals—I didn't rape her—I didn't get into the house in the night
with any such intention. Miss Catherine offered herself to me and
positively begged for my company. I couldn't create a disturbance, so
as not to disgrace Miss Catherine before the whole world. And for
that I'm a scoundrel who is to be handed over to the police?
COSTE *(slumped in his chair—expressionless)*. What was that you said?
LEGUERCHE. The truth, sir, always the truth—and you can rely on
Leguerche for that in any confounded situation. The police have never
yet crossed my path. I am honest to the marrow. But the situation I
find myself in is dishonest. Have you any use for a butcher's assistant
as a son-in-law? You'll turn that down—and I'll turn it down, if you
don't. The child ought to have a father—that is according to nature, but
I refuse to be the father according to law. It doesn't belong together—
your class and my class. It was according to the will of Heaven that I
had a child with Catherine—but no decree of God's can require me to
make the child the object of ridicule by marriage with Miss Catherine!!
COSTE. Calm yourself. What you are disclosing is shattering. Will you
give me answers to some questions?
LEGUERCHE. I was shouting, Mr Coste. I won't shout any more.
COSTE. You are in the right, Mr Leguerche, I was not sufficiently well
informed to outline my position.
LEGUERCHE. I thought you didn't know about everything—otherwise
you would have wanted our meeting sooner.
COSTE *(nods)*. How did it happen that you entered the house that night?
LEGUERCHE. An arrangement had been reached with Juliette that I
was to come that night. In any case, it wasn't the first time. When you
are engaged and are going to get married, it is not a matter of
importance. At least, not in our circles. You can't wait till the butcher's
shop is standing there ready. True love knows no time. Neither did it
ever trouble anyone in the house here that I was visiting Juliette. It's
true the gardener once kicked up a fuss the next morning because the
trellis was damaged—but I pacified him with a few chops. You see, I
always took the route up the trellis—in at a window that Juliette left
unlocked. And that is how it was that night. I climbed in—jumped
down from the window-sill on to the floor, and groped my way towards
Juliette's room at the end of the passage. Although I was creeping
along in my socks, a noise must have been noticed. For another door in
the middle of the passage was half opened—and a white arm drew me
into the room. It was Miss Catherine I found there.
COSTE. Catherine desired you?

LEGUERCHE. I resisted—for as long as one resists when kisses are like
a seal over your mouth, and body is pressed against body.

COSTE. You had to spend the night with her?

LEGUERCHE. At least until it was too late to visit Juliette. That's what
started the whole damned business!

COSTE. With Juliette?

LEGUERCHE. Naturally she asked me the next morning, when I
delivered the meat, why I had stayed away. I made excuses–finally she
cornered me with the threat to break off our engagement–and I
confessed. And I assure you, Mr Coste, with a heavy heart, for you
don't inform against a lady who has found you attractive.

COSTE. Was Catherine in love with you?

LEGUERCHE. I couldn't make it out, Mr Coste. It seemed so to me—
and at other times I felt as if I were someone quite different. In the end
I thought of Juliette while I was with her, to quieten my conscience.

COSTE. That didn't satisfy Juliette?

LEGUERCHE. She was hopping mad with jealousy. She wanted to go
running to Mr Coste to tell tales about Catherine. It took me all my
time to stop her taking this impertinent step. Then she swore she'd have
her revenge. The opportunity presented itself. Miss Catherine was
pregnant. Juliette discovered it at once—and then she never gave up
the trail. She never let go the lead she had got hold of. A lapse can be
hushed up—but not a child. I can't feel that Juliette was entirely wrong.
We have both kept silent and spared Mr Coste many embarrassments.
Would it then be so very shameless to make a claim on Mr Coste's
benevolence?

COSTE. How much are you demanding?

LEGUERCHE. I have worked it out with Juliette—in view of the fact—

COSTE. –that I in no circumstances wish the name of my niece to be
mentioned in connection with a butcher's assistant!

LEGUERCHE. Miss Catherine no doubt wishes it every bit as little.

COSTE. I have proof of that.

LEGUERCHE. That's how it is, Mr Coste. It will be the basis of a deal
which will satisfy all the parties. For Juliette and me it is a question of
our being able to get married. The setting-up of a butcher's shop of
modest proportions—or would Mr Coste be prepared to make a more
substantial sum available? We're not pressing you, Mr Coste, make no
mistake about that. But it is nice to get on in the world—if possible
at one jump.

COSTE. What do you call a more substantial sum?

LEGUERCHE *(takes two slips of paper from his pocket)*. On one sheet
I've calculated the cost of a shop with basic equipment—on this sheet
of a place with better facilities. Including working capital, of course.
(He hands him the sheets of paper.)

COSTE *(reads attentively)*. You can reckon on the better equipped
butcher's shop. *(He stands up.)* Come with me. *(He opens the door*

down right.) You must excuse me for a few moments, Mr Leguerche.
(He lets LEGUERCHE *enter—closes the door. He remains standing by the door—clasps his forehead. Then he goes quickly upstage right—opens the door.)* Mrs Jattefaux! *(*MRS JATTEFAUX *enters.)* Your defence of Catherine's veracity has meantime been shaken in the most painful fashion. You'll have to face up to the task of learning everything from the beginning again. In this school I shall be taking my place beside you on the hard bench and getting the lesson into my head that someone with the innocent face of an angel can be a more artful liar than any scoundrel with the twisted features of an ape.

MRS JATTEFAUX. What has roused your suspicions?

COSTE. They have disappeared, Mrs Jattefaux, completely wiped away—I no longer have any suspicions. I am no longer groping in the dark, where statement and counter-statement create impenetrable confusion. Until a third person comes and explains the situation—in exemplary fashion.

MRS JATTEFAUX. Who is making Catherine out to be a liar?

COSTE *(pointing downstage right).* The man waiting behind the door for compensation for this testimony of love: Leguerche, the butcher's man.

MRS JATTEFAUX. How did the fellow get—

COSTE. To Catherine?

MRS JATTEFAUX. —such ridiculous notions into his head that—

COSTE. —that fit so well with the facts that I declared myself willing to pay him for his silence! *(*MRS JATTEFAUX *lowers herself into a chair.)* Or is someone merely inventing these events which are possible in reality, but which our imaginations reject: that a young girl in a house like this lures a butcher's assistant into her room, when he is creeping along the passage to his sweetheart from the kitchen?

MRS JATTEFAUX *(astounded).* Was that here in the house?

COSTE. It took place while you were sleeping—while I was sleeping—while we believed that Catherine was sleeping as she had during all the nights before that night.

MRS JATTEFAUX. But it is impossible that I heard nothing—

COSTE. Of Catherine's cries for help? She didn't shout for help, since she was not attacked—by a ruffian finding an open door. Wouldn't she have raised the alarm if someone were trying to rape her?

MRS JATTEFAUX. Her cries would have reached me first.

COSTE. Everyone under the roof, Mrs Jattefaux. But it stayed quiet. So quiet—that the child had to appear to supply retrospective information about the events of that night.

MRS JATTEFAUX. Do you believe the butcher's assistant?

COSTE. There can be no doubts about what this man says. Leguerche is honest in his own way. It is certain that in him we have the father of Catherine's child.

MRS JATTEFAUX. Why did she name Lieutenant Marrien?

COSTE. Because she couldn't bring herself to confess to the butcher's man! A butcher's man—that is what she threw herself away on. It was to conceal that. And so the plan for a monstrous deception was coolly conceived. A lieutenant was to be the seducer—from Paris—of the most distinguished origins. She sees him in the town—knows that he is stationed here—happens to learn his name—and pins the responsiblity on him. It was excellently contrived. Except that there was a gap in the calculation: that I was not satisfied with the mere name of the lieutenant, but the lieutenant had to present himself in person. He comes and makes his protest—and Leguerche takes his place. The lie has run itself to death—and leaves behind the sullied remains of the author of all the fuss: a trollop!

MRS JATTEFAUX. What is to become of Catherine?

COSTE. That is the least worry to occupy me. Now the task has fallen to me of acquainting the lieutenant with matters for whose suppression Leguerche can be bought. Disgust will seal Lieutenant Marrien's lips. So the matter can be kept from the public, from which it must be kept for my own sake. Ask Lieutenant Marrien to come in.

MRS JATTEFAUX *rises—goes off left.* COSTE *waits—his eyes looking to the left.* MARRIEN *enters from the left.*

COSTE *(invites him to take a seat and seats himself).* My journey has become unnecessary—I shall not be accompanying you when you travel back to Paris.

MARRIEN. How am I to interpret your sudden change of intention?

COSTE *(smiling weakly).* You are no longer a wanted man, Lieutenant, the court has apprehended the real culprit.

MARRIEN *(likewise smiling).* I hope it is a transgressor on whose capture you can be congratulated.

COSTE. What do you mean by that?

MARRIEN. That the man who transgressed out of love is welcome to you as your niece's husband.

COSTE. He would not be welcome even if he insisted on marriage.

MARRIEN. Just the same the child would be legitimized.

COSTE. To be made the object of public ridicule through this legitimization.

MARRIEN. Who is the father?

COSTE. Leguerche, the butcher's assistant.

MARRIEN. A butcher??

COSTE. The butcher's assistant Leguerche, who delivers meat to the house. A course lout who takes women where he finds them. Don Juan of the suburbs. Idol of the servant's quarters. Does it matter to you? *(MARRIEN stares at him.)* It will fill you with even greater disgust when I continue: the butcher's man is the less guilty party. He has the bearing of the complete cavalier. He didn't talk. He was egged on by his fiancée, a former chambermaid of ours, whom he left in the lurch that night, so as to devote his time to my niece. For he had an appointment elsewhere. He had his Juliette—and had no need of Catherine. But Catherine wanted him to go into her bedroom. Juliette was cheated of her due. Catherine stole it from her—and so the theft was punished: she conceived the child by Juliette's fiancé. He is the real father—his name is Leguerche and he a butcher's assistant by trade!

MARRIEN *(laboured).* Why are you telling me all this?

COSTE. For reasons which are not far to seek. A Leguerche can understand them. One doesn't gossip about it. The whole thing is too gross. People would thoroughly enjoy themselves laughing at others who are dying of shame. I am among these others. I am asking for your forbearance in the use you make of your knowledge of this affair, just as the butcher's assistant is prepared to exercise it.

MARRIEN. What—is Leguerche's attitude?

COSTE. He is accepting money and keeping quiet. *(MARRIEN is silent.)* Does it surprise you that I am giving him money? He not only knows about it—he is the father. It would be senseless to proceed against him. In any case, the poor devil intends to make the best use of the money—to open a shop and marry his Juliette. What have you got against Leguerche?

MARRIEN. Nothing—

COSTE. He'll enjoy his independence and keep his mouth shut. That is fixed up. *(Pointing downstage right.)* I'll arrange the necessary details with him in my room later on. The Leguerche account will be cleared— for all time! *(He turns back towards* MARRIEN.*)* I am counting on your having forgotten all this unpleasantness that you have been subjected to here by the time you arrive at the station in Paris. At least I am putting forward the plea that you make an effort to forget. Do you give that promise, Lieutenant Marrien?

MARRIEN. There is no question of my—

COSTE. Are you refusing because you regard it as an insult that you have been wrongly accused?

MARRIEN. You misunderstand me—not a word will pass my lips. That my discretion might be held in any doubt by you is the only insult I have heard here.

COSTE *(rises—approaches* MARRIEN—*holds out his hand to him).* For that I have no cause—now or in the future. *(MARRIEN rises— takes his hand.)* It never happened, Lieutenant Marrien—and with this handshake not as far as I am concerned either. One can fill in a grave over the living too, if their actions become offensive. And by the same token she also is silenced whose allegation brought you here. Goodbye, Lieutenant Marrien!

MARRIEN *bows—does not go.* COSTE *looks at him enquiringly.* MARRIEN *returns his look—smiles.*

COSTE *(unsure).* What—

MARRIEN. I should just like to ask Miss Catherine how she knew my name.

COSTE *(astonished)*. Do you wish to speak to her?

MARRIEN. It is not curiosity—of course it is curiosity to discover in what way one can make an acquaintance without meeting.

COSTE. Why, she saw you that day in the town.

MARRIEN. But one doesn't see names!

COSTE. You can reckon that it was coincidence.

MARRIEN. It must be of such a peculiar kind that it rouses my curiosity to discover it.

COSTE *(shrugging)*. You may ask to be given an explanation. I respect your wish. *(He presses the bell. The* SERVANT *enters.)* Miss Catherine is requested to come here. *(*SERVANT *leaves upstage right.)* My business discussion summons me to Mr Leguerche. Shall we see each other again?

MARRIEN. I will take my leave now. *(He makes a formal bow.)*

COSTE. Have a good journey, Lieutenant Marrien. *(Leaves right.)*

MARRIEN *stands thoughtfully beside the chair.* CATHERINE *enters— walks without hesitation to the centre of the room—looks at* MARRIEN.

MARRIEN. Are you very surprised to find me here?

CATHERINE. Why should I be surprised?

MARRIEN. My departure was arranged with your uncle, and it should already have taken place.

CATHERINE. But you haven't left.

MARRIEN. Now neither of us is leaving for Paris—neither Mr Coste nor myself.

CATHERINE. Will you stay here?

MARRIEN. I shall go alone on the next express, which leaves in the evening.

CATHERINE. As yet you don't have leave that lasts longer.

MARRIEN. It is indeed limited to this one day—but I have no idea why, even with a more generous dispensation from duty, I should take up my quarters here.

CATHERINE. Why did you not leave at once?

MARRIEN. For that I have a reason which is sound enough to postpone my departure for a few hours.

CATHERINE. Just like when you were in the town before.

MARRIEN *(laughs)*. Then I was dependent on the time-table, which provided no better connection for Paris-but today I am acting deliberately. I want to talk to you.

CATHERINE. About all we have done together?

MARRIEN. That would be a short chapter which a few words would exhaust. I figure in it only with my name. Nonetheless it is my name, with which my existence is intimately connected. I am identical with its good or ill fortune. My interest is therefore not slight in its fate, in which it involves me. This time it seems to have played a prank on me without my noticing it. Where did my name introduce itself to you in its entirety: Jean-Marc Marrien?

CATHERINE. In the church.

MARRIEN. One doesn't speak there. Least of all about oneself. There the individual is submerged in the mass of the faithful and dissolves in the worship of all. Did my name disturb the sanctity of the place by its impious self-proclamation?

CATHERINE. It named itself to me when the organ was resounding and we were praying.

MARRIEN. Was I praying?

CATHERINE. With all who were kneeling when the priest elevated the host.

MARRIEN. At the most solemn of moments?

CATHERINE. At the most solemn moment I lowered my eyes—and read the name.

MARRIEN. Where?

CATHERINE. Your cap had been laid by you on the bench seat—and in the cap was written the name: Jean-Marc Marrien.

MARRIEN. Were we kneeling side by side?

CATHERINE. When the benediction was given we were still kneeling.

MARRIEN *(in silent astonishment. Then with a laugh)*. So it would have been enough to avoid complications if I had put my cap down with the top and not the lining upwards. Truly an action that stands in no relation to the consequences!

CATHERINE. The cap lay as it had to.

MARRIEN. Why, was I acting under some compulsion?

CATHERINE. It had to be, after we had looked at the rings in the jeweller's.

MARRIEN. I looked at the jewellery in the window—at rings too.

CATHERINE. We looked at the rings at the same moment.

MARRIEN. Were you checking to see what I was looking at?

CATHERINE. I could feel it.

MARRIEN *(falls silent again. Then amused once more)*. And this extravagance of coincidence brought us together for a third time that day—that was at the opera.

CATHERINE. In the box at the opera.

MARRIEN. Where was I sitting?

CATHERINE. On the seat in the middle against the parapet.

MARRIEN. And you?

CATHERINE. On the seat beside you.

MARRIEN. Then I left before the end of the performance and stumbled in the dark box.

CATHERINE. In the darkness you touched my arm, which was bare.

MARRIEN. I touched you?

CATHERIN *(indicating her arm)*. Just here.

MARRIEN. But that happened quite untenionally.

CATHERINE. When we had already looked at the rings together—had knelt in front of the priest—and in the evening were sitting in the festival atmosphere of the opera?

MARRIEN. What is that supposed to prove?

CATHERINE. That we were having our wedding, which had begun with the rings—received its blessing in the church—and was celebrated with music in the evening! *(MARRIEN gazes at her.)* And at night we were united, as every wedding ends.

MARRIEN *(pulling himself together).* The wedding which you believe took place did not end in the way weddings usually end, that is, with man and wife spending the wedding night together. The man who came to you that night was not the man you had married in your imagination. Are you not prepared to remember—a butcher's assistant named Leguerche? *(Her expression changes instantly-she looks at MARRIEN wide-eyed).* He is the lover of that night for whom I am being made to cover. He has presented himself. He is now discussing the matter with your uncle in the next room. He doesn't want to make a fuss—but to hold his tongue for money. You have nothing to fear from him. But steps could be taken by me to silence you, if you continue to proclaim that I am the father of your child—which you seem determined to do!

CATHERINE *(horrified).* Has someone come—who is slandering me?

MARRIEN. If the truth is slander—then slander has materialized. In person and therefore irrefutable. In the form of a butcher's man. I leave the field to my rival—Mr Leguerche!

CATHERINE *(in the greatest fear).* It isn't!!

MARRIEN. Am I to call him, so that you can recognize him again? So that the memories of that night are revived—when you decieved in the most despicable way the husband you had married with pomp and circumstance that very day?!

CATHERINE. I did not deceive you!

MARRIEN. Me??

CATHERINE. You were with me—and I conceived our child by you!

MARRIEN *(Silent. Then smiling weakly).* Confusion is created even as you speak. I was almost treating as fact what is totally without foundation. Of course you didn't deceive me, because you couldn't deceive me. And it is just as little my business to inform you of the appearance of the butcher's assistant, Leguerche. We are both on the wrong track, Miss Catherine.

CATHERINE *(hesitant).* Now you are calling me miss.

MARRIEN. How am I to address you?

CATHERINE. I have a child.

MARRIEN *(slowly).* Catherine—

CATHERINE. But I have not had a child by a butcher's man. Who is Leguerche? How did he get into my room? I didn't hear him when the

leaves on the trellis rustled by an unknown hand. The boards in the
passage creaked only from the step I was expecting. Did I push open
the door before a stranger whom I abhorred as I would any stranger
who might approach me? Did I not take into my bed the man I loved
with the bliss of my blood? Who pierced my heart with his glance as
with a red-hot needle, when a mere half-glance rested on me—at
midday outside the jeweller's shop? Who set my pulse racing under the
dome of the cathedral as I knelt beside him? Who, to the sounds of the
exulting instruments that transported me out of this world, touched my
skin and incited my surrender? What has happened beneath the
heavens that is more real than my marriage to Jean-Marc Marrien?
Was it not recorded in writing that writes itself in the books which
attest it with valid seal? Who seeks to destroy a marriage—and to kill a
child that will die if my love for its father is killed?

MARRIEN *(calmly)*. Your child will live, Catherine.

CATHERINE *(quickly)*. When do you want to see it?

MARRIEN. Is it a pretty baby?

CATHERINE. It is like you.

MARRIEN. Like me?

CATHERINE. Can it be other than like you?

MARRIEN *(nodding)*. One day, apparently like any other, cuts into
our lives. A train leaves late—and between arrival and departure a
glance into a jeweller's window—a visit to a church—going to the opera
—build up a destiny. Your destiny, Catherine. And perhaps mine, too.

CATHERINE. Is it being decided only today?

MARRIEN. I didn't know that you loved me.

CATHERINE *(goes to him and lays her hand on his arm)*. Jean-Marc-I
loved you with all my heart.

MARRIEN *(motionless, looking past CATHERINE straight in front of
him)*. And I am beginning to love you with all my heart, Catherine.

CATHERINE *(stepping back from him)*. What are you saying?

MARRIEN. I love you.

CATHERINE *(on her way to the door down right)*. Say it again.

MARRIEN. With great strength that no longer makes me uneasy!

CATHERINE *leaves.* MARRIEN *stands motionless.* COSTE *and*
LEGUERCHE *enter down right.*

COSTE *(noticing* MARRIEN*)*. You have not left yet, Lieutenant
Marrien?

MARRIEN *(turns towards him)*. I have no intention of leaving.

COSTE. Does your regiment not need you?

MARRIEN. We must wait and see.

COSTE *(to* LEGUERCHE*)*. By the way, Mr Leguerche, we can
conclude our business now. You will not have the trouble of coming
here a second time to collect the money. I will make you out a cheque
that you can take with you. That is the simplest way to settle the matter.
(He sits down at the table and writes. LEGUERCHE *looks at*

MARRIEN, *who returns his gaze.* COSTE *stands up and waves the cheque about.)* As soon as the ink is dry I'll give it to you. Don't lose it.

LEGUERCHE. One holds on to things like that! *(*MARRIEN *steps between* COSTE *and* LEGUERCHE.)*

COSTE *(tries to hand the cheque to* LEGUERCHE*)*. This is for you, Leguerche. *(*MARRIEN *snatches the cheque and tears it up.)* What is the meaning of this?

MARRIEN *(to* LEGUERCHE*)*. Nothing—*(to* COSTE*)*-and everything!

COSTE. What am I to think of you, Lieutenant Marrien?

MARRIEN. That I am the father of Catherine's child!

ACT THREE

COSTE *and* MARRIEN *seated in armchairs.* COSTE *looks at the floor, shakes his head.*

MARRIEN. Are you opposing my proposal? Catherine is not of age. You are her guardian. Your objection carries weight.

COSTE. Catherine has always acted independently. And she would not take account of the opinion of third parties this time either.

MARRIEN. I do not share your view, Mr Coste, that presumes Catherine guilty of having already taken action on her own responsibility.

COSTE. Do you believe that I am accusing her of simple disobedience? By doing so I should confess myself lacking in understanding. As a consequence, I should have to dissociate myself from these events and leave you and Catherine to yourselves.

MARRIEN *(earnestly)*. Is there still any point that has not been clarified?

COSTE. Neither shall I—nor will anyone who is informed of these events fail to recognize that a compulsion is at work here which indicates its own discernible cause.

MARRIEN. A compulsion which also gives me my orders after the event. Must I not obey?

COSTE. Since you empower me to apply the highest measure of chivalry to your person—yes.

MARRIEN *(pleased)*. You understand everything?

COSTE. You feel yourself to be the cause of the eruption of Catherine's predisposition to love? That very day found her in a state that had reached its maturity, that urged fulfilment. A spark sufficed to set off the explosion in her blood. The spark struck when your glance lit upon her.

MARRIEN. My glance!

COSTE. She loved you at once—overwhelmed by a feeling which had found its destiny. Once having succumbed, she gave further events their appropriate interpretation. The imaginary exchange of rings took place before the jeweller's window—

MARRIEN. Our engagement!

COSTE. The simultaneous visit to church was given the semblance of a wedding ceremony—

MARRIEN. The blessing was pronounced over us by the priest!

COSTE. The opera performance you both attended became the pretext for the wedding celebration—

MARRIEN. To celebrate our marriage before a thousand guests, who filled the opera-house!

COSTE. Everything is real and unreal at the same time. I am inclined to call what has brought you and Catherine together a mystical union. Doubtless of heavenly origin—doubly difficult, therefore, to establish on the firm ground of reality.

MARRIEN. As far as the world is concerned, Lieutenant Marrien entered into a legally valid marriage with Catherine Coste!

COSTE. You see no difficulties?

MARRIEN. Where could they come from?

COSTE. Catherine—is bringing a child with her.

MARRIEN. Might that displease the commandant? If so, he'll turn me out of the regiment. I'll serve at a border station—in the colonies. As a farmer I'll live in the tropics—without any uniform. With Catherine!

COSTE (shakes his head). Your commandant will do nothing against you—

MARRIEN. My family? Will they feel offended? Does it make me unfit for human society if I marry Catherine—who has a child?

COSTE. In no-one's eyes will you stand any lower because of what you propose—on the contrary: it will make the excellent qualities of your character more obvious to anyone to whom you disclose the motives which led you to marry Catherine. But do you want to run around begging for understanding that explains and excuses? Can you—for Catherine's sake as well—profane the legend of your love?

MARRIEN. I would defend the possession of this experience—as though I were tongueless.

COSTE. You remain silent—and Catherine will also keep her own counsel—a third person will talk.

MARRIEN. Who?

COSTE. Leguerche.

MARRIEN. What will he say?

COSTE. Enough to bring down in ruins your position—your relationship with your family: that your wife has a child conceived by a butcher's man. (MARRIEN sits staring.) Marrien—there are limits to all transmutations of reality, the deepest dream issues in death—you wish to live. You may obtain public pardon—they'll even pay homage to your romance!—but make sure that you are acknowledged as the undisputed father of Catherine's child!

MARRIEN. I am the father.

COSTE. You are not, Lieutenant Marrien—as long as you tear up cheques that make others silent.

MARRIEN *(looking up)*. Are you trying—to be offensive to Catherine again?

COSTE. Will not Catherine remember the night with Leguerche?!

MARRIEN. Was she not expecting me?

COSTE. The butcher's man came!

MARRIEN. To Catherine—never!

COSTE. You both deny it?

MARRIEN. Who could accuse Catherine and me of lying?

COSTE. Are these your weapons against Leguerche, who won't quit the field without desperate resistance?

MARRIEN *(calmly)*. Who else is to quit the field?

MRS JATTEFAUX *enters down right.*

MRS JATTEFAUX. Is it true that Catherine is leaving?

COSTE. Catherine?

MRS JATTEFAUX. She insists that she must leave at once. Is that your wish, Mr Coste?

COSTE. But where does she want to go?

MRS JATTEFAUX. She won't say.

COSTE. A journey without a destination?

MRS JATTEFAUX. Is that not according to your instructions?

COSTE. I have said nothing to Catherine. Does she want to go away with you, Mrs Jattefaux?

MRS JATTEFAUX. That is what I assume, though she says nothing direct. She keeps repeating: we two must leave at once. And all the time she is packing her case as fast as she can. She must really be afraid to stay here another minute. That's how she is behaving.

COSTE *(looks at* MARRIEN. *Then at* MRS JATTEFAUX*)*. Calm Catherine with this message from me: she is not to bother with her case any more—*(with a more powerful voice)*—for nowhere in the world is she more secure than in the house of which I am master! *(*MRS JATTEFAUX *leaves.)* What interpretation do you give this sudden decision of Catherine's—to set out on this journey she proposes to make with you—into the unknown?

MARRIEN. With me?

COSTE. With you, Lieutenant Marrien, she is taking flight that will end in the bramble-patch—trackless, thorny!

MARRIEN. Pursued by whom?

COSTE. By a bloodhound who will not give up the scent until he is holding the tribute in his podgy paws!

MARRIEN. Catherine will not leave—

COSTE. I can protect her!

MARRIEN. Are you alone capable of it?

COSTE. Because I am prepared to make the deal with Leguerche!

CATHERINE *(enters from the right)*. Is Mrs Jattefaux to forbid me to finish packing my case?

COSTE *(hesitant)*. It is not my order—I had Lieutenant Marrien's request conveyed to you—not to remove yourself from my care. *(Quickly to* MARRIEN*)* Didn't you say explicitly that Catherine should not leave now? *(*CATHERINE *turns her eyes to* MARRIEN.*)* Lieutenant Marrien is moved by thoroughly sensible considerations. He has asked my permission to marry you. I could have no hesitation in giving you into the keeping of the noblest of hands. There are formalities to settle. The regiment requires to be informed—the family has the same claim. Much time can be saved by giving the most careful attention to everything that is necessary. The date of the wedding is advanced. *(To* MARRIEN*)* Have you more than this one day's leave from your unit?

MARRIEN. Only one day.

COSTE *(emphatically)*. That must not be exceeded. You return to Paris immediately. By the evening you will be with your family, so as to inform them of the step you are taking—tomorrow morning you inform your commanding officer. Catherine stays with me until you send the best of news from Paris. Then I bring Catherine to you—as safe and sound as you leave her now! *(To* CATHERINE*)* Will you support my suggestion to Lieutenant Marrien, Catherine?

CATHERINE *(slowly)*. You are going away from me today-because your leave is up? *(*MARRIEN *remains silent.)*

COSTE. Lieutenant Marrien is obeying military orders when he leaves you, Catherine!

CATHERINE. Are you not worried by fear of the danger—in which you are leaving me? *(*MARRIEN *stands motionless.)*

COSTE. From what quarter should it threaten, so long as I have the will and the means—to settle certain matters in Lieutenant Marrien's absence.

CATHERINE. Won't they—when I am alone—snatch my child from me?

MARRIEN *(firmly)*. I will not return to Paris before I know that you, Catherine, together with the child, are safe!

SERVANT *enters left.*

COSTE. Who is—

MANSERVANT. Mr Leguerche wishes to speak to the lieutenant.

MARRIEN *is about to cross to* CATHERINE. *She raises her hand to stop him.*

CATHERINE *(smiling)*. You will protect the child—from him! *(Stepping backwards, she reaches the door back left and leaves.)*

COSTE *(after a pause)*. Do you wish to receive him?

MARRIEN *(to the* SERVANT*)*. Mr Leguerche! *(The* SERVANT
 leaves.)
COSTE *(beside* MARRIEN*)*. Lieutenant Marrien, let me deal with
 Leguerche.
MARRIEN. The man asked specifically for me.
COSTE. What are you going to say to him?
MARRIEN. What does one say—to a shadow?
COSTE. Are you determined to ignore his existence?
MARRIEN. Will his life be at risk if I do not know him?
COSTE. It will shatter all his hopes in life if you turn him away.
MARRIEN. Thousands could come running to me like this and collect
 their cash. I'm no public benefactor.
COSTE. He is the only one who can substantiate his demands.
MARRIEN. In my eyes?!

COSTE *shrugs his shoulders and leaves down right.* MARRIEN *leans
against an armchair. The* SERVANT *opens the door left and announces:*
Mr Leguerche! LEGUERCHE *enters. The* SERVANT *leaves.*
LEGUERCHE *coughs to indicate his presence.* MARRIEN *drops into
the chair.* LEGUERCHE *sits down on the edge of the seat.* MARRIEN
studies the tips of his boots.

LEGUERCHE *(babbling)*. I've never in my life had a couple of clouts—
 like the ones she gave me just now. There was a bang on the right, on
 the left—before I could even duck my head, I had two sets of five finger
 -marks across my face. And then I wasn't even allowed to wait until the
 marks on my skin had gone away—I had to about-turn, pick up my hat
 and prance off down the road, just the way I was with the blotches on
 my cheeks. *(*MARRIEN *coughs.)* That was the receipt Juliette handed
 me. For my account of how my visit to Mr Coste turned out at the last
 moment to be fruitless. After a very satisfactory agreement had been
 reached—between Mr Coste and yours truly. But I committed the most
 enormous bit of stupidity and spoilt everything: I wasn't smart enough.
 You were quicker than I was, lieutenant.
MARRIEN *(casually)*. In doing what?
LEGUERCHE. In grabbing. When the cheque was hovering in mid-air
 my hand twitched a second too slowly—and it was too late. You,
 lieutenant, were the happy possessor of the cheque.
MARRIEN. Which I tore up.
LEGUERCHE. In the further course of our talk I shall permit myself to
 voice my conjectures about that. To start with, I should like to express
 in retrospect my regret that as yet no agreement has been arrived at,
 since I allowed myself to be outdone by you.
MARRIEN *(ironically)*. Simply because you were not quick enough in
 accepting the cheque it has not all been settled to everyone's
 satisfaction?

LEGUERCHE. That is my opinion. It is a purely physical failing on my part, because a person like me has a bit of a problem with agility. I am a butcher's assistant. You have the benefit of a greater suppleness of limb. With your figure you have the advantage every time.

MARRIEN. Over whom?

LEGUERCHE. Me, of course.

MARRIEN. With whom?

LEGUERCHE. With your fiancee.

MARRIEN. I have become engaged to Mr Coste's niece.

LEGUERCHE. No-one could fail to congratulate you on that. An excellent match—Mr Coste's niece. There are millions there—and they've set plenty of palms itching. Suitors have been fawning around here in their dozens after that tasty morsel. One after another they've been sent packing. Until a lieutenant—on his way from Paris—turns up and comes home at a canter. What is an onlooker to make of that?

MARRIEN. Have you any particular ideas?

LEGUERCHE. When it's the usual story? A respectable girl has got herself into trouble—and now it's a question of buying the child a father out of the top drawer. For money even a lieutenant will come jumping out, once the right deposit has been put down.

MARRIEN. You think this is the case here?

LEGUERCHE. You've been bought up by Mr Coste for his niece—lock, stock and barrel. You're making the deal because you need the money. When was there ever a young lieutenant who didn't have debts? Paris —gambling—women. Perhaps you're in a real jam, it could cost you your commission—and then Mr Coste's offer comes as a light from heaven. Well and good—and sensible of you to seize it. One has to live. So get hold of the bag that spills the ducats—and give it a shake. But let others live as well.

MARRIEN. Who?

LEGUERCHE. You mustn't make the deal on your own. You must give me a share!

MARRIEN. Then—I must clear up a few misunderstandings.

LEGUERCHE. In front of me you can speak quite freely. Haven't I proved already that I can hold my tongue?

MARRIEN. Marrying a rich woman doesn't tempt me—I am very well-off myself and have no wish to extend my property.

LEGUERCHE (stares at him open-mouthed). Why—are you— marrying Catherine?

MARRIEN. I am marrying Catherine—because I love her.

LEGUERCHE. You are not—in need of money?

MARRIEN. From Mr Coste—nothing.

LEGUERCHE. You are not going—to give me—any money??

MARRIEN. Not a penny.

LEGUERCHE (mops his brow. Muttering to himself). This is a trick. Attack from the rear. Leguerche—they're trying to fool you again.

You're a bit slow in the uptake. The others are smarter. They're always ready quicker when they want to snatch something away from you that you could already have got your hands on. *(To* MARRIEN*)* Why won't you pay me anything?

MARRIEN. Do I owe you anything?

LEGUERCHE *(anxiously)*. I had to swear to Juliette that I wouldn't go back to her with empty pockets—because now we can get married— open the shop—a butcher's shop—tiles—refrigerator—meat—meat *(looking angrily at* MARRIEN.*)* Are you going to smash up my fittings before they are even installed?

MARRIEN. I have never promised you money.

LEGUERCHE. I had it, lieutenant. It was as good as mine—from Mr Coste. It was your fault I lost the money. You tore up my cheque. Now, lieutenant, make good the loss!

MARRIEN. Your claims on Mr Coste were also unfounded.

LEGUERCHE. Are you the father—*(laughing)*—of your fiancée's child?

MARRIEN *(calmly)*. I have already declared that I am.

LEGUERCHE *(sarcastic)*. So I'm not? Since when haven't I been the father? Since a lieutenant came strutting about here with his braid and his trappings. Are the sun, the moon, and the stars bursting? Nothing up there is bursting. Everything remains as it was arranged at the beginning of creation: a father is a father—and his child is his child. Who apart from the Virgin Mary does your worship think he's going to convince about the immaculate conception? *(*MARRIEN *is silent.* LEGUERCHE *steps up to him.)* Don't you like having me as a rival? A lawyer might be more acceptable—or someone or other with rank or a title. He wouldn't accept money. He would be content with the honour of having been the first. But this, damn it, this happens to be a butcher's man. A fellow of common clay. He wants money. He couldn't care less about the night with the lady. But he latches on to the consequences: a child! That's the joker I'm slipping into the pack. That'll bring me in winnings by the pocketful—will you hand them over to me, lieutenant?

MARRIEN *(has stood up—retreats behind the chair)*. Don't come near me!

LEGUERCHE. Are your fingers itching to get at my throat? Strangle me. Then I'll be silent. Then I shan't be bellowing out here—and raising the cry outside—that I am the father *(laughing again)* of your child!

MARRIEN. Go away.

LEGUERCHE. You are refraining from murdering me? Then my bill has to be paid: money—money—and more money. Don't give me your answer now—I'll give you time to think it over. Important business mustn't be settled in a hurry. You see, the amount has gone up. On your own admission you are very rich—on my admission I'm very hard up. On your own admission my existence irks you—on my admission I'm prepared to put it up for sale. For the price of a butcher's shop in a house that belongs to me. It has to be a complete house. Mine from cellar to attic. Free of all liabilities. Do you hear my offer? *(MARRIEN is silent.)* You'll have to dig deep into your pocket. There's no getting away from that. One doesn't tear up cheques. It was a piece of folly that's taking its revenge. You could have had everything cheaper—I kept my demands within reasonable limits—

MARRIEN. Get out!

LEGUERCHE. You have only yourself to blame for the increased price. But, lieutenant, don't misunderstand me: what wouldn't one be glad to pay for one's child?

MARRIEN. Get out!

LEGUERCHE. Only to return. Twenty times round the house–then I'll look back again.

MARRIEN. I'll set the dogs on you!

LEGUERCHE. They won't bite the butcher's man.

MARRIEN. The door won't be opened to you!

LEGUERCHE. I'll find a way in!

He leaves, left. MARRIEN *stares after him.* COSTE *enters quickly from upstage right.*

COSTE. You have sent him away—in a rage? *(MARRIEN turns to him.)* At the end you raised your voice—it resounded through the door. You are white as chalk, lieutenant. How did your talk with Leguerche go?

MARRIEN. He gave me—time to think it over.

COSTE. What are you to think over?

MARRIEN. Whether I choose the dogs or the whip for him.

COSTE. Have you been threatening him like that?

MARRIEN. Should I have struck him down without a word?

COSTE. You upset my plans, Lieutenant Marrien, when you declined to return to Paris. Why are you staying? *(MARRIEN looks at him.)* Are you leaving me without an answer?

MARRIEN. I did not leave—to prevent an attempt on Catherine's life being made behind my back.

COSTE. By whose hand?

MARRIEN *(seizes his hand).* By this one, Mr Coste, which up to now has showered nothing but kindness upon Catherine!

COSTE. Is it now clenched in a threatening fist?

MARRIEN. Why do you want to send me to Paris?

COSTE. I have no hesitation in replying: I propose to find Leguerche and satisfy his demands. *(MARRIEN is silent.)* Money plays a decisive part. As far as he is concerned. As far as we are concerned, Lieutenant Marrien. The power of money is raised to the miraculous— in our case, Lieutenant Marrien. A person disappears—swallowed up by the earth—the moment he feels money between his fingers. Leguerche never existed—you live in a freed world!

MARRIEN *(slowly)*. Whoever pays Leguerche—acknowledges Leguerche.

COSTE *(hesitantly)*. And whoever does not pay—has never known Leguerche?

MARRIEN. Are you prepared—with money for Leguerche—to dishonour Catherine?

COSTE *(astonished)*. Lieutenant Marrien—what are you thinking of? Do you have such confidence in the power of thought that can obliterate a human being? Does someone disappear—like a breath blown away—because someone else forgets him? In your head he is dead—probably or definitely—but outside his flesh and bones are as active as ever they were. Leguerche will exist—blustering by your side. He remains bound to you—with strong bonds, unless you sever them with a sharp stroke. It can be done: give the butcher his money!

MARRIEN *(as though awakening)*. Will he demand it from me again?

COSTE. He gave you time to think it over. How long?

MARRIEN. Not long. Minutes.

COSTE. Then it's the whip or the dogs for him?

MARRIEN. Are whip and dogs sufficient?

COSTE. To enflame—never to subdue—the uproar surrounding you and Catherine. What becomes of secrecy, if you set upon your neighbour?

MARRIEN. Is secrecy enough—to make what is done undone?

COSTE *(goes to him)*. There is one salvation in the confusion through which you must find your way: to forget yourself. To live the day that is, as if it were your first. Create a beginning—put memory aside. Are you not resolved on taking decisive action? What does the regiment matter to you now? Your home in Paris? You are prepared to make a completely new start—as through glass I can see into your inmost being. Your love for Catherine has shaken you to your foundations. I'm not attaching praise or blame to your conduct. It stands transcendent above any judgment of mine. Take thought for the realm you will settle in with Catherine. Few gain admittance to such heights in solitude—bar the way to intruders. As for this Leguerche, we will push him into the depths with money—which I will give him!

He leaves down right. MARRIEN *stands undecided. Then he runs towards the left—leaves the room—returns: bringing cap, greatcoat and sabre; he lays everything down on a chair—runs to the door down right, pulls it open:* Mrs Jattefaux! *She enters.*

MARRIEN. Where is Catherine?

MRS JATTEFAUX. She has gone to lie down to fight off a fit of faintness.

MARRIEN. Is she not able to get up again?

MRS JATTEFAUX. She is not greatly weakened.

MARRIEN. Does she hear when you speak to her?

MRS JATTEFAUX. Up to now I have received no answer from her.

MARRIEN. She must hear—that I, Lieutenant Jean-Marc Marrien—beg her to get up and come with me!

MRS JATTEFAUX. I will give her the message. *(She leaves.)*

MARRIEN *(stays near the door.* CATHERINE *enters. He throws open his arms to her).* Catherine!

CATHERINE *(in his arms).* Jean-Marc!

MARRIEN. How did it begin?

CATHERINE. Don't you know?

MARRIEN. I forget everything, so as to hear it for the first time from you. Where did we first meet?

CATHERINE. At midday outside the jeweller's shop.

MARRIEN. That was when the rings took all our attention. And then?

CATHERINE. I knelt beside you in church.

MARRIEN. For the wedding. What then?

CATHERINE. You took me to the opera.

MARRIEN. To celebrate. And now?

CATHERINE. You came to me in the night.

MARRIEN. I did indeed come to you then. I made my way through the garden—the gravel crunched—I swung myself up by the creepers on the trellis-work—pushed back the window—stood in the passage. Did I find the door?

CATHERINE. I was already opening it.

MARRIEN. I slipped into the room. You showed up white. Then I held you close against me. Was it with these hands I did so?

CATHERINE. These hands made love to me.

MARRIEN. What did I say?

CATHERINE. What did you say?

MARRIEN. Did I at least ask your name?

CATHERINE. I kept it from you during the day—in the night I betrayed myself.

MARRIEN. How does it sound?

CATHERINE *(in a whisper).* Catherine.

MARRIEN. That was how you breathed it close to my ear beside me.

CATHERINE. Then you too betrayed your secret.

MARRIEN. With my name?

CATHERINE. How does it sound?

MARRIEN. Jean-Marc.

CATHERINE. We said our own names a hundred times over, so that each should be known to the other.

MARRIEN. You—

CATHERINE. Catherine—

MARRIEN. Catherine!

CATHERINE. You—

MARRIEN. Jean-Marc! Only so do we know each other—from the first day on—when you were smitten with love—to make me the gift of a life I had never lived before! *(Changed.)* We are leaving. Are you ready?

CATHERINE. I'll shut the case.

MARRIEN. Without a case. It will hold us back. We shall lose time. I can't wait here until cases are carried out of the house. I am running away, Catherine—with you!

CATHERINE. We must run away, I know that.

MARRIEN. Where the journey leads us—shall be left to Heaven to decide over what isle it spreads its blue. Are there islands in the oceans where there are no people? Do you know of one, Catherine?

CATHERINE. We will travel across seas.

MARRIEN. Fearlessly past cliffs resembling distorted human faces. I shall spit into the most monstrous and hit—

He breaks off. LEGUERCHE *has appeared behind the french window.* MARRIEN *stares at him.* CATHERINE *follows his glance.* LEGUERCHE *opens the french window—enters—closes it behind him.* MARRIEN *places himself protectively in front of* CATHERINE.

LEGUERCHE. Twenty times round, all counted up—nothing taken off and at a steady pace. *(Advancing a couple of paces.)* At this speed. One—two. Neither a drop of sweat or an increase in heart-beat. No cheating on my part. I've kept to the agreed time. Here I am. *(Silence.)* Well?

MARRIEN. How—did you get in here?

LEGUERCHE. Over the wall—through the garden. I should know all the ways to sneak in, shouldn't I? I've used them often enough.

MARRIEN. Who—are you looking for?

LEGUERCHE. Perhaps Juliette—perhaps Catherine. Whoever's on offer. How will it turn out this time?

He steps to one side, so as to get a sight of CATHERINE. *She keeps her gaze directed towards him as though spell-bound.* MARRIEN *looks at* CATHERINE.

LEGUERCHE *(observing* CATHERINE, *nods).* So we meet again. Under different circumstances. In full daylight, that is. It was in pitch darkness then—your hand remained black before your eyes—now sunshine is blazing.

MARRIEN *(to* CATHERINE*).* Don't look at the—

LEGUERCHE *(to* MARRIEN*).* Are you ready to pay? Don't interrupt me. *(To* CATHERINE *again)* I have to refresh my memory. It would be contemptible of me not to remember—to spit as acknowledgement of favours received. I'm not a blackguard.

MARRIEN *(to* CATHERINE, *who is standing motionless).* Gather your strength—go away—

LEGUERCHE *(to* MARRIEN*).* You are not going to pay! Now I understand your protest. What sum would be appropriate? A Croesus would reckon himself poor if he were to set the price. *(Going up to* CATHERINE*)* That's style of inestimable value. *(To* MARRIEN*)* Take it from me—I have my experience. *(Taking hold of* CATHERINE*)* Clasped in these arms you lie on these breasts as if you're in the clouds. This body is a shaft from which you would wish never to emerge—and you are held a willing prisoner by these thighs as by clamps of steel. Didn't I tear myself away from you by force, Catherine, when dawn was breaking?

MARRIEN. Leave me alone with him.

LEGUERCHE. To pay me? I want no money! I'll not let you buy from me—not here *(with a sweeping gesture),* nor anywhere—what I experienced with her. There will be no deal, I refuse payment in cash. Enough of the haggling, lieutenant. Objections are a waste of time. You've frittered your time away, now it's too late: now I know Catherine for what she is! That fills my head—and leaves no room—for Juliette. Who is Juliette? A nobody. Over and done with! Where does that leave me? With you two! With you, Catherine—so as to forget nothing I'll follow the two of you. That will be my life: always on your track. I won't lose the trail. Where you are, I'll make the third. If you're sitting at table, I'll join you. If you're lying in bed, I'll be peering through the window. You travel to America—I'll be on board as a stoker. Hide yourselves in the jungle—I'll be perching in palm trees! And if anyone asks me what ties me to you, I'll spill out the whole story in his startled face: the child they're feeding is mine—she conceived it by me in an incomparable night—I, a butcher's man— name of Leguerche! The pursuit is starting now. I'll be standing at the gate—and if you leave the house, I'll hang on your heels like a burr!

He pushes open the french window—goes on to the terrace and disappears in the background. MARRIEN *stares after him.*

CATHERINE *(with a sigh).* He shan't—

MARRIEN *(crying out).* What, Catherine?!

CATHERINE. —kill the child!

MARRIEN *looks about him in the utmost confusion. With a bound he reaches the chair: he jerks the sword from its sheath and rushes after* LEGUERCHE. *A loud cry is heard in the background.* COSTE *enters down right.*

COSTE *(to* CATHERINE*).* Who was shouting? *(She is silent. He notices the open french window.)* Where is Lieutenant Marrien?

On the terrace MARRIEN *returns.*

COSTE *waits for him.*

MARRIEN *enters.*

COSTE. What—have you done?

MARRIEN. It was he I—

COSTE. What have you gained by doing that?

MARRIEN *(slowly)*. If there are actions that in their fearfulness cut us off from the world—then this is one of them.

COSTE *goes hurriedly past* MARRIEN *and out across the terrace.*

MARRIEN *(beside* CATHERINE*)*. We can live. *(They kiss.)*

THE RAFT OF THE MEDUSA

Translated by
H. F. Garten and Elizabeth Sprigge

Characters

ALLAN
ANN
FIVE BOYS
FIVE GIRLS
FOXY (dumb)
THE PILOT'S VOICE

A lifeboat in the Atlantic. 1940.

In September 1940, the liner taking children from bombed cities of England and Canada was torpedoed on the open sea. Only a few children escaped death in life-boats. What happened in one of these boats during its seven days' drifting forms the contents of the following scenes. Of the thirteen occupants eleven were eventually rescued: for the two others the plane came too late.

PROLOGUE

As it is night, only the noise and the light reveal the work of destruction. Out of the initial darkness and the almost soundless surge of the waters comes the first blinding flash of the explosion—and the crash of the bursting plates of the iron ship. The roar of the growing fire drowns the human voices, and the human figures are too small to be seen in the immensity of flame and smoke.

Only noise and light.

Lightning-pointed flames shoot up, followed by the thunder of exploding boilers.

Tongues of flame spring up from the quickly burning timber and end in a dance of sparks far above. As yet only isolated patches of fire suddenly flare up.

The whole ship has not yet been gripped by the fire.

The furious outburst even subsides again. It grows quieter and darker. During this lull comes a clatter of chains as the life-boats are lowered. This clatter cuts through the crackling of the stealthy burning.

With a resounding thud a boat hits the water.

A few more boats are lowered.

Then the heat ignites the oil. A hail of glowing iron fragments scatters upwards into the night and the void; the oil has burst the tanks and pipes. Now the gliding, liquid blaze seeps across the whole surface of the deck, leaving no gap in the fiery outline of the ship. The flaming picture of the victim is complete—now it may sink. The iron hull breaks in half and the water rushes in, dragging it down. Bow and stern rise steeply up—like whales struck by a harpoon—and dive down under a hood of smoke, deeper-deeper, until the last glimmer is extinguished, and everything that was borne on it has been obliterated by the water.

NIGHT

Deep is the darkness above the sea, murmuring dully with its
   aimless swell.
At times waves break as if hands were clapped in lament.
   Thus the sea mourns.

175

Then the wind begins its lament. First a sighing breath—rising, fading.
  Returning
with a louder moaning—meeting windy groaning
  from elsewhere. Joining with it—
    and the breeze becomes speech:

MEDUSA

MEDUSA

MEDUSA

MEDUSA

The sounds fade, and only the breath of a sigh
  lingers for a while—and dies away

THE FIRST DAY

*Out of the haze of the dawn the life-boat grows clear. Its appearance is
blotted out again by heavier mist. Once again it emerges and, clouded by
vapours, vanishes. At last the mists drift away and nothing hides the boat
any longer.*
*On its thwarts are huddled together, in crouching positions of sleep,
twelve children: six boys and six girls. Ten years, eleven years, twelve
years old. In their drab, colourless mackintoshes they all look alike. All
their heads are bare.*
One boy wears a white woollen scarf—this is ALLAN.
One girl clasps an object to her breast—this is ANN.
On the leaden sea the boat lies motionless.
It grows lighter.

ANN *is the first to wake, blinking. She peeps out cautiously between her
eyelids, only taking in what meets her eyes: the centre of the boat—no
more. Then she cannot help opening her eyes wider: the water beyond the
gunwale is reality—irrevocable reality. Now her eyes roam to the left and
survey her companions in that half of the boat. There her survey ends.
Now she feels the pressure of the object on her breast. She loosens her
grasp; it is a thermos-flask she has been guarding in this way. Soon she
unscrews the top which is also a cup—and fills the cup from the flask.
Then she drinks.*

ALLAN *wakes. He, too, becomes conscious by degrees of the boat and
his huddled companions—until his eyes focus on* ANN.

ANN *(raising the cup).* Want some? *(*ALLAN *looks at her and smiles.)*
  You don't?
ALLAN. I do. *(*ANN *pours out.)* What is it?
ANN. Milk.

ALLAN *(repeating)*. Milk.

ANN. Or don't big boys drink milk?

ALLAN. How big am I then?

ANN *(considering)*. Twelve. *(ALLAN nods.)* I'm twelve too.

ALLAN. But that's not the same thing.

ANN. What's not the same thing?

ALLAN. When girls are twelve they're older than boys of twelve.

ANN. Is that nicer or worse for boys?

ALLAN. It means they can't marry.

ANN *(amused)*. Us?

ALLAN. I mean people of the same age don't marry.

ANN *(laughing)*. But I cheated—I'm only eleven.

ALLAN. That's a very different matter.

ANN. Can you marry me now?

ALLAN. You must think it over.

ANN. Musn't you?

ALLAN. I needn't think anything over.

ANN *(holding out her arm with the cup)*. Here! *(ALLAN stretches out his arm for the cup.)*

ALLAN *(surprised)*. Warm milk.

ANN. Drink!

ALLAN *(putting it to his lips)*. Why, it's really hot!

ANN. From the thermos-flask.

ALLAN. Did you save that?

ANN. Didn't you save anything?

ALLAN *(having finished drinking)*. I saved my scarf. *(Undoing it.)* If you'd like to have it.

ANN. No.

ALLAN. You gave me a drink from your thermos-flask.

ANN. It was only a drop.

ALLAN. Now I'm warm.

ANN. I'm not cold.

ALLAN. But when you get cold, promise to put my scarf round you.

ANN. I promise.

ALLAN *(after a pause)*. And what's your name?

ANN. Ann.

ALLAN *(repeating)*. Ann.

ANN. What's yours?

ALLAN. Allan.

ANN. Really?

ALLAN. You mean they go well—Allan and Ann.

ANN. You say it as though we were . . .

ALLAN. Alone in the world—Allan and Ann.

Now there is a short silence during which they both look out at the sea, away from each other. Then the rigid figures of the other inmates of the boat come to life.

SECOND BOY *(rubbing his eyes, rising).* Where's the liner?

THIRD BOY. What liner?

SECOND BOY. Our ship.

FOURTH BOY. Why, it was torpedoed.

FIFTH BOY. It can't float any more when it's been torpedoed.

SIXTH BOY. It went up in flames directly after it was torpedoed.

FIFTH BOY. The oil caught fire.

FOURTH BOY. If it hadn't been for the wind which blew away the smoke.

THIRD BOY. We'd have been choked by the smoke.

SECOND BOY. So we haven't got our ship any more. *(He sits down again and buries his face in his hands. There is a silence.)*

ALLAN *(handing the cup to ANN).* The milk will get cold if you don't screw it up again.

ANN *(taking the cup and looking round the boat).* Anyone thirsty?

SECOND GIRL *(raising her hand).* I am.

ANN. Any others?

THIRD GIRL. There won't be enough for us.

ANN. If we share it.

ALLAN. I've had some already.

ANN. So have I. How many of you are there?

FOURTH GIRL *(counting).* Five boys.

SECOND GIRL *(doing the same).* And five girls.

ANN. That makes ten. For ten, ten half cups. Keep still in the boat, or I'll upset it. *(She pours out.)* Who's number one?

SECOND GIRL. I'm one. *(She takes the cup, drinks and returns it.)*

ANN *(pouring out).* Who's two?

THIRD GIRL. I'm two. *(She drinks and returns it.)*

ANN *(pouring out).* Who's three?

FOURTH GIRL. I'm three. *(She drinks and returns it.)*

ANN *(pouring out).* Who's four?

FIFTH GIRL. I'm four. *(She drinks and returns it.)*

ANN *(pouring out).* Who's five?

SIXTH GIRL. I'm five. *(She drinks and returns it.)*

ANN *(pouring out).* Who's six?

SECOND BOY. I'm six. *(He drinks and returns it.)*

ANN *(pouring out).* Who's seven?

THIRD BOY. I'm seven. *(He drinks and returns it.)*

ANN *(pouring out).* Who's eight?

FOURTH BOY. I'm eight. *(He drinks and returns it.)*

ANN *(pouring out).* Who's nine?

FIFTH BOY. I'm nine. *(He drinks and returns it.)*

ANN *(pouring out).* Who's ten?

SIXTH BOY. I'm ten. *(He drinks and returns it.)*

ANN *(shaking the thermos-flask).* Now twelve have drunk from one flask and it's not empty yet. The rest is for whoever gets weak first.

SECOND GIRL *(anxiously).* Why should we get weak?

SECOND BOY. If it's a long time.

THIRD GIRL. If what's a long time?

THIRD BOY. Before we get to shore.

FOURTH GIRL. Are we very far from the shore?

FOURTH BOY. There's nothing but sea, is there?

FIFTH GIRL. The middle of the sea?

FIFTH BOY. As we sailed three days ago, there's no land anywhere.

SIXTH GIRL. But why did we sail?

SIXTH BOY. Children are not supposed to stay in bombed cities.

SECOND GIRL *(after a silence).* We are just children. The whole ship full of children. We play and we sing, and we don't hurt anybody. And if we did, they could punish us. They oughtn't to drop bombs on us. Are we so wicked? Are we grown-up already? We only want to escape from the terrors of the grown-ups. Grown-ups are so terrible. We're children who never do such wicked things. They might put an end to cruelty if they could see us. If they could just see how one of us shares out her drop of milk, although she needs it so much herself, and lets everyone have a drink. *(Bursting out.)* It ought to be printed in all the newspapers in the world how children behave to each other if they're allowed to **be** children. Why do the grown-ups do such cruel wicked things?

The SECOND GIRL *weeps, her head on her arms. Sobs shake her shoulders. Silence.*

ALLAN *(loudly).* Let's search the boat. In every life-boat there are emergency rations that are supposed to last the grown-up crew for ages. We are still children and need less to eat. I can eat just a little and feel quite full, as if I'd eaten a lot. Whoever wants half my share can have it.

SECOND BOY. I wouldn't take it. Honest I wouldn't.

THIRD GIRL. Anyone who took that from someone else, wouldn't be behaving right.

THIRD BOY. No, he'd be behaving rottenly.

FOURTH GIRL. He couldn't expect any of the girls in the boat to take any notice of him.

FOURTH BOY. The girls should have more to eat than us boys.

THE GIRLS *(jumping from their seats).* No—less!

THE BOYS *(doing the same).* No—more!

ALLAN. The boat's rocking—don't upset it! *(At once they are quiet and everyone sits down.)* Now we'll get out the oars. The provisions are stored underneath. Give a hand all of you!

With a common effort the children pull the long oars-four of them-from under the thwarts and lay them along the gunwales. They rest, panting.

ALLAN *(bringing out a pole)*. The boat hook. When you want to land, you hold the boat in with that. It's essential then. Take care of it. *(He passes it to the other children; bending down in the bows)* I can see something here. *(He pulls out a sail. Calls.)* Bags—tins! Biscuits— sugar—ham! And lots of water in tins! Nothing's been forgotten. There's food enough if we're careful. We won't begin till noon and we'll hold out without another meal for as long as we can. *(He puts back the sail. Turns and surveys the boat.)* And what's in the stern?
SECOND BOY *(in the stern)*. Here?
ALLAN. What's that covered up?

The SECOND BOY, *helped by the other children, pulls away a crumpled sail.*

SECOND BOY. There's someone else! *(All the children turn their heads in that direction.)*
THIRD GIRL. Is he dead?
FOURTH GIRL. He's got his eyes open.
THIRD BOY. He's alive.
FOURTH BOY. Why don't you get up?
THIRD GIRL. Can't you get up?
SECOND BOY. Have you hurt yourself?
FOURTH GIRL. If he had, he'd cry.
SECOND BOY. We'll put him on the seat and ask him how he got into the boat.

It is a boy of nine with red hair and a freckled face in a rust-red sweater whom they lift on to the thwart. A torch on a string hangs round his neck.

FIFTH GIRL *(exclaiming at the sight of him)*. Red as a little fox. *(The* CHILDREN *laugh.)*
SECOND BOY. Well then—you are Foxy. We've dug you out of your hole. You might have been suffocated. Why didn't you crawl out yourself? *(FOXY stares silently at the children.)* Can't you talk? *(FOXY stares silently.)* Are you still frightened because we were torpedoed and everything burnt? *(FOXY stares silently.)* That's all over now—the bangs—the explosion—the fire. Or do you still see sparks in front of your eyes? *(FOXY stares silently.)* I suppose you ran off straight away and climbed into this boat? Without a coat— with your torch. Does the torch work? *(He switches it on.)* It does— and yet you're miserable. There's no reason to be. I'd be jolly glad to have a torch with a good battery. *(He switches it off. To the other children)* Now, who doesn't envy Foxy such a torch?
THIRD GIRL *(after a pause)*. We ought to give him a drink.
FOURTH GIRL. There was still some warm milk left.
THIRD GIRL *(to* ANN*)*. Give me the thermos-flask.
ANN. Can you open it?

THIRD GIRL. Don't you want to?

ANN. You can do it.

The THIRD GIRL *takes the flask, unscrews the cup and fills it.*

THIRD GIRL. Now then drink, Foxy. *(*FOXY *clutches the cup and empties it.)* Now we've all drunk the same milk—now the flask is empty! *(To* ANN*)* Here's your empty flask back.

ALLAN *(clapping his hands).* We'll row!

SECOND BOY. Where to?

ALLAN. The nearest shore.

THIRD BOY. But we're in the middle of the sea.

ALLAN. How do you know? The ships go on a zig-zag course to make it less dangerous. Maybe we aren't far from land. Perhaps we shall even reach it today. Get the oars into the rowlocks.

SECOND BOY. The oars are too heavy for children.

ALLAN. If three of us row with one oar, it will work.

SECOND GIRL. We'll have a competition with the boys and see who holds out longest.

Now the GIRLS *sit on one thwart and the* BOYS *on the other. With difficulty the long oars are put in position.*

ALLAN. We must keep time by counting: one-two. At one, dip in—at two, lift out. All of you count: one—

ALL *(joining in).* One-two-one-two-one-two-

The strokes of the oars set the boat in motion. On the after-thwart FOXY *sits rigidly. Now the boat disappears and the* One-Two *of the* CHILDREN'S *voices dies away.*

THE SECOND DAY

The swathes of mist drift away. The boat with its cargo of sleeping children comes in sight. The oars are shipped and lie along the gunwales. A whining and barking-like the yelping of a puppy-is heard in the boat. This wakes the CHILDREN *and they straighten up from their crouching positions.*

SECOND GIRL. Has a puppy got into our boat?

THIRD GIRL. In the night?

FOURTH GIRL. From the ship?

FIFTH GIRL. There, it's barking again.

They all listen.

FOURTH BOY. A dog couldn't swim for a day and a night.

FIFTH BOY. And then climb over the edge of the boat?

SIXTH BOY. Perhaps it's a sea-dog.

SECOND BOY *(lifting the sail in the stern).* It's Foxy. He's crept back under the sail. Foxy—wake up! No dogs are chasing you. Nobody's biting you. *(He shakes him.)* There! Now you're awake. Here, sit up! It's morning.

FIFTH GIRL. He never gets up by himself.

SECOND BOY. We'll lift you on to the seat. *(With the aid of the* FIFTH BOY, FOXY *is lifted on to the after-thwart.)* That must have been a horrible dream. Who was after you? Hounds with mouths like this, gnashing their teeth to tear you to pieces? Where are they now? They've gone. It's us you see now. Are we savage hounds who'd chase you and bite you? You're not afraid of people's faces, are you? Of the faces of children who aren't real people yet? Are you afraid of us?

THIRD GIRL. Let him wake up properly first.

FOURTH BOY. Leave him in peace till then.

They turn away from him.

ALLAN *(in the bows).* We'll start the day with a bag of biscuits. *(He gets it out.)* This is a damned knot. I can't undo it. Who's got quicker fingers?

ANN *(seizing it).* Me.

ALLAN *(watching).* How clever you are! I've never seen such fingers. Like a fairy's.

ANN. I am a fairy too.

ALLAN. How do you mean a fairy?

ANN. Because I . . . *(opening the bag)* because I've undone the knot.

ALLAN *(still looking at her).* No—you are one even without your nimble fingers. I wouldn't be surprised if you—could fly.

ANN. Then I'd fly off and come back with the big plane that will save us all.

ALLAN. I know you would.

ANN. I'll do it too if we're to have biscuits now.

ALLAN *(taking his).* If we each have two, the bag ought to go round.

He passes the bag on. In this way the bag goes from one child to another and each takes two biscuits. The FIFTH GIRL *holds the bag out to* FOXY.

SECOND BOY. You must give it to him. He won't take anything himself.

FIFTH GIRL. Here, Foxy—one in each paw. Now eat. Eat with us. So we all eat. Now we all eat together.

FOXY *follows the example of the others who are entirely absorbed in eating their biscuits.*

ANN *(stopping suddenly).* Thirteen! *(The attention of some of the* CHILDREN *is drawn towards her.)* We are thirteen! *(Other* CHILDREN, *however, are not disturbed.)* Didn't you hear? You mustn't go on eating. We are thirteen!

SIXTH BOY. There's room for thirteen.

ANN. There's room for more. For fourteen—fifteen—sixteen. But there mustn't be thirteen.

FOURTH BOY. Who says so?

THIRD GIRL (laughing). Who says so!

FOURTH BOY. Well, yes—I'm a town boy. I don't know anything about seafaring.

SECOND GIRL. This hasn't anything to do with seafaring.

FOURTH BOY. With what, then?

ANN. With Christianity.

THIRD GIRL. Aren't you a Christian?

FOURTH BOY. Of course I am.

ANN. Who isn't a Christian in the boat?

SECOND BOY. Why, we're all Christians.

ANN. There you are! We are thirteen Christians—and now we're lost! (Silence.)

THIRD BOY. It doesn't follow . . .

THIRD GIRL. What doesn't follow?

THIRD BOY. That thirteen always . . .

SECOND GIRL. Thirteen Christians—not thirteen heathens.

FOURTH GIRL. It doesn't apply to heathens.

THIRD GIRL. Heathens aren't like us. They're just heathens.

THIRD BOY. I'm only talking about Christians. I don't know any heathens.

FOURTH GIRL. And what do you know about Christians?

THIRD BOY. Well, thirteen Christians may ride on a bus—and does the bus overturn?

ANN. They just ride—there's no need for the bus to overturn.

THIRD BOY. So what?

ANN. They don't eat. There's no table on a bus to eat at. But in the boat we eat. That's the difference.

THIRD BOY. There isn't a table here either.

ANN. And drinking from the same flask—eating from the same bag— isn't that even worse? Not even Jesus did that—and yet He was crucified.

THIRD GIRL (after a pause). Yes—it comes from Jesus.

ANN. It comes from the Last Supper—and that's the highest thing you can think of. Or don't you think it applies to us, because we are better than Jesus and His disciples?

THIRD BOY (shyly). I never said I thought I was better.

SECOND GIRL. It sounded like it.

THIRD BOY. I pretend sometimes.

FOURTH GIRL. You won't get away with that before Our Lord in Heaven.

THIRD BOY. But I do believe what you believe.

SECOND GIRL. Now you're just being a coward.

THIRD BOY. Me—a coward? *(Facing the other boys)* If anyone says anything against Jesus and laughs at His Supper, I'll . . . *(He shakes his fist.)*

ANN. I suppose you're converted now. You don't seem to learn much at your school. But Jesus leads everybody into temptation, so that they will believe in Him. That's why we're in this boat. The liner would never have been torpedoed if you'd had more respect for Jesus and His twelve disciples, who make thirteen altogether. So we owe it to you that we're here on the sea and will sink when the storm comes. The storm comes when there are thirteen. *(There is silence in the boat.)*

ALLAN *(confidently)*. There won't be any storm.

ANN *(pointing at him)*. There's a heathen!

ALLAN. My baptism was just as Christian as anybody else's in the country.

FOURTH GIRL. Then you've got to believe.

ALLAN. But not in the storm.

ANN. The storm is just the result of true faith.

ALLAN. Is it true faith?

THIRD GIRL. What else could it be?

ALLAN. Superstition.

THIRD GIRL. Let me tell you what my parents did once. I mean—grown-up people. You ought to see my father. He isn't afraid of anybody, and my mother is as brave as my father. But once we had a party and I was already in bed. Then suddenly my mother rushed into my room and shook me, crying: 'You must get up at once—one of the guests hasn't come, and now we are thirteen.' No one would have sat down at the table—all the lovely food would have been wasted, if I hadn't been there. The guests were white as ghosts, and their knives and forks shook—just because they would have been thirteen if my parents hadn't counted carefully. That's why the guests kept thanking them all the evening—and the next day one aunt even came and gave my mother a present for being so observant. They take it as seriously as that not to have thirteen eating at one table.

SECOND GIRL *(sighing)*. Yes—it's frightfully serious.

FOURTH BOY *(after a pause)*. I know a case too.

GIRLS. What case?

FOURTH BOY. I overheard it. I have grown-up parents too who are never afraid. I was ill and couldn't get up, or they would have fetched me in the same way. My room was next to the hall and I heard the visitors arriving. All the time the door was opening and shutting; soon they would all be there. But next time the bell went, I heard my parents come out into the hall and open the door themselves. My father and mother were talking in turns: 'My dear doctor, you must go away again. Goodness knows how this can have happened! We must have counted wrong—we are thirteen.' Then I heard the doctor say in a terrified voice: 'Don't tell the others about your mistake. It might have consequences.' 'Heaven forbid!' my mother whispered. 'We won't have seen you for days.' Half the night after that I could hear them enjoying themselves. They weren't even allowed to say that the thirteenth had nearly turned up—and I kept my mouth shut.

THIRD BOY *(leaning his head on his hands)*. That could have had a horrible ending.

ALLAN. Well, you can't tell how it would have ended.

SECOND GIRL. Of course nobody can tell, because they were careful.

ALLAN. Would it have had to end so horribly? We haven't any proof, that's what I say.

ANN. No proof? All right then, I'll give you the proof. My uncle has a big estate—as big as a country with no end. I went to stay with my uncle in the holidays, and I was allowed to ride and swim and do whatever I liked. Now, my uncle was a great hunter. He has even hunted dangerous animals in another continent. I think he has killed snakes too. That's a most daring thing to do. Yet he never boasted about what he had done. But he did sometimes talk about his gardener who had eleven children. And that was not too many for my uncle. He said: 'If there only were twelve, they wouldn't always be sitting thirteen at table. As long as they are thirteen, there'll be no end to their misery.' Then, one child died, and my uncle was really glad for the sake of his gardener's family: now at last the spell was broken—the dead one had saved the living. From then onwards there was peace and happiness in the gardener's cottage. But only after the thirteenth had died.

SIXTH GIRL *(after a pause)*. Your uncle hunted lions and snakes?

ANN. That's why it's a proof, because a man like that knows what's dangerous and what isn't. The snakes and lions are less so than thirteen people eating the same food and drinking the same drinks.

Now the CHILDREN *sit dejectedly and hesitate to bite the biscuits in their hands.* FOXY *does not eat either, as the others are not eating.*

ALLAN *(jumping up)*. Let's go on rowing. Somewhere there is land— there is an island, only a few strokes will get us there. Then we'll lie under the palm-trees and let ourselves be fed by the natives. We'll each have a hut and eat and drink to our hearts' content. Come on—let's row! *(He climbs over the thwarts in order to sit opposite* FOXY.*)* Foxy—you count. Can you count like this: one–two?

ANN. Foxy can't do anything. We've got to do everything ourselves.

Again the long oars are pushed into the rowlocks. The CHILDREN, *this time boys and girls mixed, ply the oars and, counting in time, drive the boat forwards. Fading:* 'One–two–one–two–one–two–one–two–'

THE THIRD DAY

The early mist melts away. In the boat crouching CHILDREN *are asleep. Only the* SECOND GIRL *is sitting up, awake. She pulls her handkerchief from her coat pocket, fumbling clumsily with her left hand in her right pocket, while she carefully holds out her right hand. Having pulled out the handkerchief she moves to the side of the boat and leans far over to dip it in the water. She slowly pulls it out again and sits up. She wraps her right hand in the wet cloth, working clumsily with her left hand. Next moment a shrill scream pierces the silence. The scream changes into a wild howl—the girl writhes with pain.*
The CHILDREN *start from their sleep and turn their heads towards the crying girl.*

SECOND GIRL *(shaking her right hand)*. Pull it off! Pull it off! I'm burning.

THIRD BOY. How do you mean, burning?

SECOND GIRL. Oh, you want to leave me to burn! You are beasts!

FOURTH BOY. Do you want to get the handkerchief off?

SECOND GIRL. Before my hand is burnt—take it off!

THIRD GIRL *(taking it off)*. What was it?

SECOND GIRL *(whimpering)*. What was it—what was it—why, it was salt water. I hadn't thought of it, that seawater is salt. And salt on open wounds—it's as though you'd touched fire!

SIXTH BOY. How could you bear it?

SECOND GIRL. I couldn't bear it. I couldn't bear it even before. I couldn't sleep. I've been awake the whole night, and I was afraid I'd fall out of the boat if I leaned over the water in the dark. Then in the morning—when at last it was clear daylight—I pulled my handkerchief out of my right coat pocket with my left hand—like this—as it wasn't as bad as the other one—and dipped it in and wrapped it round the worst hand. Now it's bleeding. There! You can all see the blood running. *(She holds up her right hand.)*

FOURTH BOY. If it bleeds, it's getting better.

SIXTH BOY. The salt will run out.

FIFTH BOY. Let it bleed freely.

THIRD GIRL *(covering her eyes)*. I can't look at blood.

SIXTH GIRL *(doing the same)*. Awful—human blood.

THIRD BOY. It's dripping into your sleeve.

FOURTH BOY. You've made quite a mess of yourself.

SECOND GIRL. Where?

FIFTH BOY. Because you touched your face.

SECOND GIRL. When I was crying. One can't help crying, when it hurts like that.

ALLAN *(after a silence)*. Does it still hurt very much?

SECOND GIRL *(sobbing)*. Tears are salt too—like the sea.

ALLAN *(lifting an empty biscuit bag)*. That's what this bag will do for. I'll make some bandages out of it. Both hands?

SECOND GIRL. The other one isn't bleeding yet, but it could bleed if I knocked it.

ALLAN. Two strips, then. Now I'll soak them—with better water. *(He gets out a tin.)*

CHILDREN. Drinking water!

ALLAN. Can't I use my share the way I want to?

FIFTH BOY. Do you want to die of thirst?

ALLAN. Die of thirst? I don't get thirsty very soon if I don't want to. *(Now he soaks the strips of linen in the tin. To the SECOND GIRL)* Hold out your hands—let me bandage them. Does that feel cool? *(She nods.)* That's what it's for. And if afterwards you hold your bandaged hands in the wind, it'll feel like ice. For moisture grows colder in the wind, remember that.

SECOND GIRL *(smiling)*. I'll remember.

ALLAN. That's how you learn things on a voyage of adventure. *(He returns to his thwart in the bows.)*

SECOND GIRL *(looking round)*. Do I look very untidy?

THIRD GIRL. Wipe the blood off.

SECOND GIRL *(lifting her bandaged hands)*. I haven't any fingers.

THIRD BOY. Never mind that bit of blood.

FOURTH BOY. We don't look too tidy ourselves.

SIXTH BOY. As we don't wash any more.

FIFTH BOY. Only Foxy doesn't get dirty—he's always got his freckles. *(He stoops and helps FOXY on to the thwart aft.)* It's morning again, Foxy. Show us your freckly face. How many are there? Haven't you ever counted the freckles? Shall we guess? The one who guesses right, wins—the torch. Ping—it's still working! It's a glittering prize. I'd give anything in the world for that torch.

THIRD GIRL. You can't possibly count the freckles.

FOURTH BOY. If Foxy keeps quite still.

FIFTH BOY. I'll try.

He kneels in front of FOXY and silently counts, surrounded by the other children. ALLAN and ANN are alone in the bows.

ALLAN *(taking one of ANN'S hands and opening it)*. Are your hands still alright?

ANN. I'm not so thin-skinned.

ALLAN. Are fairies so tough?

ANN. I've rowed a lot in my life.

ALLAN. Where?

ANN. On my uncle's estate which has its own lake.

ALLAN. Among swans?

ANN. Black Australian ones.

ALLAN. Black-Australian ones . . .

ANN. Don't you believe there are black ones?

ALLAN. I'm just imagining—how lovely!—you rowing among the black swans—

ANN. In a white frock of course.

ALLAN. I couldn't see it any other way.

ANN. Riding, too, makes one's hands tough. Don't you believe that?

ALLAN. I believe everything you say.

ANN. It's the reins that do it. Of course you wear gloves, but that only partly protects you. The leather straps press through just the same. That's how one's hands get firm.

ALLAN *(looking at the inside of her hands)*. They're not like any other hands—your hands.

ANN *(withdrawing them)*. I could still row for twenty more days—but the others couldn't.

ALLAN. Which others?

ANN. The other children. They've already got blisters on their hands, which will be bleeding tomorrow. *(Calls out)* Who hasn't got any blisters? *(Now they all turn away from* FOXY.*)*

THIRD BOY. I can't row any longer. *(He holds up his hands.)*

THIRD GIRL. I hardly did yesterday—today I can't take hold of anything any more.

FOURTH GIRL. Until my hands bleed? No—no more rowing.

ALL *(in a babel of voices)*. No more rowing.

ALLAN *(jumping up)*. But then we shan't move from this spot. We can't dawdle about here until the food gives out. We haven't inexhaustible supplies in the life-boat. And there are thirteen mouths to feed.

ANN *(after a silence, calmly)*. One mustn't eat any more.

ALLAN. What—do you mean?

ANN. I say: one of us mustn't eat any more.

ALLAN. How do you make that out?

ANN. Well, that's the atonement for our guilt.

ALLAN. What guilt?

ANN. We were thirteen eating and drinking together. We found that out yesterday—and today it will be worse if we do it again, when we know there are thirteen of us.

ALLAN *(turning to the others)*. Who agrees with this?

ANN. Who agrees that their hands will be bleeding tomorrow and that they will be whimpering just as she is whimpering again now?

ALLAN *(to the* SECOND GIRL*)*. Is it burning?

SECOND GIRL *(writhing)*. Like fire.

ALLAN. Then it must be put out again.

SECOND GIRL *(shaking her head)*. No more water—that's for drinking.

ALL *(grumbling)*. It's drinking water!

ALLAN. I've no right to command you. I can only give mine up.

THIRD BOY. You've done that already—**your** share.

FOURTH BOY. It was your ration for today.

ALLAN. I don't need any.

THIRD GIRL *(after a pause)*. Who is not going to eat any more?

ANN. Who volunteers? Who will save us from our plight and swear a solemn oath not to take another bite or another drink until we are rescued? Even if he had to die—without complaint like our holy Jesus died for the salvation of mankind, which finds eternal life through His death on the cross? *(There is a deep silence.)* I can't do it either. Nor do I blame any of you. We are still in our childhood and we couldn't do anything so tremendous that would be told of afterwards in books. We're only children—and if we have to fulfil the Christian commandment—then let's draw lots.

SECOND BOY *(after a pause)*. He hasn't got to starve, has he?

ANN *(shrugging her shoulders)*. Not if land is sighted in time.

FIFTH GIRL. Shall we be allowed to eat at once—on land?

ANN. On land it will all be over.

FOURTH GIRL. Some get less hungry.

THIRD BOY. We're all weak already.

FOURTH BOY. Not one bite?

ANN. Drawing lots will decide. *(Silence.)*

SECOND BOY. I'll give up my note-book. I know how to draw lots. I'll put a circle on twelve pages and on the thirteenth a cross. Whoever gets a circle can be happy. The one with the cross—

ANN. Is lost.

The SECOND BOY *tears thirteen pages from his note-book and marks them. Then he screws the pages into small rolls.*

SECOND BOY *(to* ALLAN*)*. Have you got another empty bag in the boat?

ALLAN *(passing it)*. I won't spoil the game.

ANN. It's not a game—it's a matter of life and death.

Now the lots are put into the bag which is shaken vigorously.

SECOND BOY. And who's going to begin?

THIRD BOY. The one who suggested drawing lots.

ANN. Me. *(She takes the bag.)*

SECOND BOY. Don't open it till we all have our lots.

ANN. All right, I'll wait.

The bag is passed round. Finally it is held out to FOXY *who does not take it.*

SECOND BOY. There, Foxy—grab the last one! *(*FOXY *stares without moving.)* Shall I draw for him?

ANN *(clapping her hands)*. Everyone must draw for himself.

While she is speaking, her own lot rolls from her lap. ALLAN *picks it up and opens it quickly. He starts.*

THIRD BOY. But he doesn't know what he's meant to do.
ALLAN *(loudly)*. He mustn't either!
ANN *(startled)*. Where's my lot?
ALLAN. I'm throwing it into the water here—with mine. *(He climbs along the boat and snatches the lots from three of the* CHILDREN.*)* All into the water! *(Throws the bag overboard too.)* It won't bring our rescue for one of us to stop eating and drinking. Our rescue—now that our sore hands can't hold the heavy oars any longer—will come from making a flag—so we're spotted from far off. They won't spot us without a flag. Now I'll rig up a mast and let a flag fly.

He climbs forward again and firmly lashes the boathook upright to a thwart. Then he takes off his white scarf and fastens it to the top of the boathook.

ANN *(calling out)*. It's getting foggy. They won't see the flag in the fog. For all your flag we're completely lost!

A curtain of fog draws near and covers the boat and the children in its thick folds.

THE FOURTH DAY

The fog is billowing across the light of day. The hour is uncertain. Nothing is visible. Then a throbbing sound penetrates the fog; it is like a muffled drum, beaten at different speeds.
When the fog clears in whirling vapours, the boat is revealed.
The CHILDREN *are sitting on the thwarts, awake.* FOXY, *too, in his stony rigidity, on his thwart aft. The* SIXTH BOY. *noticing nothing, keeps on beating with an iron rowlock on an empty tin, placed on a thwart.*

SECOND BOY *(loudly)*. We're out of the fog now! *(The* SIXTH BOY *keeps on drumming.)*
SECOND GIRL *(seizing his arm)*. You needn't drum any longer.
SIXTH BOY *(stopping)*. Why not?
THIRD BOY. Because there is no more fog.
SIXTH BOY. I couldn't have gone on any more. *(He throws down the rowlock.)* Anyhow, it was all nonsense.
ALLAN. It wasn't nonsense. If there had been a ship close by, they couldn't have seen us in the fog, but they could have heard us from far away. For fog carries sound.
SIXTH BOY. Fog as thick as that?
THIRD BOY. Yes. According to certain laws of physics.

THE RAFT OF THE MEDUSA

SIXTH BOY. Do they hold good everywhere?

THIRD BOY. Where shouldn't they hold good?

SIXTH BOY. In our case when we're drumming and waiting for help.

THIRD BOY. There's no difference.

SIXTH BOY. Then it's a good thing there are such laws. *(Silence.)*

THIRD GIRL. The flag!

All the CHILDREN *look up at the top of the boat-hook which has no flag.*

FOURTH GIRL. The flag has disappeared.

FIFTH GIRL. The wind has blown the flag away.

SIXTH GIRL. Who could find us on the wide open sea without a flag?

THIRD GIRL. The flag was to be our rescue.

ALLAN *(after a pause)*. I'll make another flag.

ANN. Have you got another scarf?

ALLAN. I'll tie two shirt sleeves together; they're even longer than the scarf was. I can always find a way out.

ANN *(shaking her head)*. You can't find a way out for us.

ALLAN. Why not?

ANN. You could tie shirt sleeves a yard long to the hook—it still wouldn't be any good.

ALLAN. Of course it will be good for us all if my shirt sleeves are seen. They won't only save me, but the whole boat.

ANN. The boat won't be saved.

ALLAN. They're sure to see us one day or hear the drumming. We'll drum on two tins if the fog comes back.

ANN. The drumming's no good and the flag's no good, and from rowing we've got nothing but sore hands. All this has a deep reason. That's why the flag has blown away too. Why, there hasn't been any wind! And yet the flag blew away. If this isn't a sign, I don't know what a sign would look like.

ALLAN. I didn't fasten it properly.

ANN. That's just an excuse. But the real reason's still there.

FIFTH BOY *(after a pause)*. What is the reason of our not being saved?

ANN. Count again—how many we are. *(The* CHILDREN *look round at each other.)*

SECOND BOY. We haven't grown any fewer.

SECOND GIRL. Nor more either.

ANN. We can't grow more—only fewer. *(Silence.)*

THIRD GIRL. Have we got to wait—until one of us dies?

ANN. Not one dies—we all die while we are still thirteen. *(Silence.)* We weren't allowed to draw lots. Somebody snatched the lots away and threw them into the water. Maybe he had a good reason.

ALLAN *(smiling)*. Maybe.

ANN. If he had the cross himself on his lot and opened it secretly before we others were allowed to.

ALLAN. Me?

ANN. The one who asks is usually the one meant.

ALLAN. I swear I didn't open my lot.

ANN. Why did you stop us then?

ALLAN. Because one mustn't gamble with life. Life is a serious matter.

ANN. Now you're saying it yourself. And twelve lives are twelve times more serious than one life. *(To the other* CHILDREN.*)* Isn't that child's play—just mental arithmetic. *(Capping it)* And when there are thirteen lives, one is too worthless not to be sacrificed for twelve. *(Calmly)* As we're not to draw lots-we've got to use force. *(Silence.)*

THIRD BOY *(hesitating).* Force?

FOURTH GIRL *(to* ANN*).* What do you mean-force?

ANN. One of us must get out of the boat. One of us mustn't eat and drink and sleep with the others any longer. One who is still living with us is our Judas—like Judas who betrayed his Lord. *(Silence.)*

ALLAN. There is no Judas here.

ANN. In every thirteenth person Judas comes back, and unless he dies the boat will upset. We've already stayed in one boat with him too long. We mustn't stay thirteen any longer—that is tempting God. And God won't stand that—specially not from children. Even grown-ups take care not to make up the Judas-number. Remember the examples we've told—they could be multiplied by a thousand and more, if you asked everybody. By a hundred thousand. So long as these people were Christians—like us.

THIRD GIRL. I was got out of bed so that there should be fourteen.

FOURTH BOY. I was listening when they sent one away so as to make it only twelve.

ANN. Only when one child had died could happiness come to the gardener's cottage. There had been thirteen before. *(Silence.)*

FIFTH GIRL. Are we tempting God now?

ANN. In his kindness He is still warning us.

SIXTH GIRL. How does He warn us?

ANN. The flag blew away without any wind and the fog came. That is the last warning—now the storm will break loose.

SECOND BOY. A storm will upset the boat.

ANN. It's bound to. *(Silence.)*

ALLAN *(undoing his coat. Loudly).* Now I'll make the flag!

ANN *(just as loudly).* Now we'll do what we have to do.

ALLAN. What do you have to do?

ANN. Use force—as we're not to draw lots.

ALLAN. You mean to kill someone in the boat?

ANN. The thirteenth!

ALLAN. Who is going to let that happen to them?

ANN. Foxy! He couldn't do anything; not row, nor count when we were rowing—nor drum. Nothing-nothing-nothing. He was lying in the boat and would have died long ago if we hadn't found him. He can't blame us if we choose him. He won't feel anything as he goes down. At the first gulp of water his breath will go. He's no use here—that's why it must be him. *(The* CHILDREN *turn towards* FOXY.*)* One push and he'll have gone. Give him a push!

ALLAN. Whoever pushes Foxy—whoever even tries to push Foxy . . .

ANN *(violently).* Heathen!

ALLAN. Then I am a heathen.

ANN. And with a heathen we're to . . . *(her voice fails her.)*

ALLAN. A heathen who knows the Christian commandments. Better than you do. One says: Thou shalt not kill. *(Silence.)* There's nothing to be said against that, is there? It's as clear as daylight, isn't it? A deaf man can read it and a blind man can feel it. How can it not be understood by anyone who has all his senses? This is our religion which we preach to heathens. These are the proudest words our lips can say: Thou shalt not kill! *(Silence.)* These are God's words, crystal clear. I say it once more: neither the blind nor the deaf can escape this truth— on no pretex can they deny their knowledge, even if they coil round the truth like a snake—it's known to everyone who calls himself a Christian! Thou shalt not kill! *(Silence.)* Or are there any of you with duller senses than the deaf and the blind? *(Silence.)* Then obey this commandment and act like Christians: Do not kill!

ANN *(after a pause).* You don't need to be blind and deaf to understand—that that only holds good in church. In life it's quite different.

ALLAN. But isn't the Church our life?

ANN. Then we wouldn't need any church—no churches where God's word is preached. What would they preach about if everything happened in life as we hear it in church? Who'd keep on going to church if they only heard there what was happening anyway? Then the preacher would have nothing more to say and could disappear from the pulpit. There'd be no need for the whole Church and everything that goes with it. Why, there's a great army of preachers which wouldn't exist if the commandments were obeyed—especially this commandment: Thou shalt not kill. You can't ever have seen our preachers blessing the weapons with which more people are killed than ever before. Even the bombs that drove us away and the torpedo that sank our ship may have been blessed—if the preachers were allowed in to do the blessing. They're quite willing to do it. That's how it is in all countries where there are Christians . . .That's why they are Christians, because they only kill with weapons that have been blessed. But kill they must—and if they didn't, there wouldn't be anything to talk about in our churches. That's the difference—that's what you've got to understand: commandments are made for Sunday's sermon and they sound terrific in church—but outside everything's different— there the greatest evil is thirteen.

ALLAN. That's a difference you're making up.

ANN. Between Church and Life?

ALLAN. One day the commandments will be obeyed.

ANN. And no churches be needed?

ALLAN. Jesus will live once more.

ANN. Jesus lives in heaven.

ALLAN. I mean He will return to our earth and not be crucified any more.

ANN. On doomsday. Then He'll sit in judgment. And woe to him that has failed. Be his sin great or small.

ALLAN. Killing is the greatest.

ANN. Who's asking you to do it? *(She turns away from him.)*

ALLAN *jumps from the thwarts and climbs to the stern. There he picks up* FOXY *in his arms and carries him through the boat, putting him down in the bows.*

ALLAN. Now I'll build a tent for us, Foxy. We'll live in it just as we please. And no one else shall be allowed in. That's the way it's to be and I vouch for your safety. *(Skilfully he fastens the sail to the point of the boat-hook, thus forming a tent in which* FOXY *is concealed. Fresh banks of fog roll towards them.* ALLAN *is hardly visible in front of the opening to the tent.)* We must drum. If we don't try hard, nothing will come to our rescue. The rescue depends on us—don't let yourselves be deceived! Drum—drum—drum!

The fog engulfs the boat. Only the drumming announces its existence. But it sounds like negro drums in the jungle, making the blood freeze.

THE FIFTH DAY

Foggy air and leaden water. The only sound is the drumming—regular, metallic. Until the haze thins out and clears. There is the boat, with the tent in the bows, concealing ALLAN *and* FOXY.

The THIRD GIRL *puts down the rowlock and sinks on to a thwart, exhausted like the other children.*

ALLAN *(stooping to come out of the tent).* Now I must drum. Why don't you call me when it's my turn? *(Looks up.)* I see—no more fog! *(Now he sits down so that he is facing* ANN. *She wipes the moisture from her face with her hands.)* You can be in the tent, Ann. It's drier in the tent. There's room for three.

ANN. I don't sleep in the tent with boys.

ALLAN *(after a pause).* You were in the tent, though.

ANN. I haven't moved from my seat.

ALLAN. I don't dispute that. But there are meetings when no physical movement is necessary.

ANN. In dreams.

ALLAN *(nodding)*. I've been dreaming about you. Do you want me to tell you about my dream?

ANN. Dreams are forgotten when one wakes up.

ALLAN *(violently)*. Not this one, Ann. Ann—I firmly believe there are events that determine one's whole life—and they happen so suddenly, as things only happen in dreams. If we couldn't dream, life would not mean anything to us. I wouldn't want to go on living without this dream.

ANN. Did you dream of a golden castle?

ALLAN. Of you.

ANN. Nothing very nice about me as you see me here.

ALLAN. But it wasn't here.

ANN. Where was it then?

ALLAN. With your uncle on the estate. Do you remember how you described staying there?

ANN *(hesitating)*. Yes—I remember.

ALLAN. The pond—the black swans—Australian ones.

ANN. It wasn't any use—my telling you all that.

ALLAN *(eagerly)*. It wasn't the swans, though, circling under the willows—swimming among the waterlilies.

ANN. But have you been there?

ALLAN. Why?

ANN. Because it is just as you described it.

ALLAN. Now you see how powerful dreams are. They're more powerful than any reality. You'll know that very soon. How old are you now?

ANN. I've told you already.

ALLAN. Twelve or eleven?

ANN. That's my secret.

ALLAN. In my dream you were grown up. That's why it doesn't matter whether you're twelve or eleven. That's what my question means.

ANN. I'm nearly twelve.

ALLAN. That doesn't alter the vision I had of you. I think I shall always see you like that. Eighteen.

ANN *(amused)*. Me—eighteen? I suppose you were nineteen then? *(ALLAN shakes his head.)* Twenty? *(He shakes his head again.)* How old then?

ALLAN *(solemnly)*. Twenty-one.

ANN. And you want me to believe that?

ALLAN. You will believe it when I tell you how I went to your uncle, to ask him . . . *(He checks himself.)*

ANN. To ask my uncle what?

ALLAN. If I might kiss you.

ANN. And—did my uncle scold you?

ALLAN *(dreamily)*. It was wonderful. It was very bright in that room. Usually rooms with a great many bookshelves are dark, and in this room there were rows of books to the ceiling. They gave out so much greatness—so much silence that time ceased to exist. As though the eternal stillness had swallowed up all noise and had changed our knowledge into something we cannot understand. One could feel a different glorious kind of striving—in which the deeds we do now are strictly forbidden. That was wonderful: to be outside oneself and at the same time to reach more deeply into oneself.

ANN. My uncle really has got a great many books.

ALLAN *(joyfully)*. Was that right?

ANN. And what did you talk about?

ALLAN. We talked about you. Your uncle talked. There was no need for me to explain anything. He said: 'When you kiss my niece, you will never forget the time you spent in this room. For it is through this room that the way leads—there is no other that makes one worthy and immortal.' *(After a pause, looking up)* By immortality he meant love, didn't he?—And one becomes worthy when one . . . *(Sighs)* To become worthy, that's the most difficult thing . . . *(Breaking off, he leans his head on his hands.)*

ANN. And—did we kiss?

ALLAN *(looking at her)*. As grown-ups kiss—so we kissed each other.

ANN. Holding each other close?

ALLAN. Together for ever.

ANN *(after a pause)*. That's what one dreams.

ALLAN. Yes—that was my dream . . . Are you angry?

ANN. Why should I be angry?

ALLAN. Because I kissed you.

ANN. But my uncle allowed you to.

ALLAN *(hesitating)*. And would you kiss me . . ?

ANN *(looking round the boat)*. If the others allowed it. *(She laughs. Suddenly checks herself, then claps her hands.)* We are going to get engaged! *(The other* CHILDREN *are now roused and turn towards the pair. To* ALLAN*)* Or wasn't this a proposal?

ALLAN. I have told you that this dream is going to be my very life.

ANN *(to the others)*. You see. His dream has ordered him to kiss me. And if you kiss you're bride and bridegroom.

ALLAN. It really is like that.

ANN. Then kiss me.

ALLAN *(hesitating)*. In front of the others?

ANN. Where else then?

ALLAN. In the tent.

ANN. Where Foxy is? *(ALLAN silently takes her in his arms and kisses her.)*

SECOND GIRL *(waving her bandaged hands)*. Now we have a pair of lovers in the boat!

SECOND BOY. Kiss again! *(ALLAN and ANN kiss again.)*

THIRD BOY. Each boy shall take a bride!

THIRD GIRL. Each girl a bridegroom!

ANN *(loudly)*. No! Just me and him!

FOURTH GIRL. Why do only you two want to kiss?

ANN. Because we are going to get married. We shall have the wedding tomorrow. Only one couple can have a wedding. I'll explain that afterwards. There's no room in the boat for so many couples.

SIXTH BOY. But there's been enough room for everyone till now.

ANN. Not for getting married, though. Getting married is a different matter. Do wait till I explain!

ALLAN *(surprised)*. Ann—are you really serious?

ANN. As surely as I kissed you—I shall marry you.

ALLAN *(bursting out)*. This is even more beautiful than dreaming. To prove that this isn't a dream I must . . . *(He ponders, stoops and gets out the thermos-flask.)* Everyone must sign their names to show that this didn't stay just a dream. We'll send a message to the world so it knows that this came true. The world in its trouble needs messages like this. *(To the SECOND BOY)* Have you got any paper left?

SECOND BOY *(pulling his notebook from his pocket)*. Yes.

ALLAN *(unscrewing the thermos-flask. To ANN)*. You offered me a cup of milk and I looked at you. I loved you at first sight. It was meant to happen like this. Now we're going to get married—and it will be testified here. I shall write it. *(He tears a page from the note-book, writes, and hands it to ANN.)* Now sign. *(ANN reads, signs, and passes it on. Then all the CHILDREN sign. ALLAN receives the page back.)* And Foxy.

ANN *(abruptly)*. Foxy too?

ALLAN. Foxy mustn't be left out.

ANN. But Foxy can't write.

ALLAN. Then I shall write for him: 'And Foxy'. *(Having written, he folds up the page, stuffs it into the thermos-flask and screws it up again. Then he stands up in the boat and with a wide sweep flings the thermos flask far out.)* The mesagge with an unknown destination. Whoever picks it up shall announce: 'Allan and Ann are one in life and death!' *(The CHILDREN follow the flask with their eyes.)*

FOURTH BOY. That will never sink.

FOURTH GIRL. Red can be easily seen.

FIFTH BOY. Will anybody see it?

ANN *(loudly)*. Now we've got to prepare for the wedding. There must be a ceremony.

ALLAN. What are you planning?

ANN. Something you mustn't know about. *(To the other CHILDREN)* No, Allan mustn't know beforehand. Allan must go into the tent and let us talk it over alone. So help me make him go to his Foxy.

SIXTH BOY. You are to go to your Foxy.

SIXTH GIRL. To Foxy!

SEVERAL. To Foxy!

ALL *(raising their fists threateningly)*. To Foxy!

ALLAN *smiles without understanding and stoops to re-enter the tent.*
The CHILDREN *keep their eyes on the opening of the tent.*

FIFTH BOY *(to* ANN*)*. You were going to explain to us . . .
SECOND GIRL. Explain what?
THIRD BOY *(turning round)*. Look at the fog!
ANN. Come close so that I can whisper—and then I'll explain to you
   what this wedding . . .

While the CHILDREN *crouch round* ANN, *the fog envelops them.*
Out of this fog ANN'S *voice can no longer be heard. But another sound*
emerges with growing strength. It is just a 'Yes' *pantingly repeated*
and ending in complete assent.
Then the drumming starts again, savagely as if in triumph.

THE SIXTH DAY

Stillness over the motionless water. Dense sluggish fog. The silence is
first broken by the sound of bells. Then the fog parts and the boat is seen.
ALLAN *and* ANN *are sitting on the fore thwart. In the stern the other*
CHILDREN *are crowded round the tin, which a* BOY *is beating. His*
regular beats accompany the CHILDREN; *the 'ding-dong' of whose*
voices imitates bells.
This continues until ANN *raises her hand. Silence.*

ANN *(to* ALLAN*)*. Now we have arrived in the church.
ALLAN. How beautiful it was driving through the streets with the bells
   ringing!
ANN. And in bright sunshine.
ALLAN. Did you see the crowd at the church door?
ANN. That's what you'd expect.
ALLAN. As Ann and Allan are getting married.
ANN. Hush! We mustn't talk any more. Now there'll be singing.
   (Once more she makes a sign over her shoulder. The CHILDREN *sing*
   in their pure children's voices.)
CHILDREN. *Praise the Lord! ye heavens, adore Him,
   Praise Him, Angels in the height;
   Sun and moon, rejoice before Him,
   Praise Him, all ye stars and light:
   Praise the Lord! for He hath spoken,
   Worlds His mighty voice obey'd;

---

*Translators' note: In the original: *Lobe den Herren, den machtigen König*
                der Ehren! As the English version of this hymn is not familiar
                to children, *Praise the Lord! ye heavens adore Him* is suggested
                for use instead.

Laws, which never shall be broken,
For their guidance He hath made.

Praise the Lord! for He is glorious;
Never shall His promise fail;
God hath made His Saints victorious,
Sin and death shall not prevail,
Praise the God of our salvation;
Hosts on high, His power proclaim;
Heav'n and earth, and all creation,
Laud and magnify His Name.

ANN *(in an undertone to* ALLAN*)*. After the singing the preacher
appears. You must imagine everything. You have been to a wedding,
haven't you?
ALLAN. I didn't pay much attention.
ANN. Then watch me. *(Looking ahead)* There he is. Watch him as I am
doing. He's speaking to us. Of course the sermon isn't so long as for
grown-ups. We are just children.
ALLAN. But he is speaking as solemnly as he does to grown-ups.
ANN. That's just habit.
ALLAN. But it makes me feel hot and cold all over.
ANN. Shut up! Now he's marrying us. Give him the ring . . . Now put
it on my finger . . . The blessing comes next. *(She bows her head.)*

ALLAN *too, after carrying out* ANN'S *whispered directions, stays
with his head bowed. Then* ANN *straightens up again.*

ALLAN *(doing the same)*. Are we . . . ?
ANN. We are still in church. Another hymn! *(She makes the sign.)*
CHILDREN. *Praise, my soul, the King of heaven;
To His feet thy tribute bring;
Ransomed, healed, restored, forgiven,
Evermore His praises sing.
    Praise Him!   Praise Him!
    Praise Him!   Praise Him!
Praise the everlasting King.

Father-like He tends and spares us:
Well our feeble frame He knows;
In His hands He gently bears us,
Rescues us from all our foes:
    Praise Him!   Praise Him!
    Praise Him!   Praise Him!
Widely yet His mercy flows.

*Translators' note: In the original: Beethoven's *Die Himmel rühmen des Ewigen
Ehre.* As that song is unfamiliar in English, this or any other
traditional hymn may be used.

ANN *(turning round on the thwart)*. Now we'll have the wedding-breakfast. Here are our guests!

CHILDREN *(holding out their hands to* ANN *and* ALLAN*)*. Congratulations! Congratulations!

SECOND GIRL. Your lovely wedding-dress!

THIRD GIRL. Silk?

ANN. Brocade. It was badly creased in the car. Never mind, one only wears it once.

FOURTH GIRL. Your lace veil.

ANN. Old lace.

FIFTH GIRL. It looks quite new, though.

ANN. Old lace is more precious.

FOURTH GIRL. That's how it is with lace.

FIFTH GIRL. How should I know that?

ALLAN. We mustn't let our guests starve.

ANN. The wedding-breakfast is ready.

SIXTH BOY. What is there to eat?

ANN. Oh—it's a long menu! We must hurry if we want to eat it all. *(To* ALLAN*)* Give me a bag. *(*ALLAN *bends down and brings out a bag of biscuits.)*

ALLAN. Are these delicacies from the Far East?

ANN. Much nicer. It's what nobody has ever eaten. Imaginary fruits.

CHILDREN. Oh—they should taste good! *(*ANN *opens the bag—takes two biscuits and passes them to* ALLAN*.)*

ALLAN. Two each?

ANN. Do you want more than me?

ALLAN. Do you want mine?

ANN. Each his share. *(The bag passes from hand to hand and returns to* ANN, *not yet empty.)*

ALLAN *(seizing it)*. Give it to me. *(He takes out the last two biscuits and puts them into his coat pocket.)*

ANN. There—you **are** taking more than me.

ALLAN. These are not for me.

Immediately the CHILDREN *undergo a visible change. They bend over, and with furtive glances nibble their biscuits.*

ANN *(jumping up)*. The wedding-breakfast is finished. What's next, Allan?

ALLAN. Next?

ANN. Don't you know?

ALLAN. What should I know?

ANN. What two people have to do after the wedding.

ALLAN. I'll do anything.

ANN. They have to sleep in one room.

ALLAN. Would you sleep in one room with me?

ANN. I must.

ALLAN. You can't imagine a room.

ANN. A room may be a tent.

ALLAN. Well, there really is a tent.

ANN. Then let's go into the tent. *(She opens the entrance to the tent and steps back.)* We aren't alone.

ALLAN. Foxy is there.

ANN. I'm not interested in Foxy—I'm just saying that we must be alone.

ALLAN. But it's only Foxy.

ANN. I tell you I can't go into the tent with you, if I'm not going to be alone with you. If that's what you want, I needn't have bothered about the wedding dress and the veil and everything. The bells have been rung and they have sung twice—it was as solemn as all that, and you said yourself you felt hot and cold all over. Then has all this been a lie? Tell me yourself—it will teach me a lesson for the rest of my life—what I am to think of you—and of your love

ALLAN. Crying makes you even more beautiful.

ANN. Do you think I'm crying for that?

ALLAN. Now you're like eighteen.

ANN. And mustn't be alone with you?

ALLAN. But we are alone.

ANN. And Foxy?

ALLAN. Shan't be in the tent. *(He looks at her lovingly.* ANN *offers him her lips.* ALLAN *kisses her.)*

ANN *(to the* CHILDREN*).* Now get Foxy.

The SECOND *and the* FIFTH BOYS *cross the boat, enter the tent and come back with* FOXY *between them.*

ALLAN. He is still going to have what I've kept for him! *(He takes the biscuits from his coat pocket and holds them out to* FOXY.*)*

SECOND BOY. These are yours—they belong to you.

FIFTH BOY *(taking the biscuits away).* He doesn't want to eat them now.

SIXTH BOY. Can't we use his torch?

FIFTH BOY. We could give signals with it at night.

ALLAN *(violently).* Don't do that! The ships sail under black-out, you know. A small light gives away a whole ship. They might take our boat for a trawler and fire at our light. That's certain death. *(Seizes the torch.)* Give me the torch! I want to make sure that none of you waves it and shows the target to an enemy. *(He puts the torch in his pocket.)*

ANN. Look—the fog!

ALLAN. Darker than ever!

FIFTH BOY. We'll drum—stay in the tent!

ANN *(pulling* ALLAN *with her).* Into the tent!

The wall of black fog closes in and covers the boat. Savage blows beat on the tin and the din rises, drowning every other sound.

THE SEVENTH DAY

The fog lies heavily on the sea, blotting out the day. The mist thins slowly—until the last strands have lifted from the boat.
Between the thwarts the CHILDREN *squat, listless and silent. Then a roar is heard high up in the air.*
The SIXTH BOY *wakes, listens. Suddenly he throws up his arms.*

SIXTH BOY. A plane! *(Gradually the other* CHILDREN *straighten themselves and look up.)*
SECOND GIRL. I can't see it.
THIRD BOY. It can't be seen yet.
FOURTH BOY. There's still fog up there.
SECOND BOY. It's above the fog.
FIFTH BOY. The fog must clear first.
SIXTH GIRL. Then he'll see us.
FOURTH GIRL. Then the plane will rescue us!
CHILDREN *(in an outburst of joy)*. The plane! The plane! *(ALLAN crawls out of the tent.)*
SECOND GIRL *(to* ALLAN*)*. A plane is coming to rescue us.
SIXTH BOY. I heard it first.
ALLAN *(anxiously)*. I hope it won't fly past.
FOURTH GIRL. Our plane?
CHILDREN *(in a fresh outburst)*. It's our plane—our plane! *(ANN crawls out of the tent.)*
ALLAN. Ann—we can hear a plane! Maybe this is the rescue.
ANN. This **is** the rescue.
ALLAN. How do you know?
ANN. I just know. *(To the other* CHILDREN*)* Or can't I know? *(In silence the* CHILDREN *bow their heads.)* The others know, too. This is quite certainly the rescue.
THIRD BOY *(after a pause)*. I can see the plane!
FOURTH BOY. A sea-plane!
SECOND BOY. It's circling over us.
FIFTH BOY. Now the pilot has sighted us.
GIRLS *(clapping their hands)*. Now the pilot has sighted us!
ALLAN. . . . He's coming down in wide circles—that's a sure sign he means to rescue us . . . There's room for everyone—in that huge fuselage. *(To the other* CHILDREN*)* Who's to get in first . . . Foxy must get in first. He's the smallest . . . Where is Foxy? *(Again the* CHILDREN *are silent.)* Is he under the sail—sleeping through the rescue? *(The* CHILDREN *are silent and do not move.)* Pull the sail away! *(The* CHILDREN *stay as they are.)* Why don't you do what I tell you?
FIFTH BOY *(defiantly)*. He—isn't under the sail.

ALLAN. Where is he then? *(Deep silence. Realizing)* What have you done with Foxy? *(Faltering.)* You haven't . . . *(Turns to* ANN.*)* They have thrown Foxy out of the boat . . . *(His voice fails.)*

ANN *(firmly)*. And now we are saved. *(*ALLAN *stares at her.)* That's how I knew we were being saved.

ALLAN *(with an effort)*. I wasn't to look after Foxy in the tent—is that why? . . .

ANN. That's why. That's one reason.

ALLAN. Ann—it isn't true. Say it isn't true, Ann. You didn't deliberately—you didn't do this to me—you didn't, when I believed you—I do believe you, Ann. You must tell me you didn't go into the tent with me just to get Foxy out of the tent. You did love me, Ann.

ANN. I did love you.

ALLAN. But now you don't love me any more?

ANN. I can't quite say.

ALLAN. Don't—so long as Foxy didn't die that way.

ANN. What way?

ALLAN. By a murder.

ANN. I haven't murdered.

ALLAN. The others did with your help. *(To the* CHLDREN*)* Aren't you murderers?

FIFTH BOY. Do you mean to tell on us?

ANN. Sneaks are traitors.

ALLAN. Do you mean to deny that Foxy was in the boat with us?

SECOND GIRL. Who knows that we were thirteen?

THIRD GIRL. Who counted us?

ALLAN. You counted yourselves. The note is floating in the thermos-flask. And at the end of it I wrote: 'And Foxy'.

ANN *(fiercely)*. We ought to spit at you!

SIXTH BOY *(yelling)*. The plane is on the water!

The roar of the engines has ceased—now the floats and one wing of the high plane glide on to the scene.

The PILOT *remains invisible, but his voice is clearly heard.*

PILOT. Hullo, there! Have you got the boat-hook ready? The boat-hook, do you understand? The boat must be held fast to the float with it. Which is the strongest of you? He must hold on as hard as he can. Otherwise we shan't get you out of your boat! *(*ALLAN *quickly removes the sail and undoes the boat-hook; from now on he holds the boat fast to the float.)* We're going to lower a rope-ladder-we shall have to swing it well out. Take care! *(Noises in the plane above.)* You've been lucky, children! A patrol boat picked up your red thermos-flask. That note was a good idea. It's already being printed in the papers, I may tell you. You're quite famous now. Specially the youngest married couple in the kingdom. They're the most admired. Those two have become an example to the whole country of how to behave in danger. Not to think of danger, but to dedicate yourself to life as if it were a wedding-day. And each of the others who signed is a little hero! *(Noises in the plane.)* And where's Foxy . . . Your puppy who's on the list too . . . A nice idea to include your puppy among the humans . . . Isn't it in the boat? Starved? . . . Couldn't it survive? Or did it jump overboard? . . . Don't take it to heart; a puppy is only a puppy—and you are safe. After all that's more important than Foxy. *(The rope-ladder is lowered from the plane into the boat.)* Now you can climb up—one after the other. Don't wait till the others have got to the top. The ladder is very strong and you're no weight. Really, seven days on the open sea have done their work. You look like wicked little devils. One would be quite frightened if one wasn't so sorry for you. *(The* CHILDREN *throng to the ladder.)*

SIXTH BOY. Girls first!

PILOT. Bravo, youngster!

ANN *and the five* GIRLS *disappear above the wing of the plane.*

SECOND BOY. We'll climb faster!

The five BOYS *also disappear above.* ALLAN *still holds the boat fast.*

PILOT. You can let go now—the boat won't drift off before you've saved yourself.

ALLAN *(with a cry).* I won't save myself!

PILOT. What won't you do?

ALLAN. I won't . . . I won't . . . I won't be in the world without Foxy!

PILOT. Did he belong to you?

ALLAN *(beside himself).* He didn't belong to me—he belonged to the whole world. The whole world is guilty of Foxy's death.

PILOT. Don't forget that men die too.

ALLAN. Yes. They kill—kill—kill. They have chosen to do at any time and for any reason what they shall not do.

PILOT. Men will become better one day—and be like children.

ALLAN. Children will be like grown-ups–for as children they are already like grown-ups.

PILOT. Do children kill then?

ANN *(invisible above).* Allan—you must save yourself!

ALLAN. Is that you calling, Ann?

ANN. I was serious about the wedding.

ALLAN. I was serious when I saved you. You drew the lot with the cross. I looked at it secretly and threw it into the sea with the other lots.

ANN. You're telling me this so late!

ALLAN *(tears streaming down his face).* Because it's the last thing I wanted to tell you. Now I have nothing more to say! *(He unhooks the boat-hook and flings it into the water.)*

PILOT *(very loud).* We're receiving a message. We're being followed. We can't stay here any longer. We're pulling up the ladder. Hang on!

(The rope-ladder disappears above. ALLAN *remains in the boat.)*
After such an ordeal a mind can grow confused. Pity! It seemed a good mind.

The engines start roaring. The sea-plane glides from the scene and soon roars above.
It grows dark. In the darkness another plane approaches from the opposite direction. ALLAN, *clearly visible in outline, climbs on a thwart and pulls the electric torch from his coat pocket.*
When the enemy plane is quite close ALLAN *waves the lighted torch to and fro above his head. It does not take long for the plane to discover its target. A volley from the machine-gun stretches* ALLAN *out in the boat.*
The plane moves off.
It grows darker.

EPILOGUE

A blood-red light rises above the sea
staining the water's path like blood
On this tide of blood the boat is drifting
Its sides being pierced by bullet-holes
it is already half-sunk.
Allan lies with his head and his outflung arms
on the centre thwart:
AS IF CRUCIFIED.
Rising, the seeping water laps over
Allan's body.
The boat sinks deeper.
With a great surge the waves
submerge the boat.
When the waves subside, the boat
and Allan have vanished.
ONCE AGAIN
IT IS FINISHED.